Nonprofit Boards:
A Practical Guide to Roles, Responsibilities, and Performance

Nonprofit Boards:
A Practical Guide to Roles, Responsibilities, and Performance

by Diane J. Duca

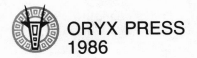 ORYX PRESS
1986

The rare Arabian Oryx is believed to have inspired the myth of the unicorn. This desert antelope became virtually extinct in the early 1960s. At that time several groups of international conservationists arranged to have 9 animals sent to the Phoenix Zoo to be the nucleus of a captive breeding herd. Today the Oryx population is over 400, and herds have been returned to reserves in Israel, Jordan, and Oman.

Library of Congress Cataloging-in-Publication Data
Duca, Diane J.
    Nonprofit boards.

    Bibliography: p.
    Includes index.
    1. Corporations, Nonprofit—Management. I. Title.
HD62.6.D83   1986   658'.048   85-43487
ISBN 0-89774-231-1

I dedicate this work to all executive directors of nonprofit organizations and their board members. I have the greatest respect for all of them—they have not an easy task but a most admirable one.

Contents

Preface ix

Chapter 1: The Board's Legal Responsibilities 1
  Legal Obligations 2
  Moral Obligations 4
  Rules and Regulations of Tax-Exempt Status 5
  Charitable Giving and Solicitations 10
  Voluntary and Involuntary Dissolution 12
  Summary 14

Chapter 2: Organizing Your Board for Maximum Effectiveness 15
  Size of a Board 15
  Board Models 16
  Types of Boards 18
  Working Structure of a Board: Committees 23
  Committee Responsibilities 26
  Responsibilities of Board Officers 32
  Summary 35

Chapter 3: Policy Management and Planning 37
  The Nature of Policy 37
  The Nature of Planning 44
  Summary 53

Chapter 4: Recruiting and Sustaining Board Membership 55
  Recruitment of New Board Members 55
  Why People Say Yes 67
  Motivating Your Board 69
  Summary 74

Chapter 5: Orientation and Training of Board Members 76
  Orientation of New Members 76
  Board Training Programs 83
  Summary 89

Chapter 6: The Board's Fiscal Responsibilities 91
  Financial Development 91
  Budgeting and Fiscal Management 99
  Summary 106

Chapter 7: Holding Effective Board Meetings *by John E. Tropman and Diane J. Duca* 108
  Deterrents to Effective Meetings 108
  Principles for Effective Meetings 112

Rules for Effective Meetings 115
Minutes 122
Summary 125

Chapter 8: The Board's Evaluation Responsibilities 127
Program Evaluation 129
Evaluation of an Executive Director 133
Evaluation of a Board 136
Summary 142

Chapter 9: Building Working Relationships 144
Board/Executive Relations 144
Maximizing Participation 149
Human Relations Aspects of Board Management 154
Summary 158

Appendices: Sample Documents 161
University of Utah National Advisory Council Bylaws 163
Bylaw Section on Committees 170
Board Member Job Description 172
Nominating Committee Form for Board Recommendations 174
Planning Documents 176
Trustee Workshop Agendas 201
Annual Operating Budget 204
Board Self-Evaluation Instrument 205
Minutes Using Paragraph Heading Format 210
Minutes Using Narrative Format 214

Annotated Bibliography 217
Index 223

Preface

Boards of nonprofit organizations define their responsibilities differently. In many cases, the responsibilities that a board assumes are simply a continuation of how the organization's past boards of directors have functioned without any thought to why. For example, if board members historically have assumed the role of strategic planners for the organization, then planning becomes a specific board responsibility. In other cases, the responsibilities assumed by a board depend on *who* serves on that board. A small neighborhood organization is unlikely to have wealthy board members or members with access to wealth. A metropolitan art museum may have a board roster that reads like *Who's Who*. In the first situation, fund raising may seem an impossible task for board volunteers; therefore, fundraising responsibilities are not delegated to the board. In contrast, the museum board has easy access to wealth; it is expected to raise large sums of money, and fund raising becomes a natural board responsibility.

Whether the scope of a nonprofit board's responsibilities is extensive or limited, a board must be well managed. It is imperative for the organizations, associations, and institutions that make up the independent sector to have responsible, effective, and knowledgeable boards of directors.

Unfortunately, many potentially good boards are ineffective due to a lack of leadership, a lack of management skills, or just a lack of knowing what to do. By applying sound management practices, by seeking out leaders of integrity and by learning what a board's functional responsibilities are, most boards should discover a dramatic and productive change in their effectiveness. The individual board member stands to gain. He or she will feel better that his or her time is put to use more effectively. Individual organizations stand to gain, too. But, the most important and ultimate beneficiary is our society. Nonprofit organization efficiency that springs from an effectively managed board of directors can't help but enhance the quality of educational, health, and welfare services that nonprofits provide.

The nine chapters of this book discuss the various functions of a nonprofit board—its roles and the performance of its members. The complexity of the legal responsibilities associated with volunteer board service pointedly illustrates that serving on a nonprofit board should not be taken lightly. Organizing a board for most effective performance is best accomplished by setting up various board committees to support the functional program and administrative areas of an organization. When individual board members assume specific tasks as committee members and actively participate in the areas of policy setting, planning, financial development, fiscal control, and evaluation, they are exercising "due care"on behalf of the nonprofit organization.

The difficult part for most members of a nonprofit board is understanding what it is they are supposed to do, and even when that understanding is reached, how they might go about it. This book was written to help volunteer board members not only understand the roles they should play in a nonprofit setting but also to learn the processes for implementing their responsibilities. Additionally, I have drawn on the experiences of a number of organizations from various fields to illustrate how nonprofits have effectively put their boards of directors to work for them.

Much of the action taken by a board eminates from its board and committee meetings. If these meetings are ineffective, it follows that the work of the board may also be ineffective. I have asked John E. Tropman, Ph.D., professor of social work at the University of Michigan in Ann Arbor, to contribute his expertise on how to make meetings work. Tropman is an authority on effective group meetings; he has published many books and articles on this subject; and is frequently asked to provide training to nonprofit organizations on effective boards and effective meetings. In Chapter 7, he offers rules that can help boards of directors focus their meetings and aid in the decision-making process.

Whether a nonprofit organization is private or public, has a large or small budget, has many or few board members, is rural or urban by location, or has local or national programs, the precepts in this book are relevant to its responsible management and effective performance and are transferable to most situations. The quality of any board of director's performance is enhanced by its sense of a shared purpose and the satisfaction individual members gain from helping a charitable nonprofit organization and their community.

ACKNOWLEDGEMENTS

My special thanks go to John E. Tropman for his contribution to Chapter 7 and to Nancy K. Buchanan for her editorial assistance.

Chapter 1
The Board's Legal
Responsibilities

Volunteer board members are trustees with legal and fiduciary responsibilities to a charitable nonprofit organization. State laws recognize this position of trust and, to varying degrees, regulate the fulfillment of this trust. In some states the laws regulating charitable and nonprofit organizations are mainly registration and reporting acts; in other states, laws also attempt to define the ethical responsibilities connected with solicitation and the management of charitable funds.

Entrusted with the management and care of an incorporated nonprofit organization, trustees must maintain certain standards in carrying out their functions. Certain actions on the part of a nonprofit board of directors are prohibited. Because legal responsibilities and liabilities are inherent to board membership, one should not look upon his or her role as a member of a nonprofit board lightly. In agreeing to serve on a charitable board, one should be prepared to attend to the affairs of the corporate body and devote energy to fulfilling the responsibilities of this position of trust.

In examining the powers, duties, and liabilities of a nonprofit board of directors, Howard Oleck gives us several points to consider:

- Routine affairs are for the board of trustees or directors to decide.
- Extraordinary affairs are for the members to decide.
- Fundamental changes in policy or purposes must be approved by the general membership.
- An honest director who uses reasonable care and diligence has no personal liability for corporate debts or obligations.
- Directors guilty of fraud or bad faith are personally, jointly, and severally liable.
- Insist on written records of objections or doubtful decisions or acts.
- Be sure to prepare and file at least an annual report on the organization's finances and affairs.

- Provide in the bylaws for compensation of directors and officers. Provide also for reimbursement of litigation expenses.
- Do not give compensation to trustees of charitable organizations, directly or indirectly.
- Include power in the bylaws for directors and officers to deal with the corporation but include protective restrictions. Generally discourage such transactions.
- Do not allow use of the organization as a tax dodge or business holding device by anyone or any group.
- Do not allow trustees or officers to make the organization a proprietary device. Use trustees' and/or members' proper powers to prevent abuse.
- Remember that directors and trustees often must serve as financial experts. If they are not such experts, they must obtain expert guidance and assistance or face personal liability.[1]

LEGAL OBLIGATIONS

Not only is a board of directors necessary for a nonprofit organization's existence, but it is also responsible for a number of legal matters. The first of its legal requirements begins with the incorporation of the nonprofit organization in its state. To incorporate in any state, one to three people must be listed on the incorporation document as the initial board of directors. As an organizing instrument, a board is necessary before applying to the Internal Revenue Service (IRS) because a list of board members must be included with the application for recognition of exemption. The existence of a board must be verified for the purpose of executing contracts and conducting other business of the corporation.

The courts have found the nonprofit board to be responsible for an organization's activities, thus board members must behave in a prudent manner. Boards must practice a certain degree of "care, skill, and diligence" in managing the affairs of the organization. They must ensure the "safety" of the corporation's legal documents and act in a professional manner. Boards, by law, must exercise "good faith" and "due care"; they are obliged to act in a bona fide manner for the benefit of the nonprofit organization. As long as a director acts in good faith and in the best interests of the corporation, he or she is generally protected from personal liability for any errors in judgment. However, the consequences of "negligence or willful mismanagement" rest with those ultimately responsible for the organization—its board of directors. To ensure that the statutory standards of care for boards of directors are met, it is critical for board members to be informed, and this requires regular attendance at board meetings. Personal liability is incurred through nonmanagement—by not attending meetings and by ignoring the corporation's affairs.

In applying for tax exemption with the IRS, an applicant organization must give assurances that no member of its board of directors is "unduly compensated by virtue of his or her involvement." This relates to the matter of conflict of interest or self-interest, which is frequently an ethical question but can also be a question of liability. A conflict of interest exists when a board member stands to gain personally from a transaction made by the corporation, such as the purchase of property; when a board member sells something to the nonprofit organization at a price higher than market value; or when a board member conceals, by remaining quiet, an adverse interest. If conflict of interest is even remotely suggested, a prudent director should refrain from voting on the issue. However, in those states where corporate law applies to nonprofit organizations, "self-dealing" is allowed if the transaction is fair. "Although New York law provides that an interested director may vote on a transaction in which he or she has an interest, the corporation may avoid the transaction if the interested director's vote was necessary for its authorization, unless the parties to the transaction can demonstrate affirmatively that the transactioin was 'fair and reasonable as to the corporation at the time it was authorized'...[Not-for-Profit Corporate Law§715(b)]...Similarly, although an interested director may be counted for the purpose of determining whether a quorum is present at a meeting at which a transaction in which he or she has a personal interest will be considered, a prudent and interested director may desire not to be counted for that purpose."[2]

New York's Not-For-Profit Corporate Law, Ohio's, and other state statutes prohibit the nonprofit corporation from making loans to directors or officers. If an illegal loan is made, all directors of the board are liable unless some members vote against it and the minutes reflect those dissenting votes. If a director is not present at a meeting where a prohibited loan was authorized, he or she may send by registered mail his or her written dissenting vote to the secretary of the board for inclusion in the minutes. This action, taken within a reasonable time after a director learns of the loan, protects him or her from personal liability by making sure minutes accurately indicate his or her "good faith."

Legal action can be brought against a board of directors, or an individual director, if there is any neglect or "violation of due care" in handling the organization's assets. Directors may be required to pay back to the corporation funds wasted or lost through neglect. However, charges of financial mismanagement must be supported by factual documentation if they are to stand up in court. Directors are not liable for a corporation's bankruptcy or to unpaid creditors—liability extends only to those negligent acts that injure the nonprofit organization or its public.

To protect itself from future liabilities, a board should ensure that its bylaws are carefully written and frequently reviewed, as this document can have important legal ramifications. Bylaws should serve as the rule book for the board of directors and serve to guide directors in their transactions on behalf of the organization. If directors ignore reasonable precautions stated in the bylaws, they may be grossly negligent and, therefore, can be held personally liable. Boards should consider purchasing errors and omissions insurance, also called officers and directors insurance, in order to protect themselves from a potential lawsuit for mistakes made in the course of conducting board business. Additionally, a board may also consider fidelity bonding for everyone in the organization (staff and volunteers) who has access to the corporate funds and assets.

Bylaws can have important legal ramifications.

MORAL OBLIGATIONS

A nonprofit board of directors must make every attempt to see that organization program dollars are spent efficiently and that as many constituents as possible are helped by the services of the organization. With the tax-exemption status a nonprofit organization receives along with other related special benefits, constituents and the general public have a right to expect board members to behave competently and with diligence.

A board is morally responsible to use all means at its disposal to conduct its business in a competent manner. It must ensure that the organization hires the best possible people to conduct the organization's programs and that the staff employ professional standards in implementing services. A board is accountable to the organization, its clients and constituents, and the general public. (Chapter 8 discusses a board's role in evaluation and related accountability functions.)

RULES AND REGULATIONS OF TAX-EXEMPT STATUS

The advantages of tax-exempt status with the IRS are obvious: the organization is able to accomplish more things if it does not have to spend funds on income taxes, and tax-deductible dollars can be raised to support the organization's work. It is assumed that most readers are already part of an established nonprofit, charitable, and qualified tax-exempt organization. For those who may still be in the organizing stages, look at the references listed in the Bibliography at the end of this book for guidance in setting up a tax-exempt organization. For those who may be associated with a nonprofit, tax-exempt organization that is less than two years old, your status is probably not yet final.

Refer to IRS Form 1023 packet and U.S. Government Publication No. 557 for specific information on filing. Form 1023 [or Form 1024 if you are a nonprofit filing under Section 501(c) other than 501(c)(3)] notifies the IRS that you are applying for recognition of tax-exempt status on the basis of the supporting financial data you submit. It also notifies the IRS that your organization claims it is *not* a private foundation. Some 501(c)(3) organizations such as churches, hospitals, and schools are automatically excluded from private foundation status at the time of their initial filing for exemption.

Reporting Requirements

Unless an organization makes substantial changes in its purpose or operations, its determination as a tax-exempt organization remains unchanged. The annual filing of Form 990 (or 990–PF for private foundations) and Schedule A [for 501(c)(3) organizations] with the IRS is an organization's primary means for accounting to the federal government. Other governmental entities, like the local secretary of state office, may also require annual reports. There are penalties for late filings and for incomplete filings, and your tax-exempt status is jeopardized by not filing.

If your organization claims it is not a private foundation and the IRS has declared that you are publicly-supported, this status must be verified annually by reporting your sources of income on Schedule A (of Form 990). The board of a nonprofit organization must continually be alert to whether the organization meets the "one-thirds" test of a "public charity." "Your group can qualify as being publicly supported if it normally gets a 'substantial' amount of its support from government or foundation grants or from contributions from the general public. In this context, 'substantial' means one-third, and 'normally' means a four-year average up to and including last year, unless your funding has changed substantially this year (in which case this year gets averaged in as well), or unless you are a new organization, in which case you average in all the years you've got."[3]

The rules regarding public support can be confusing. If an organization doesn't automatically qualify because less than 33⅓ percent of its total support is "public" support, the organization may meet the IRS's "facts and circumstances" test. Certain sources of revenue, like unrelated business income or certain contract fees, do not qualify as "public" support. If an organization receives an unusually large donation one year, it can fail to meet the test; however, the IRS allows certain exclusions of one-time large grants. Other factors that help to muddle the computation of an organization's public support percentage include gifts from "disqualified persons," bequests, gifts other than cash, related business income, and more. With so many opportunities for interpretation, a board that has the slightest question about the organization's "thirds-test"should consult with an attorney who specializes in tax-exempt law.

Unrelated Business Income

Despite its tax-exempt status, a nonprofit organization can be taxed on any unrelated business income. This has been a feature of federal law since 1950, although its significance is felt more today with an increasing number of nonprofit organizations turning to entrepreneurship. The objective of this tax has been to help eliminate unfair competition with other corporate businesses.

A nonprofit organization can operate a business if it furthers the organization's tax-exempt mission. "For example, an organization that purchases and sells at retail products manufactured by blind persons was held by the U.S. Tax Court to qualify as a charitable organization because its activities result in employment for the blind, notwithstanding its receipt of net profits and its distribution of some of those profits to qualified workers."[4]

Incidental business activities conducted by a nonprofit organization will not alone be reason for the loss of tax-exempt status, but the income from those activities is taxable. The IRS can decide to point to some revenue-generating aspect of an otherwise exempt activity. For example, an organization may publish a newsletter which furthers its tax-exempt goals by informing the public about its services. If that newsletter is sold, the income from subscription sales is usually nontaxable. If, however, the newsletter carries paid ads, that advertising income may be taxed.

Some business-related activities are clearly nontaxable. An obvious example is that of a thrift shop that sells only donated goods, is run entirely by volunteers, and whose proceeds support a charitable, tax-exempt organization. The earnings from a nonprofit's investments are not considered business income, and the courts have ruled that investing is not a business activity in a tax context. Businesses carried on primarily for the convenience of an organization's constituents, employees, or patients, like a hospital's gift shop, are called "substantially-related activities" and are not taxed. An occasional bingo game sponsored by a nonprofit organization would be a fund-raising event, but regularly scheduled bingo games are considered "unrelated business income" and can be taxed.

Licenses and Regulations

Licensing is the government's primary way of supervising corporate operations. Despite general complaints about too many government regulations, nonprofit organizations have, so far, escaped close government scrutiny. However, as our national deficit continues to increase and the government is forced to look for additional revenues, the tax-exempt benefits of charitable organizations are likely to become a target for reform. State and local governments forfeit millions of dollars each year in property taxes because of the large holdings of tax-exempt colleges and universities, churches, and other institutions. Licensing is also a source of revenue for local governments, and the trend toward increased supervision and licensing of nonprofit organizations will undoubtedly continue.

Specific activities of nonprofit organizations must be licensed or require a permit. A few of these activities are listed below:

Ticket Sales—Certain information, such as pricing and liability, must be printed on a ticket to a public event. When an agent outside the organization is used as a ticket outlet, other liabilities are incurred and additional regulations may apply.

Food Sales—Incidental food sales on your organization's premises to your own members or constituents (e.g., a camp canteen, vending machines) rarely require special licensing. However, if food sales involve meal preparations, are available to the general public as in museum cafes, involve government funding of the food program, or use USDA commodities, licensing from your local city health department will be necessary.

Alcoholic Beverages—Serving alcohol at functions held at your agency is a matter of internal policy; many nonprofit boards prohibit, by policy, serving alcohol on the organization's premises under any circumstance. However, if you sell alcoholic beverages, even on one occasion only, a permit is required by most local governments' liquor licensing commission. Nonprofit organizations may apply for a liquor license in order to sell alcoholic beverages at regular functions and, generally, must comply with the same regulations, including zoning waivers, as any other business establishment.

Mailing—There are special postal rates for "authorized" non-profit organizations for bulk mailing. An annual permit is required; postal regulations must be followed or permit privileges can be cancelled.

Building Permits—Nonprofits are not exempt from local housing and building department permit regulations.

Boxing and Wrestling—Amateur athletic associations, boys clubs, and any other organization conducting a boxing or wrestling exhibition must apply to their state and city boxing and wrestling commission for a license. Provision of proper facilities, medical supervision, and other liability coverage must be met.

The more technical the organization's services, such as medical or mental health care, research, handicapped job training, or physical rehabilitation, the more likely the organization will need licensing. A board must be aware of all local, state, and federal regulations governing the provision of its organization's services. In many cases, a nonprofit organization may not legally commence operations until it has obtained certain statutory approvals. If an organization is considering expansion into a new program area that requires licensing, its board will need to judge whether the organization can meet and maintain mandatory licensing requirements. Government departments usually supervise licenses and permits. A school, for example, would make inquiries at the local or state department of education, or a social services agency at the local department of social services.

Lobbying

Each organization has an interest in the legislation that affects activities in its field, in laws that affect charitable giving, in regulations affecting its responsibilities as an employer, and in other referendum matters. Any direct or indirect effort to oppose or support a referendum is lobbying. Letter writing by members to congressional leaders on behalf of some issue and testifying at a public hearing are legislative activities. If an organization itself undertakes legislative activities, it can lose its tax-exempt status. For example, if a university student newspaper takes a position for or against a referendum or an election, that activity is not ascribed to the university. Similarly, student demonstrations and electioneering are not considered official acts of the institution on whose campus the demonstration was held.

In 1972, the U.S. Court of Appeals for the Tenth Circuit gave a new dimension to the concept of "attempting to influence legislation" when it upheld the revocation of tax-exemption of the Christian Echoes National Ministry. [*Christian Echoes National Ministry, Inc. v. United States,* 470 F. 2nd 849 (10th Cir. 1972) cert. den. 414 U.S. 864 (1973).] The court, after holding that the pertinent income tax regulations properly interpret the intent of Congress (before enactment of the elective rules), found the following "substantial" legislative activities: articles constituting appeals to the public to react to certain issues, support of or opposition to specific terms of legislation and enactments, and efforts to cause members of the public to contact members of Congress on various matters. Of particular consequence was the court's explicit rejection of a percentage test in determining "substantiality," which was dismissed as obscuring the complexity of balancing the organization's activities in relation to its objectives and circumstances. Said the court: "The political (i.e. legislative) activities of an organization must be balanced in the context of the objectives and circumstances of the organization to determine whether a *substantial* part of its activities was to influence or attempt to influence legislation."[5]

The 1976 Tax Reform Act recommended that nonprofit, charitable, tax-exempt organizations be allowed to engage in legislative activities, if such participation relates to matters of direct interest to the organization and its membership. The act did not change the concept that legislative activities cannot constitute a substantial portion of the nonprofit organization's efforts. Nonprofits may elect, on a year-to-year basis and by filing Form 5768, to come under the act's standards. The act prescribes levels of expenditures for legislative activities. In one year, an organization cannot spend more than one million dollars, or a given percentage of the organization's exempt-purpose expenditures, on legislative activities. (See Figure 1.) Specific limitations are also imposed on "grass roots" (general public) lobbying. An organization can lose its exempt status if its expenditures on lobbying activities exceed by 50 percent over four years, the amounts permitted under P.L. 94–455.

As late as 1983, no court decision or IRS public rulings had been made on these new rules. However, some private letter rulings regarding the "degree of allocations" required in determining lobbying expenses suggest the IRS will be strict in its interpretation. It is wise for a board to pay attention to its lobbying and legislative activities and their related costs and to ask for a regular accounting in order to avoid tax penalties. When in doubt, a board should secure professional counsel.

Figure 1. Lobbying Expense Limits (P.L.94–455)

If total exempt-purpose expenses are:	*Lobbying Nontaxable Amount:*
$500,000 or less	20% of exempt-purpose expenses
More than $500,000, but less than $1,000,000	$100,000 + 15% of the amount of exempt-purpose expenses over $500,000
More than $1,000,000, but less than $1,500,000	$175,000 + 10% of the amount of exempt-purpose expenses over $1,000,000
Over $1,500,000	$225,000 + 5% of the amount of exempt-purpose expenses over $1,500,000

(Grass roots nontaxable amount = 25% of an organization's nontaxable lobbying amount.)

CHARITABLE GIVING AND SOLICITATIONS

Although not intended to affect the nonprofit sector, the Economic Recovery Act of 1981 has consequences for charitable nonprofit organizations and institutions and a board of directors needs to be aware of these. Historically tax reform bills have done little to benefit charitable giving. Tax reform bills are primarily aimed at "tax simplification," which tends to reduce the value of all deductions, including charitable donation deductions. Even though the new act contains some provisions that are intended to benefit philanthropy, for example, the charitable contributions deduction for those who do not itemize, the fact remains that tax-motivated giving ranks very low on the list of reasons why people give. Additionally, philanthropic statistics show that those middle and lower income people who do not itemize deductions on their tax returns (and are now able to take charitable gift deductions), more frequently give to churches rather than to other nonprofit organizations. The tax benefits of charitable contributions are of more concern to the large donor than to the average $25 to $100 donor, and most often relate to the potential tax savings on the transfer of property or other noncash assets. The new act has reduced capital gains/taxes and estate tax rates, which diminishes the appeal of those types of gifts to a charitable organization.

Boards of nonprofit organizations need to be aware of these more significant aspects of the 1981 act that are applicable to nonprofit organizations:

- above-the-line charitable deductions for those who do not otherwise itemize their deductions
- corporations are now allowed to deduct up to 10 percent of their PTNI (pretax net income) for charitable contributions (increased from 5 percent)
- deductions for gifts of new manufactured equipment or scientific property used for research
- deductions for gifts of copyrighted works of art
- reduced unrelated income tax rates
- increased investment tax credit for rehabilitation of qualified historical structures
- investment tax credit for certain rehabilitated buildings leased to nonprofit organizations
- revised rules for transferring real property when it relates to purposes of conservation
- expansion of windfall profit tax exemption for child care agencies
- reduced payout requirement of private foundations by requiring only the minimum investment return be distributed in grants

The early predictions on the impact of this act were that nonprofit organizations—philanthropy—could stand to loose billions of dollars in donations. Over the long term, the real dollar loss may prove to be less dramatic. In the meantime, nonprofits have adjusted their approach to deferred giving fund raising and have generally been forced to reexamine their attitudes about philanthropy and government support.

Regulation of Fund-Raising Activities

There are no federal laws regulating charitable solicitations; however, fund-raising activities are regulated at the state and local government levels. The more common statutes governing a nonprofit's solicitation activities deal with the issues of disclosure of fund-raising costs or limits on fund-raising expenditures. Statutes relative to disclosure frequently require an organization to provide potential donors with specific information. A summarized financial disclosure statement printed on donor's receipts with a notation that complete information can be obtained by contacting the named organization at a given address and phone number is acceptable in many instances.

In 1982, two states, Arkansas and Kentucky, removed provisions that limited the amount of total contributions that could be spent on fund raising. It is believed the U.S. Supreme Court's ruling on the Schaumburg case (*Village of Schaumburg v. Citizens for a Better Environment* voided a city ordinance that prevented nonprofits from fund raising if expenses exceeded 25 percent), which stated that nonprofit organizations cannot be denied the right to solicit despite the costs, has influenced state legislators to remove "caps" (percentage limits). Since 1982, the trend has been to abandon the percentage limits; however, only 13 states are known to have no cost limitations.

In December 1983, the American Association of Fund-Raising Counsel, Inc., reported that Indiana, Kentucky, and Nevada were the only states that had no registration or licensing requirements regarding nonprofits' solicitation activities. Thirty states are known to require licensing or registration for "fund-raising counsel," and all but three (Indiana, Kentucky, and North Dakota), plus the District of Columbia, require fund raisers' bonding in amounts ranging from $2,500 (Oklahoma) to $20,000 (South Dakota).

States' agencies responsible for charitable solicitations' regulations differ, but the common ones are secretary of state offices, attorney general offices, and departments of consumer affairs; the state of Pennsylvania has a Commission on Charitable Organizations and New York has an Office of Charities Registration. When in doubt about where to go for information, begin with the local secretary of state office.

VOLUNTARY AND INVOLUNTARY DISSOLUTION

Some small nonprofit organizations may disband informally by simply stopping their operations. This is not troublesome if no parties, such as constituents, are injured or raise objections and if there are no unpaid creditors. However, ceasing activity, the sale of all assets, or appointment of a receiver are not, in themselves, legally considered as dissolution. Therefore, informally disbanding is not wise because sometime in the future an objection can occur and board members may find themselves liable for "improper conduct."

Dissolution of a nonprofit organization should be carried out with the appropriate formality, and it is a board of directors' responsibility to see that this is done. Most state statutes specify not only how a nonprofit corporation can voluntarily dissolve, but also what percentage of the membership must agree on dissolution. For example, in California and Ohio a majority vote of the board of directors is sufficient; a two-thirds vote is mandated in Delaware, Minnesota,

New York, South Dakota, and Colorado. An organization's bylaws should also specify conditions and procedures for dissolution, and they must at least parallel a state's statutes.

Typically, voluntary dissolution is initiated by the required vote of an organization's membership and/or board of directors. A *Certificate of Dissolution of: (name of organization)* is filed with the secretary of state and approval of the dissolution from the state Supreme Court (or other appropriate administrative body) should be attached to the *Certificate.* (This "approval" may be in the form of a separate document.)

Nonprofit organizations can be dissolved by the following:

1. Repeal of the enabling statute under which they were incorporated.
2. Death or withdrawal of substantially all the members without replacement by new members.
3. Surrender of the charter by voted action of the members (with or without court supervision) in accordance with statutory procedures.
4. Expiration of the stated period of duration of the corporate existence, without extension or revival.
5. Annulment of the charter by the state authorities for improper corporate conduct.
6. Court order, on the application of creditors or members, in accordance with statutory procedures.[6]

Forfeiture of a nonprofit's charter, or involuntary dissolution, can occur when the corporation abuses or neglects its powers, privileges, or duties. Common grounds for involuntary dissolution are misuse of powers; fraud and criminal conduct; failure to file required reports; failure to pay taxes; and conducting improper activities or those activities considered injurious to the public, especially ones related to health and safety standards. Forfeiture action against a nonprofit corporation can only be effected by a state's attorney general.

Results of Dissolution

Formally declaring (voluntary or involuntary) dissolution is not the end of the process. The organization's assets must be liquidated and distributed. (In the case of involuntary dissolution, the court designates a "custodian" or "receiver" to dispose of assets rather than the organization's trustees.) During this winding-down period, which according to some state statutes cannot exceed three years, the board of directors meets and votes on matters related to the organization's liquidation proceedings. The assets of a dissolving charitable organization must go toward charitable purposes and, according to some state statutes, to a similar charity; the board, or officers appointed by the board, are responsible for appropriate transfers. The organization may continue to accept donations and bequests during this winding-down phase; is still responsible for its taxes and debts; and is liable for damages from any breach of contract, such as leases and employee contracts.

Properties held in trust are subject to special rules of distribution. Unfortunately, there is a lack of conformity and some confusion among state statutes regarding nonprofit property transfers for religious and charitable organizations.

SUMMARY

The nature of the legal responsibilities associated with serving on the board of a nonprofit charitable organization varies from state to state. Most statutes require board members to act in good faith and state that it is unlawful for members to have a conflict of interest. Board members also have a moral obligation to act competently on behalf of the organization. It is up to individual members to be informed about personal liabilities and the consequences of negligence for both the organization and the individual member.

Some activities conducted by a nonprofit organization require licensing and all nonprofits are required to file annual reports with the IRS. Unrelated business income, lobbying, and charitable solicitation activities are all subject to special rules and regulations. And, when a nonprofit organization elects to disband, certain formalities must be followed. It is important for board members not only to be aware of the laws, rules, and regulations governing nonprofits but also to ensure that the organization fulfills its responsibilities in these areas.

NOTES

1. Volunteer Urban Consulting Group, "The Legal Responsibilities of a Board Member," in *Resource Materials for Girls Clubs of America Fall Training Seminar, Girls Clubs: Design for Growth*, ed. Joseph Weber (1975), p. 8.

2. Howard L. Oleck, *Nonprofit Corporations, Organizations, and Associations*, pp. 647–48.

3. Arnold J. Olenick and Philip R. Olenick, *Making the Nonprofit Organization Work*, p. 1121.

4. Bruce R. Hopkins, *The Law of Tax-Exempt Organizations*, p. 615.

5. Ibid., p. 235.

6. Oleck, *Nonprofit Corporations, Organizations, and Associations*, p. 1088.

Chapter 2
Organizing Your Board for Maximum Effectiveness

The Denver Area Council of Boy Scouts' board of 75 members might seem cumbersome to other organizations, but for the Boy Scouts it works and has worked for over 30 years. This large board is a highly sophisticated organization in itself. Tacoma (WA) Rescue Mission's board structure is the result of three years of deliberate culling and consolidation. Board reorganization started when its new executive director demanded changes that would produce a working board to help the agency better serve the community. Craig Rehabilitation Hospital's (Denver, CO) two-board structure is relatively new and evolved, with some struggle, from an effort to meet more effectively the financial needs of the institution. The Colorado Association of Fund Raisers, a four-year-old organization, has not yet developed to the point where it can support a full-time staff to manage its affairs, so the board administers all the association's programs.

Each of these organizations illustrates a different board structure. There doesn't seem to be one right way to structure the board of a nonprofit organization. What is important is flexibility. As an organization grows, or, in some cases contracts, it changes, and its governing body should reflect those changes. When an organization finds that its board no longer helps the organization meet its goals, has become stagnant, or is not up to the task of meeting new challenges presented by the organization, then the structure and composition of the board need to be reexamined.

SIZE OF A BOARD

There is no one correct response to the question of how many should serve on a nonprofit's volunteer board of directors. The 164 respondents to a survey done in November 1984 of Colorado's nonprofit boards of directors revealed that boards range in size from 3 members to 59 members. Eighteen members was the most common response. A trend toward small-sized boards was evident: 71 percent of all responding organizations have boards of 20 or fewer members. Organizations in small communities (those with population under 25,000) tend to have few large boards and most frequently reported a board size of five. Organizations in cities with a population over 100,000 showed not only many large boards but also a great disparity in the sizes of their boards. In this survey, youth/family service agency boards average 20 to 24 members and are most inclined to have large-sized boards of 34 to 59 members. Hospital boards are more likely to have 7 to 9 members; museum and zoo boards have 8 or 9 members; and the majority of other human service agencies report 13 to 15 members on their boards of directors.[1]

BOARD MODELS

Boards can be grouped into three primary models: large, medium, and small. A large board consists of more than 30 members; a medium-sized board has 20 to 30 members; and a small board has less than 20 members.

The argument for a large governing body is based on the idea that there are greater opportunities for solving broad community problems when interaction among many different representative constituencies occurs. Proponents of large governing bodies rationalize size as a necessary means to rational decision making. (A rational decision-making model suggests that a large number of people representing different sides of an issue can contribute ideas, weigh alternatives, and thus arrive at a more cost-efficient resolution.)

For a large board to work, there must be some established procedure for managing the input and reporting processes. Committees commonly provide a means for individuals to offer their ideas and suggestions. Full meetings of the board are a forum for reporting. Since one purpose of a large board is maximum participation, board meetings can run several hours if members are to discuss issues, respond to committee reports, and share new ideas. Inactive members on this type of board defeat the purpose of a large board. Large boards should have a bylaw stipulating attendance requirements and the action to be taken when these requirements are not met. For example, a member who misses three consecutive meetings will be removed from the board (some exceptions may be stated).

Other organizations find that a large board of directors helps create a sphere of influence. The 75-member board of the Denver Area Council of Boy Scouts has, in effect, 75 different points of access. This board is predominantly composed of business leaders, but it also includes educators, professionals, and other civic leaders. The executive director says if there is some problem or particular need in a scouting district, he knows his board can access someone who can help. For example, when the agency needs publicity for some event, the board has access to the media and to advertising and public relations firms. The board can open the proper doors. When bids were needed for capital improvements for scouting facilities, the board had representative access to architects and contractors as well as building material suppliers. The executive director also lists specific items the organization may need (e.g., chairs, typewriter, microwave oven for the employees' lunchroom, etc.) on the back side of each board meeting's agenda. His board invariably responds by either giving the item(s) or putting the organization in touch with someone who can. The majority of businessmen who serve on this Scout board mandate short meetings of an hour and a half. Committees are used extensively and the full board acts on committee recommendations at regular monthly meetings.

A large board created only to "link important names" with the organization can compromise the effective governance of the organization. Names can be important in establishing credibility, especially to a new organization. However, if names are just names, and not participating members, the effect can be more harmful than helpful. Imagine the following scenario: A foundation is considering a sizable grant to an organization and notices several bigwigs on the board. A foundation trustee knows two of these bigwigs and calls on them for information. These members have never attended a board meeting and rarely find the time to read the organization's minutes, which are mailed to them. This organization's credibility will diminish as the foundation realizes its bigwig board members are affiliated in name only.

Enlisting the support of influential community leaders is viable, but building a large board on this premise usually doesn't make sense. An advisory body of important names may be an alternative—putting names on a board is not the only way to bestow recognition to the organization. This alternative is based on the assumption that the most influential people in town are the busiest and, therefore, the least likely to be working board members. Of course, the ideal is to have influential people on your board who also are active members. Unfortunately, this seems to be a reality for only a few organizations in any given community. However, when your organization needs the special influence a bigwig can bring to bear on a situation, you are more likely to get a commitment if he or she is a member of the board of directors and has a stake in the outcome. Remember, board members have a vote in the affairs of an organization; advisers typically do not.

Joseph Weber favors a medium-sized board model because large boards are not, in his opinion, the answer to responsible member participation. He prescribes a formula for filling board seats based on the six basic managerial functions of most organizations: personnel, administration, finance, program, public relations, and community relations. He says three to five members representing each of these areas, plus 12 or so seats to meet other needs, would lead to an optimum-size board of 30 to 36 members. Weber suggests that a medium-sized board will invariably result from such a deliberate method of board recruitment.[2]

The third model is based on the principle of the least number involved. One assumption underlying this principle is that growth brings about a disproportionate increase in complexity as well as more and more specialization. This, in turn, leads to the estrangement of individual participants. Another assumption is that too many heads only confuse discussion on issues and muddle decision making.

Even though some organizations have medium- to large-sized boards, they may actually operate on the principle of allowing a few to make decisions by relying heavily on an executive committee. The Gilpin Elementary School (Denver, CO), a small private alternative school, illustrates another extreme. Its board of directors has two members—the founding director and his wife. These two members do not function as a board per se; they simply exist to fulfill legal incorporation requirements for tax-exempt purposes. They do, however, use an advisory body composed of parents who assist in formulating some of the school's policies.

The Tacoma Rescue Mission case illustrates consolidation that resulted in a smaller board of directors. It shrank to its present size of 15 members from about 30. The executive director reports they now have a "workable-sized" group.

The size of any nonprofit board should reflect the nature of the organization, its business, and the available personnel in its community. The effectiveness of an organization's board is not a function of size. The quality of its leadership, the dedication of individual board members, member access to resources to help solve problems, and other factors are, by far, more important. Nonetheless, organizations still need to deal with the question of board size when setting up a new agency or reviewing their present structure. If there is no perfect size board, then it is more useful for an organization to consider the purpose and type of board most appropriate for achieving its mission.

TYPES OF BOARDS

Three common types of boards are policymaking, administrative, and advisory.

Policymaking

A policymaking board acts as the governing body for an organization and typically makes decisions on the direction of its programs, the allocation of funds, and other administrative policies. (Chapter 3 discusses the policy-setting role of a board in detail.) Policy boards have the authority to hire and fire the executive director who reports directly to them. Its volunteer members do not receive any type of compensation.

Administrative

An administrative board is a managerial type of board whose members may or may not receive compensation, depending on the organization's "Articles of Incorporation" and its state's statutes that address the issue of compensation for nonprofit board members.[3] In addition to making policy and program decisions, members of administrative boards are directly involved in the management of the organization because typically it has no paid staff. This type board does the work of staff.

The Colorado Association of Fund Raisers, Inc., provides an example of an administrative board. Its board meets monthly to set policies on the expansion and recruitment of membership; to approve new members; to approve all educational programs to be presented to the membership; to receive and distribute funds; and to conduct all other business of the corporation. The board has contracted with a secretarial service to disseminate information about the association and provide a contact point for its members and other interested persons. This board does all the work of the association and uses a membership committee structure to help meet its objectives.

Advisory

An advisory board usually exists alongside an organization's governing board. It is an ad hoc group of individuals assembled for a particular reason, and it meets infrequently or is called together in a crisis. It has no real authority. An advisory board may make recommendations upon request of the executive director or other department head regarding new or special programs, or it may be called on for advice in problem solving or planning. The executive director and other managers are not responsible to their advisory board, nor are they required to heed their recommendations.

Typically, advisory boards are used in the area of financial development. Their involvement in fund raising may be direct or indirect. An organization may create a business advisory board composed of key corporate executives. Busy executives often prefer to play the role of an adviser rather than to serve as a board member; it takes less of their time. Organizations may use these advisers to assist in opening doors and identifying prospects for solicitation purposes.

The *Bylaws* of the University of Utah's National Advisory Council state that its fiduciary responsibilities are "to aid the University in connection with its financial and fiscal matters and needs, such as rendering assistance in obtaining funds and gifts from the private sector, including individuals, business organizations and foundations; and by way of specification but not in limitation, to assist and support the University of Utah's Permanent Endowment Fund."[4] The university uses the council as a vehicle to get alumni and other prominent people on campus twice a year for one-and-a-half-day meetings where department heads present reports of new programs requiring financial support. Council advisers are thoroughly educated and updated on the university and enjoy a round of social activities during their campus visits. In their own communities, advisers act as ambassadors of goodwill for the university. (See Appendix for a copy of the University of Utah's National Advisory Council *Bylaws.*)

Advisory boards are directly involved in fund raising when their responsibilities in solicitations are defined, and advisers are recruited for such specified purposes. Advisory boards are indirectly involved in fund raising if they are part of a group of individuals assembled to lend their prestigious names to an institution and are so listed. They are recruited for that name-lending purpose only. It is assumed their connection with the organization will attract attention and perhaps provide leverage for contributions.

Another common use of advisory boards is specialized counsel. The AMC Cancer Research Center (Denver, CO) has created an advisory body, separate from its institutional board of trustees, for a new Home Health Care Program. The 16-member group is made up of representatives from outstanding community organizations working in the field of home health care or related activities, three trustees, medical personnel, and the head of a regional public relations firm. These advisers are called on individually to advise staff on program direction, and they provide an evaluation and program review function. They are also in a position to make referrals to the program. As a body, they get together as needed but do not hold regular meetings.

Advisory boards can behave as general counsel or can be a sounding board. There is a tradition of dialogue between the University of Utah's president and its National Advisory Council. When the council is on campus for its biannual meetings, a half-day session with the president is always on the agenda. Because council members have different backgrounds, different perspectives, and represent different industries from different cities, the president of the university solicits their viewpoints. He may ask their opinion on a new direction for the university or seek their collective counsel on a particular problem area. Off campus, council members also take the initiative to contact the university with ideas, suggestions, and prospective contacts. This kind of exchange between an institution and its advisers doesn't happen just because the structure is there. It occurs because a deliberate effort is made.

Organizations can easily be drawn into the trap of creating structures but not using them effectively, if at all. Unless there is some written document defining an advisory board's purpose and objectives, it is easy to lose sight of why it was created. If your organization has an advisory board, it is important to look periodically at its activities and examine its usefulness. If there is no significance to this board's existence, if your organization doesn't really use or need that pool of talent, or if your advisers have no talents, then the board should be disbanded.

When an advisory board does have a meaningful mandate, it must be integrated with the total organizational structure. The effectiveness and potential of any ad hoc group is diminished if it exists outside the agency's organizational framework. The best way to ensure integration is to make sure at least one member from the board of directors sits on all advisory boards. The liaison can report back to the board of directors on the advisers' activities, but more importantly, he or she can help keep the advisory group operating within the organization's scope. Advisory boards and other ad hoc groups such as auxiliaries should not be relegated to a secondary status. All are important in helping an organization achieve its goals; they deserve the same cultivation and nurturing that a board of directors might receive.

Other Board Structures

In addition to these basic board structures, there are foundation boards and national boards. These types of boards may not differ in their organizational pattern, but they do have distinctive characteristics that warrant mention.

In addition to a governing board, many organizations set up a separate foundation board with its own trustees and a separate set of bylaws. This dual structure is most common among hospitals and institutions of higher education, especially state-supported colleges and universities. In most cases, the foundation board is a conduit for raising and receiving funds. Hospitals frequently establish a foundation to circumvent state regulations that may prevent them from receiving rate increases. A hospital must show a need for a rate increase and that is difficult to justify if the hospital is sitting on a three million dollar endowment. Thus, when a hospital foundation is created, the hospital's endowment fund is transferred to the foundation, and the hospital corporation's financial statements no longer show a surplus.

Colleges and universities frequently establish a separate foundation board to provide a structure for enlisting the active support of business people and people of wealth. College boards of trustees have unique and academically oriented responsibilities such as curriculum building and student and faculty recruitment, in addition to the other responsibilities of any nonprofit board. These specialized functions call for different talents that may or may not be compatible with the institution's need for funds. The ability to give and get money is not necessarily found in the same person who has an intimate knowledge of higher educational practices. In setting up a separate foundation, institutions of higher education are able to satisfy their need for a group of people who can not only give money and raise large sums of money but also know how to effectively manage the funds raised. And, with trustee status, they have authority. State-supported colleges and universities use the foundation board to circumvent some private sector funders' policies and practices of "nonsupport to tax-supported institutions." A gift can be justified to a university's private foundation.

Nonprofit organizations in other fields find that the foundation structure is useful under other situations: (1) When an existing board of directors is program-oriented, competent, and hard working but refuses to raise money, a separate foundation may be established for the singular purpose of raising funds, and its members are recruited for that purpose; (2) when an organization receives more than 50 percent of its operating budget from government sources, a separate foundation can be a useful vehicle not only for attracting private sector dollars but also for keeping its funds from intermingling; and (3) some organizations, by their business and geographic location, should be and are governed by a representative community-based board of directors. This does not necessarily allow for ties to the business community, which are helpful in leveraging private funding. In most cases, we find that the reason for setting up a foundation board is financial development.

National boards of directors are large because they need representatives from different groups that have an interest in the decisions and policies made at a national level. In *Effective Leadership in Voluntary Organizations,* Brian O'Connell says 100 members are about maximum—beyond that, participation isn't significant enough to create a feeling of honor and responsibility. The committees of a national board are characteristically made up of individuals who are experts in the field of the committee's purpose.

One final type of board structure, one incorporating voting memberships, merits attention. A nonprofit organization may have different classes of members with or without voting rights as defined in its articles of incorporation or its bylaws. The common membership structure is one that solicits individuals to join the organization for the purpose of creating a broad base of support. However, the focus here is on membership classifications that are granted powers similar to those normally given to the board of directors, such as members with voting privileges. Some organizations' articles of incorporation identify a body other than its board of directors that has the ultimate responsibility or authority for the organization—a voting membership.

O'Connell believes in a "process of maximum feasible involvement" where the largest possible number of members vote on the major issues concerning the organization. A voting membership is used to accomplish this. "If an organization is dealing with a major public problem, maximum participation in defining the problem and its solution represents the shortest route to community action."[5] He proposes that a voting membership, a cross-representation of the community, should be at least four times the size of the organization's board of directors. He feels the benefits derived from an informed and supportive public overrule the problems of managing a large group of people; this support constituency ultimately becomes a resource to be tapped for further financial and human resource contributions.

Another voting membership model is found among national umbrella organizations like the National Mental Health Association. Its voting membership is composed of delegates from the various states' mental health associations. Members meet once a year and are empowered to vote on policy issues such as standards of affiliation, bylaw changes, program initiatives, fiscal practices, and other matters. The voting membership provides guidance to the board of directors.

WORKING STRUCTURE OF A BOARD: COMMITTEES

A board's responsibilities vary from organization to organization but generally can be divided into eight broad categories:

1. to clarify the organization's mission
2. to interpret the mission statement to the public and enhance the organization's public image
3. to approve goals and objectives/set long-range plans
4. to establish policies and other guidelines for agency operations
5. to be legally responsible for all aspects of the organization's operations
6. to ensure the organization's financial stability and solvency
7. to hire and support the executive director and assess his performance
8. to evaluate the performance of the organization and of the board itself

Not only must a board understand and accept these responsibilities, but it must also have some operational structure for accomplishing these things and conducting its business efficiently. Committees are one means to that end.

Not all boards have a committee structure. Some are too small to be subdivided; some prefer to form task forces as needed; and others prefer to behave as a committee in the whole. However, most nonprofit boards do use committees and define a basic committee structure in their bylaws. Typically, there is a bylaw empowering the president of the board to name other committees as needed, thereby giving the committee structure essential flexibility and the potential to change and grow with the organization. (See Appendix for sample bylaws with a description of committee structures.)

Benefits of Committees

The use of committees to accomplish organizational objectives is based on the premise that smaller groups of individuals can conduct themselves more efficiently than the whole and that a definitive structure is required to operate efficiently. Committees provide a function of economy for the organization by providing a vehicle for parceling out the agency's work and removing more mundane tasks from the full board's consideration. They provide a means for in-depth board participation, as individuals contribute their specific talents and knowledge to committee assignments. Furthermore, a committee structure encourages broader participation on the part of board members.

Committees also play an advisory role. They meet separately from the full board to discuss agenda items assigned by the board president, the full board, or the committee chairperson. They report to the full board with their findings and recommendations on action(s) to be taken. It is in this advisory capacity that committees may initiate board decisions, if not board policies. These little administrative bodies must function effectively or the quality of the organization's services may be adversely affected.

A committee structure is effective when several elements are present. First, it is imperative that all committees have definite tasks. They should know the limits of their authority, their responsibilities, and their potential. Second, committee chairpersons must be capable of leading committee members through a rational decision-making process in order to reach appropriate decisions. Third, each committee should include at least one key program director or manager from the organization's staff. Fourth, committee members must be willing to give whatever time is required to their fact finding, evaluation, or other activities. Last, committees must conduct their business in a timely fashion. This latter point is more significant than it may appear. Committees are notorious for their inability to make up their collective minds. A decision or recommendation stalled in committee can destroy an important timetable for the organization.

Types of Committees

Before describing the responsibilities of some common board committees, a distinction should be made between standing committees and ad hoc committees. Standing committees are permanent committees established in an organization's bylaws. They are expected to meet regularly and conduct activities that will lead to accomplishing a set of prescribed objectives. Ad hoc committees differ in that they are assembled for a specific purpose for a limited period of time and are disbanded when their job is done. Except for mention under the president's authority to assemble, ad hoc committees usually are not described in an organization's bylaws. (The Interfaith Counseling Service of Scottsdale, AZ., distinguishes between standing committees and special committees. See Appendix.)

The Maricopa (Phoenix, AZ) Camp Fire Council's bylaws do not offer a distinction between standing and ad hoc committees. Instead, all committees of the council are standing ones. "The board of directors, by resolution, shall establish and determine the functions of such standing committees, as it deems necessary, to assist the board in carrying out its functions."[6] Despite the use of the word "standing," the implication and intent is to permit the open-ended formation of committees as needed.

Ad hoc committees should be used with discretion and should not supplant the work of an organization's standing board committees. When a problem or new business arises, the board should consider the ability of an existing standing committee to handle the matter before forming a new ad hoc committee.

A committee, whether standing or ad hoc, serves one of four purposes for an organization: administrative, liaison, study, or project. Administrative committees deal with the operational and procedural matters of the organization. A liaison committee promotes communication between the organization and other community groups. Study committees focus on new directions and programs that may be required to respond to problems. (These are most often ad hoc because they are formed to review a specific situation.) Project committees pick up where study committees leave off by monitoring and/or evaluating program services.[7] When a committee's assigned project or problem is large in scope, the committee may subdivide. Subcommittees report to the full committee with their findings and recommendations.

COMMITTEE RESPONSIBILITIES

Executive Committee

With few exceptions, nonprofits are authorized in their bylaws to form an executive committee to function on behalf of its board of directors in emergencies and/or interim situations. In most cases, an executive committee can exercise all the powers given to the board except the right to make bylaw changes. The executive committee is powerful by definition and poses a danger if it usurps the board of directors—if it makes all the board's decisions and relegates the full board to rubber-stamping. While some organizations use their executive committee excessively, most rely on it to move things along in lieu of taking all matters before the full board. If an organization finds it is relying on its executive committee to do all the work of the board, perhaps it should reexamine its organizational structure and, more pointedly, the purpose of its board.

Bylaws should limit the power of the executive committee by stating that its authority shall not circumvent the responsibility and authority placed on the board of directors. It is up to a board to maintain control.

The executive committee is always a standing committee but it may have more diverse functions when it meets regularly. In this case, it may review or prepare board meeting agendas to ensure all matters coming before the board are relevant and appropriate. It may plan the board's work. It may interpret board policies to staff, oversee policy implementation, and refer questions to other committees or to the full board. It reports its activities at each board meeting.

Executive committees are typically composed of the officers of the board and may include the chairpersons of board standing committees. Since the president of the board appoints committee chairpersons, an executive committee that contains only committee chairpersons may lead to biased actions from a group that thinks alike. It is wise to balance the executive committee with other board members or to select committee representatives other than chairpersons. Past board officers may be included on the executive committee and the executive director is an ex-officio member. On the one hand, this committee should represent the best of the board—its leaders—because it has the authority to act in crisis and interim situations. On the other hand, it should also be representative of the full board in order to review more objectively matters that come before it. An executive committee behaves as a miniboard, so it is proper for it to be a microcosm of its board of directors.

Program Services Committee

All social service agencies should have a program committee. Hospitals may have a medical services committee, and colleges and universities may have an academic committee. Whatever you call it, all nonprofit organizations and institutions should have a standing committee related to its mission, and its function is similar in all cases.

Major policy recommendations emerge from this committee because its primary duty is to study how the organization can continually best serve identified community needs. It must not only review the organization's program but also keep abreast of trends in the field and of the community's changing needs. It needs to ensure that programs expand or contract in proportion to changes in membership or clientele. The program services committee has an evaluation and forecasting responsibility. It schedules programmatic growth for the organization and recommends new activity areas to the board. It sets short-term, intermediate, and long-range service objectives. This committee works closely with the finance committee to determine the resources needed to support the organization's programs. Because it projects future staffing patterns that will be required by expanded programs, this committee is closely linked to the personnel committee, and it alerts the public relations committee to program changes requiring interpretation to the organization's public.

This committee is staffed by the executive director and other key program managers. Its members include persons with experience in program planning, forecasting, organizational development, and at least one expert in the field of the organization's business. If an organization's program is complex and many outreach services are offered, this committee will likely be broken into subcommittees. A comprehensive youth service agency offering employment training, tutoring, substance abuse counseling, and clinical services may have a program subcommittee addressing each of these major service areas.

Finance Committee

A finance committee is not responsible for raising money. Fund raising and funds management require different talents and a different focus. This standing committee's chief responsibility is to oversee the agency's finances and assets, including the allocation of its total resources. With assistance from the board treasurer and executive director, it prepares the organization's annual budget for approval by the board. In larger organizations staffed with a controller or accountant, this committee will more likely review a budget drafted by these professionals on staff. The committee should see that a monthly (or at least a quarterly) financial statement is presented to the board; normally the board treasurer gives the report. It must ensure that the agency's bookkeeping practices are in accord with standard accounting procedures for nonprofits and that its financial records are accurate. In smaller organizations, the finance committee may actually prepare financial reports, approve the payment of bills, and perform other bookkeeping functions. It is not enough to simply present a financial statement; the committee and board treasurer also advise the board when income and expenditures are less, or more, than projections and report on cost-efficiency. It periodically evaluates the organization's sources of revenues, its income structure, its investments, its assets and liabilities position, and it should make policy recommendations when changes are indicated. Nonprofit organizations should have an annual audit conducted by an independent accountant, preferably a certified public accountant. This committee hires the auditor and supervises the audit process. (See Chapter 6 for more on the fiscal responsibilities of the board.)

The finance committee is composed of the board treasurer, who may or may not be the chairperson, an accountant familiar with nonprofit accounting principles, and other board members with appropriate experience and knowledge. It is staffed by the executive director and the agency controller or bookkeeper. Depending on the size of the organization and whether it is facility-oriented, the finance committee should be authorized to establish subcommittees for functions such as property and facility management, portfolio investments, or endowment management.

Personnel Committee

The personnel committee recommends policies and procedures regarding the organization's hiring and firing practices, salaries, benefits, working hours, and working conditions. Its primary charge is to ensure that the agency's working environment is conducive to attracting and keeping quality personnel. While the full board actually hires the executive director, the personnel committee often recruits, screens, interviews applicants, makes a recommendation concerning the top candidates, and evaluates the executive director's performance. Once personnel policies are established, this committee periodically reviews them; keeps the board updated on future personnel requirements; ensures that the executive director or personnel director is aware of current laws and regulations governing personnel practices; reviews new staff positions, terminations, and resignations; advises on staff training and development; formulates grievance procedures; and guides all other relevant personnel policy matters. Large nonprofit institutions with union employees may also charge this committee with labor relations issues like collective bargaining.

This committee is commonly identified as a standing committee in the organization's bylaws. However, organizations with fewer than 20 employees will find that this committee need not meet regularly. Since personnel management is becoming an increasingly complex issue, large organizations with a personnel department will find it helpful to have their personnel director sit on this committee or serve as an adviser to it. It is also recommended that an executive director of another nonprofit of comparable size and mission serve on this committee. It can be particularly supportive to the executive director to have a colleague present who has firsthand understanding of the personnel problems in a nonprofit agency. An organization's executive director should always sit on this committee as he or she is the spokesperson for other staff members. The executive brings personnel grievances and suggestions or requests to the board's attention by way of the personnel committee.

Resource Development Committee

A resource development committee is always a standing committee unless an organization doesn't need to raise annual funds. Some organizations earn their annual operating budgets from service fees or other income-producing activities. Public nonprofit organizations receive their annual budgets from a local, state, or federal entity. In such instances, a resource development committee would be assembled only if there is a special program or capital improvement project that requires new or supplemental funding.

The resource development committee is responsible for recommending a philosophy of fund development to the board. While the entire board is responsible for the organization's solvency, this committee ensures that the funds necessary to conduct its business are raised. The broader title of "resource development" implies that its charge includes not only cash but other resources such as donated goods and services. (See Chapter 6 for a board's role in fund raising.)

Nominating or Board Development Committee

Most nonprofits name a standing nominating committee in their bylaws. Unfortunately, too many organizations use this committee as an ad hoc committee, thereby limiting its effectiveness. It is not uncommon for a nominating committee to meet one month before the board's annual meeting and hurriedly prepare a slate of nominees. When inadequate attention is given to the selection of new board members, inappropriate board membership may be the result. (See Chapter 4 on recruiting.)

Instead, a board development committee is responsible for maintaining a current file of prospective board members. This enables it to bring a list of carefully selected nominees to the board whenever a vacancy occurs. However, there is a trend to enlarge this committee's responsibilities to include providing orientation to new board members, arranging annual board planning retreats or other board education programs, and alerting board members to other volunteer training opportunities in the community. If a nominating committee adopts the name "board development committee," it is more likely to broaden its responsibilities to include supervising the board's education and training activities. (Chapter 5 gives a more detailed discussion on board development activities that may be promoted by this committee.)

The executive director is an ex-officio member of this committee. Other members should have wide or varied contacts in the community and a good ability to judge others' potential. Committee members with like interests tend to know the same people, thus a representative composition is important.

Public Relations and Community Relations Committees

Large organizations with professional marketing and public relations staff have little need for a public relations committee. A small organization without this expertise on staff should have a standing public relations committee charged with interpreting the organization's program, services, and mission to its publics.

A public relations committee sets specific and general public relations objectives: themes to be communicated, target audiences, methods to be used, and timetables for accomplishment. Unless there is a marketing staff, this committee helps to identify the organization's various publics to whom different messages are targeted. It may assist in accessing media representatives, but it should not get involved in routine staff tasks like writing and placing press releases. It may advise on contracting with advertising and public relations counsel, advise on expanding the organization's sphere of influence and/or publics, make suggestions regarding mailing lists, or direct demographic research on the agency's publics. This committee works closely with the board's program, finance, and resource development committees. It reviews and evaluates its activities for its publicity impact and recommends to the board any necessary changes. It is alert to organizational problems that may require a more sensitive interpretation and reviews the organization's literature to ensure consistent messages. The public relations committee is also concerned with internal communications and ensures that the organization has some regular vehicle for communicating with its members. When there is no public relations committee because professional staff perform these functions, all board members are responsible for spreading the organization's story at appropriate times and ensuring that the organization has a good public image.

A community relations committee may be a subcommittee of a standing public relations committee, or it may be a separate standing committee. Whether it is a subcommittee or a separate committee, its job is to oversee the organization's interaction with other community groups. It ensures that the organization assumes a coordinated approach to the resolution of community problems. It may provide access to other agencies in the community, advise on communication techniques, assist in planning and implementing activities that involve other community groups, and ensure that the organization is appropriately represented at major community events or public hearings. As limited resources force more organizations into mergers and consolidation, the responsibilities assumed by this community relations committee carry increasing importance.

The functions of public relations and community relations committees vary significantly and so does their composition. A public relations committee requires skills and knowledge in media relations, advertising, marketing, and external communication planning. A community relations committee requires a broad knowledge of other community services, organizational development skills, political savvy, and, possibly, knowledge of consolidation planning.

Other Committees

So far, only the common board committees of a nonprofit organization have been described. Discussion of long-range planning as a standing committee has been intentionally omitted. Long-range/strategic planning is best accomplished by a task force or ad hoc committee. This does not imply that planning is a temporary preoccupation but rather that an ad hoc status encourages a change of membership and, therefore, a regular infusion of new ideas. Actually, once an organization creates its strategic plan, further board planning responsibilities are focused on evaluation, review, and updates. If all board committees take their responsibility for evaluating and forecasting in their respective areas seriously and do a competent job, a planning task force should be able to manage updating the organization's plans in relatively short order. (See Chapter 3 for a board's planning responsibilities.)

RESPONSIBILITIES OF BOARD OFFICERS

President/Chairperson

The head of the board of directors, who shall be called president in this section, is naturally the most important officer. The president provides direction to the board and must be a strong, effective leader who is skilled in group processes and knowledgeable about people. He or she has six main responsibilities.

1. The president is the general manager of the board and sets goals and objectives for the board. All boards should have goals and objectives that are separate from organizational goals. Boards should determine what they are going to do and what they hope to accomplish within a year on behalf of the organization and in accordance with the organization's strategic plan. These goals and objectives must be effectively communicated by the president to the rest of the board so that these members can carry them out.

2. The president organizes. He or she divides board tasks into manageable assignments and structures them for committee assignment. The president names committees and appoints their chairpersons and is responsible for selecting the best person(s) for a job and for ensuring that assignments are carried out in a timely fashion.

3. The president is a motivator—he or she instills activism. A critical job of the president of any board is the creation of a team out of its members. The president must constantly communicate with fellow members, clarify members' roles, make appropriate assignments according to individual interests, and respect each members' individual needs—what they hope to gain from their board experience.

4. The president is responsible for measuring and evaluating the board's performance. This does not mean that a score card is kept on members' performances. Rather, the president helps set the standards and procedures whereby board self-evaluation can occur on a regular basis.

5. The president of a board of directors is a catalyst for change. He or she starts projects and then lets other members complete them.

6. The president calls meetings of the board and presides over them and is responsible for maintaining agenda integrity and keeping meetings focused. (See Chapter 7 on effective meetings.)

Vice-President

Too often the vice-president of a board has no responsibility other than conducting and presiding over meetings in the president's absence. The vice-president of a board should be selected on the basis of strong leadership potential and the vice-presidency should be a training ground for the presidency. If the vice-presidency is to be a true grooming position, it must carry with it further responsibilities. These responsibilities could include the responsibility for board development—the ongoing education of all members and orientation of new members. When there is a board development committee, the vice-president could be its chairperson. In this capacity, the vice-president would plan annual board retreats, special planning work sessions, and/or special board meetings where a program of boardsmanship education is offered.

The vice-president should also chair at least one committee of the board and serve on at least one other board committee. He or she should work closely with the board president in board performance evaluation and provide direct input to the agenda-building process.

Secretary

In most organizations, the secretary of the board is responsible for taking minutes of board meetings. This task should be assigned to someone else because it prevents the secretary from taking an active role at meetings; he or she is too busy taking notes on the discussion to join in the discussion. Some organizations assign a staff secretary to take minutes. If confidentiality of board meetings is a concern, the meeting can be taped by the board secretary.

Writing up the minutes and mailing them out to members is a clerical task that is best carried out at the staff level. In small organizations the board secretary usually performs these traditional minute-taking and minute-transcribing functions out of necessity.

The secretary acts as an adviser to the staff person assigned to record the minutes. He or she should be able to discern the high points of any discussion, the most important points to be recorded, and share this expertise with the minute-taker. The secretary should be fully familiar with the proper format for writing up board and committee minutes and instruct responsible staff on that format. (See Chapter 7 for a discussion of minutes.)

The secretary reviews all board minutes for accuracy and completeness before they become a permanent record of board proceedings. The secretary maintains written copies of all board business and transactions, is responsible for their completeness, is knowledgeable about their content, and is therefore able to retrieve information about the board's business when requested.

The secretary acts as parliamentarian for the board of directors and needs to be familiar with *Robert's Rules of Order*. Few boards have an official or separate parliamentarian anymore, as most board meetings are not conducted in strict accordance with *Robert's Rules* (and do not need to be). However, situations do arise when parliamentary procedures are needed, for example, the passing of complicated motions, withdrawing motions from the floor, and so forth. When meeting discussions get out of hand, using *Robert's Rules* can help pull people back on track by advising a call for a motion or vote.

The secretary may be called upon for other traditional secretarial matters: correspondence on behalf of the board or signing corporate papers. It is useful if the secretary of the board is also a notary. In addition, some board secretaries act as the board's historian.

Treasurer

The treasurer is responsible for overseeing the organization's finances in the broadest sense. Although the treasurer presents the monthly (or quarterly) financial reports at board meetings, he or she is not the organization's bookkeeper. However, in some small organizations he or she may take part in bookkeeping activities. Today's nonprofit organization is more likely to employ a computer accounting service to prepare its financial reports, and many organizations have their own in-house computer to provide financial data. Even the requirement that a board treasurer must be an accountant or CPA is no longer as essential as it was 7 to 10 years ago. However, accounting skills or knowledge are very important to help interpret financial statements and advise on budgeting processes to other volunteer board members.

The treasurer should also be knowledgeable about investment opportunities and, with the finance committee, assist in managing the organization's portfolio. This does not mean the treasurer makes investment decisions. Those are board decisions, and they are best handled by an independent broker, bank trust department, or securities firm. The treasurer (with the finance committee) reviews whatever investments are made, is responsible for ensuring that the organization's investments are sound and appropriate, keeps track of investment earnings that are reported to the board, and recommends any adjustments.

SUMMARY

The rationale for a board of directors with over 30 members is based on the notion that the more diverse the people involved in decision making are, the more democratic decisions will be. Medium-sized boards with 20 to 30 members often result from recruiting individuals with expertise that complements an organization's basic managerial/functional areas. Small boards with less than 20 members are most common.

Boards can be characterized by type. Policy boards set the direction of an organization. Administrative boards also set policy but, unlike policy boards, they are involved in an organization's managerial decision making. Advisory boards have no decision-making authority and are called on to give advice in specialized areas. A foundation board is a special board structure most often created for the purpose of raising money. It usually exists in addition to an organization's governing board of directors. National boards have unique characteristics and so do "voting memberships."

Committees provide an operational structure for carrying out the responsibilities of a board of directors. When an organization complains of an ineffective board, it probably means that its board committees aren't functioning. The significant role committees play reminds us that committee appointments and assignments must be made carefully. Only people appropriate to the task and only those necessary to do the job should be assigned to a committee. Most board committees are prescribed in an organization's bylaws; however, ad hoc committees may be formed as needed to consider special problems.

Despite the structures a board may devise to manage its operations, it may or may not meet with success. In the final analysis, success depends on capable leadership. Active leadership can help eliminate negligence or indifference among (board) members and raise the performance level of the entire board of directors. While each officer of a board is responsible for certain board management tasks, all are responsible for motivating the board's membership.

As a colleague said, "Good structures don't make an organization work, good people do. Give me a group of good people and they'll find a way to get the job done."

NOTES

1. Diane J. Duca, "Survey Report on Colorado's Nonprofit Boards of Directors" (Paper written for the University of Colorado/Denver, Graduate School of Public Affairs, Denver, May 1985).

2. Joseph Weber, "Resource Materials for Girls Clubs of America Fall Training Seminar: Design for Growth" (Workshop manual prepared for Girls Clubs of America, Inc., 1975).

3. Internal Revenue Service, *How to Apply for Recognition of Exemption for an Organization,* 1977 ed. (Washington, DC: IRS).

4. University of Utah, "Objects and Purposes," Article III, Section 3.1— In General A through E, *National Advisory Council Bylaws* (Salt Lake City, UT: University of Utah).

5. Brian O'Connell, *Effective Leadership in Voluntary Organizations,* p. 71.

6. Maricopa Camp Fire Council, Inc., "Standing Committees," Article X, Section 1a., *Bylaws* (Phoenix, AZ: Maricopa Camp Fire, Inc.).

7. Tracy D. Connors, ed. "The Board of Directors," in *The Nonprofit Organization Handbook,* Chapter 2, pp. 35–64.

Chapter 3
Policy Management and Planning

While many opinions exist about the roles of a nonprofit board of directors, there is little disagreement that it is an appropriate and primary responsibility of the board to set policy. Unfortunately, there is a great deal of confusion surrounding the meaning of policy. Various policies exist, and differences between types of policies are not always clear. It is sometimes difficult to distinguish policy setting from other elements of strategic planning and to differentiate policies from objectives or strategies. Because policies are so important to the management of any corporation, profit or nonprofit, it is important to define what a policy is and to look at its characteristics.

THE NATURE OF POLICY

A survey of corporations conducted by the National Industrial Conference Board came up with several definitions of the term "policy": "a broad interest, direction or philosophy; an expression of the corporation's principles and objectives; guides to thinking and action; general standards not subject to frequent change; and procedures and practices."[1]

Policies focus on the issues critical to an organization and unquestionably are a matter for board concern and decision making. Policies are guides to action and are intended to result in the achievement of the organization's mission. They may be broad, such as "It is the policy of this organization to be a good community citizen," or more definitive, "It is the policy of this organization to encourage its employees and volunteers to participate in community council meetings." Policies set limits; they help to resolve questions that may arise on how the organization conducts its business. Without policy directives, an organization's operations may flounder in inconsistency. It is the board's responsibility to ensure that policy statements are thoughtfully derived and consistent with the organization's mission.

Policies usually have a long life. In fact, too many organizations fail to evaluate and revise their policies periodically until some crisis occurs. Policies should be framed with an eye to their long-term applicability. The policy manual of one company says, "A policy is a statement of management's intent with respect to matters of broad and long-range significance to the company."[2]

Policy and planning activities are frequently confused because a policy is a type of plan by definition. An organization may have one without the other. "It is the organization's policy to vigorously support a program of staff development" is a policy statement; the organization may not yet have planned a course of staff development. Or, an organization's five-year plan may include conducting annual training programs or retreats for staff, but no policy statement such as the one cited above may exist. However, the existence of a major policy statement can force a plan. A key point to remember is that policies can be either guides to planning or a derivative of planning.

"The organization will increase its services to the elderly by 10 percent this year" is a proper objective statement. When a policy includes a means to an end, it may become an objective; it is no longer a "pure" policy statement. However, policy statements and objectives can be interchangeable. "It is our policy to increase services to the elderly by offering additional programs" is both a policy statement and an objective; it states an intent and specifies a means of achieving that intent.

Another distinction needs to be made between policies and strategies. Strategies usually refer to the deployment of the organization's resources. For example, a strategy to gain neighborhood support for a new service center would be to hire neighborhood residents as staff. Policies are larger in scope than strategies because they cover entire management processes.

Finally, operating procedures, rules, and regulations differ from policies. They all offer guidance and specify a course of action. The difference is a matter of degree. Operating procedures are commonly a series of steps to be followed, such as procedures for ordering supplies. Rules also describe a specific course of action but allow minimum flexibility. "Each department will order its own supplies from central purchasing" is a rule. Strategies, procedures, and rules are rarely a matter for board consideration.

Types of Policies

A look at Steiner's three types of policies—philosophical, resource development, and working—may help clarify what policies are. He includes ethical and moral policies in the first type, policies relative to the allocation of major resources in the second, and operational matters in the third group. Another way of grouping policies, according to Steiner, could be corporate, divisional, and departmental. Obviously, the latter grouping would not fit a small organization with a single program.

The chart that follows is adapted from Steiner's "Pyramid of Business Policies."[3]

Figure 1. Pyramid of Policies in Nonprofit Organizations

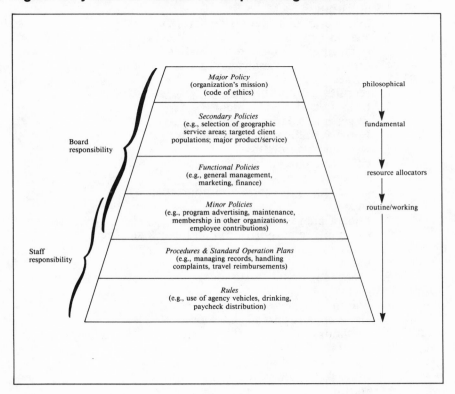

The pyramid structure illustrates the descending importance of types of policy decisions. The lower end of the pyramid encompasses operational concerns, while the top addresses priority policies affecting the purpose of the organization and the way it conducts its business. Note that the area of minor policies may, or may not, fall under the board's purview. Larger, more complex organizations tend to defer minor policy decisions to administrative staff. Smaller organizations' boards are more likely to make minor policy decisions.

Policies emerge from a number of functional areas. A board does not need to set policies for all the areas illustrated in the following outline. In fact, the principle of the fewest applies. Policies should be set only if they are clearly needed, can be stated without confusion, and are likely to have an impact on the achievement of the organization's goals. However, a board needs to be aware of these common areas for policy consideration.

Classification of Policy Areas[4]

    I. Administration
       1. managerial distinctions and responsibilities
       2. growth
       3. strategic planning and forecasting
       4. other (e.g., data management, evaluation)
    II. Personnel
       1. recruitment and hiring
       2. training and development
       3. wages and salaries
       4. Equal Employment Opportunity
       5. work environment
       6. collective bargaining
       7. fringe benefits
       8. other (e.g., grievances, reimbursements)
   III. Finance
       1. budget planning and control
       2. expenditure authorization and check signing
       3. capital assets
       4. audits
       5. other (e.g., loans, insurance)
   IV. Program
       1. planning
       2. size—expansion and outreach
       3. methods
       4. referrals
       5. quality control and evaluation
       6. other (e.g., safety, research)
    V. Marketing
       1. product/service
       2. pricing/service fees
       3. promotion/publicity
       4. place/distribution
       5. other (e.g., timing, client relations)
   VI. Facility
       1. location
       2. maintenance and repair
       3. other (e.g., expansion, subleasing)
  VII. Public Relations

1. internal/family
2. external/publics
3. other (e.g., affiliations, memberships)
VIII. Legal
1. contracts and agreements
2. licensing
3. other (e.g., bonding, compliance with regulations)

Setting Policy

Understanding the nature and purpose of policies is the first step in developing appropriate ones. If policies are to be designed to meet specific needs, then the best persons qualified to identify them are those with the most intimate knowledge of the organization—staff. It is highly appropriate for staff to make policy recommendations, and the need for a policy statement, and a subsequent directive, may emerge from any level in the organization. It is the job of the executive director to assess that need and to determine if it might be addressed under existing policy. The executive director should analyze the perceived policy need and decide if it deals with an issue that should be brought before the board of directors or if it can be appropriately addressed with a procedure or rule set by management. If a matter is to go to the board for policy consideration, the executive director should carry the recommendation to them.

While it is proper for a nonprofit board to receive policy recommendations from the organization's administrative staff, the board should be in control of policy-setting procedures. (The board advises staff on the format of policy presentations, the channels or committees to which policy recommendations should be submitted, timing, and so forth.) A board must not allow its responsibility for policy setting to be totally relegated. Karl Mathiasen wisely advises, "Whenever a board is engaged in review or revision of staff proposals, it must be careful not to give in to the temptation to change things just in order to have the feeling of doing something."[5] He also warns boards not to jump on the bandwagon to set policy on the basis of a few members' objections or suggestions. A quick response is inappropriate considering the time and energy that staff have put into a thoughtful proposal. A board that capitulates to such tendencies can undermine staff confidence and enthusiasm. Policy setting is a shared responsibility that demands a balance between staff and board influence.

The lines of authority for issuing different types of policies should be designated in some written document: the organization's bylaws, manual of operations, or board manual. Policies should be based on facts, not opinion. They should be comprehensive and stated in broad enough terms to encompass a number of situations and activities, present and potential. An organization should not require a new policy statement each time there is some new program development.

Policies should be clear in their intent. Coming up with the appropriate language to achieve the clarity necessary to an effective policy statement can be time consuming. However, it probably requires less time than might be spent on resolving some future dispute stemming from vaguely stated organizational policies.

In addition to structure, there is another important aspect to consider when setting policy—environment. A board must be alert to the changing political, social, and economic climates in the community where it has operations. It needs a comprehensive view of all these matters as they may have an impact on the organization. It is advisable for any board to seek the opinions and counsel of experts outside the organization when considering questions of major policy.

A board has an obligation to be accountable to its primary publics, such as funding sources and clients, but it also has a responsibility to consider the larger general public when making policy. For instance, a national research institute has a policy of not disclosing its list of donors. This policy was appropriate 10 or 20 years ago when the institute's primary donors were individuals, but its donor base has changed over the last five years to include more foundations, corporations, and government support. The development staff is handicapped by this outdated policy as they are unable to respond to the common request from corporate and foundation prospects who ask to see "who else" is supporting the institution. It seems somewhat suspect to reply "twenty local foundations, five national corporations and dozens of local companies." This policy is difficult to explain in a time when nonprofits' accountability to the public is an important issue, and competition for the charitable dollar is keen. Perhaps more important, such a policy can be misunderstood as inappropriate and deliberately secretive. The institution's board of directors is either unaware or unresponsive to the changes that have occurred, and are occurring, in the field of philanthropy.

Policies need to be in writing. A policy manual, in addition to an operations or procedures manual, is a good idea. The manual should be kept in the organization's administrative office and should be available for review by all management staff. The board needs to periodically review the organization's policies to determine which have become obsolete. When the board updates the organization's long-range plans, it is appropriate to review policies. The older a policy statement is, the greater the likelihood that it will be blindly accepted or, even worse, steer the organization in the wrong direction. Too often organizations fall into the trap of inexplicable behavior because "it's our policy." Strict adherence to policies out of step with the environment in which the organization operates can be disastrous. It is the board of directors' responsibility to see that this does not happen.

Policy Implementation

Responsibility for policy implementation, unlike policy setting, is subject to disagreement. Some of these varying viewpoints are cited below.

Brian O'Connell takes the position that in voluntary organizations, board and staff together establish policies, and the board, with the help of staff, carries it out.[6] Conrad and Glenn view policy as a circular process: Beginning with board and staff consideration of policy alternatives, policy decisions are made by the board; staff implements them; and monitoring is conducted by board and staff.[7] A well-respected Denver philanthropist, active on many profit and nonprofit boards, says it is the board's job to set policy and make certain that staff carry it out. Joseph Weber says staff have the responsibility for implementing policies adopted by the board, and the board should hold staff accountable for implementation.[8]

The majority of opinion favors staff dominance in policy implementation. When friction exists between a board and staff, it often stems from not understanding the differences between policy formulation and administration. Policy administration, according to management experts, is clearly an administrative task and, with rare exception, not an area for board involvement. It is in the nonprofit sector that some exceptions exist.

Board members who meddle in the day-to-day operations of an organization invite greater problems than just the annoyance they may be to professional staff. This practice diverts members from their more important responsibilities and hampers the efficient management of the organization by muddling its lines of authority. A primary exception would be the administrative type of board that manages all the organization's activities when there is no staff. The case of a youth employment center in Seattle provides another exception. It is the policy of this organization to provide employment training, counseling, and job placement for underprivileged youth. Its staff provides training and counseling; board members actively solicit jobs for the youths.

The exception in the first instance is obvious. The exception of board implementing policy in the second case involves a different set of circumstances. The staff and board members have jointly come to an agreement that board members will participate in this aspect of policy implementation. Also, this board has another policy to limit the size of the organization. This latter policy in fact mandates the other; with a staff of three and an ambitious caseload, it would be difficult for the organization to achieve its goal without direct board participation in some areas of operation.

Acknowledging that there are situations where members of a non-profit board may properly be involved in policy implementation, organizations should otherwise adhere to the major case rule: board and staff formulate policies, board sets policies, staff implements policies, and board and staff evaluate the results. This partnership is not only proper but most likely to result in efficient operations. As in all management areas, clear lines of responsibility enable the worker, staff member, or volunteer, to focus his or her energies and maximize achievement.

THE NATURE OF PLANNING

Planning has been defined as a rational and systematic deter-mination of where you presently stand, where you hope to be, and how you will get to that point. Objectives are set and resources are allocated to support the activities that will take you to that desired place. It is a process that concerns itself with the future impact of decisions made in the present.

Peter Drucker feels that the notion of planning rests on a number of misconceptions. The time span is not the determinant of short-range or long-range planning. A plan is not short-range because it takes only a few months to implement. Rather, he says, the important consideration is the time span over which it is effective. Long-range planning answers the question, "What should our business be?" and prevents an organization from assuming today's services and markets will be those of the future. However, management experts say that skills are needed in strategic planning rather than in long-range plan-ning. Managers often have difficulty distinguishing between long-range and strategic planning and claim the difference to be one of semantics. Drucker says it is important to note what strategic plan-ning is not before looking at what it is.

1. *It is not a box of tricks, a bundle of techniques.* It is analytical thinking and commitment of resources to action....Model building or simulation may be helpful, but they are not strategic planning; they are tools for specific purposes and may or may not apply in a given case....

2. *Strategic planning is not forecasting.* It is not masterminding the future. Any attempt to do so is foolish; the future is unpredictable. We can only discredit what we are doing by attempting it....

3. *Strategic planning does not deal with future decisions. It deals with the futurity of present decisions.*...The question that faces the strategic decision-maker is not what his organization should do tomorrow. It is, "What do we have to do today to be ready for an uncertain tomorrow?" The question is..."What futurity do we have

to build into our present thinking and doing, what time spans do we have to consider, and how do we use this information to make a rational decision now?"

4. *Strategic planning is not an attempt to eliminate risk.*...The end result of successful strategic planning must be capacity to take a greater risk....To extend this capacity, however, we must be able to choose rationally among risk-taking courses of action....[9]

For a definition of what strategic planning is, we turn again to Drucker. "It is the continuous process of making present entrepreneurial (risk-taking) decisions systematically and with the greatest knowledge of their futurity; organizing systematically the efforts needed to carry out these decisions; and measuring the results of these decisions against the expectations through organized, systematic feedback."[10]

While strategic planning focuses on the organization as a whole, there are other levels of planning: program planning, budgeting, operations planning. These specific levels deal with individual responsibilities, resource allocation, and control. They respond to such questions as: What programs and projects should be considered? Which of these programs and projects best reflect the organization's uniqueness (to give it a competitive edge)? How shall funds be spent on programs? What short-term activities should be employed to move the organization closer to its goals? Who should do what? Who should be responsible for motivating and controlling behaviors?

Strategic planning, if it is to be effective, must incorporate all these levels of planning. These levels also need to be mutually supportive and reinforcing.

Characteristics of Planning

Several features set planning apart from other managerial tasks. Planning needs to be a creative process that draws on both the present and the past of an organization. It is futuristic in that it involves a shared vision of what the organization wants to be and deals with future consequences. According to George Steiner, it is characterized by its simplicity, comprehensiveness, major import, confidentiality, and qualitativeness. A plan needs to be rational and flexible, in writing, and formally prepared.[11]

Conceptually, planning is philosophically based and arises from three main premises: the values of top management, societal expectations of the organization or its socio-economic environment, and data from the organization's environment. Planning deals with a broad spectrum of alternatives; it deals with an entire organization; and it requires large amounts of information.

Essentially, strategic planning is a decision-making tool. It allows a manager to evaluate alternatives and to look at the total organizational picture; it forces specific objectives to be set and boosts other management functions such as evaluation and resource control.[12] Strategic planning deals with anything relevant to the success of an organization.

Resistance to Planning

If planning is good for an organization, if in today's world it may be synonymous with survival, why does there remain a resistance to planning? A primary antiplanning bias lies with one's natural desire to avoid uncertainties, and strategic planning deals with uncertainties. As a result of planning, personal relationships may change; decision makers and the whole power structure of an organization may change. Strategic planning requires risk-taking that can result in either success or failure. Some executive directors have learned from experience that planning is also threatening because it can expose conflicts between departments in the organization or between staff and the board of directors; it places new demands on a manager and is reminiscent of childhood authority conflicts.[13]

In *Corporate Planning for Nonprofit Organizations,* Dr. James H. Hardy attributes this resistance to planning by nonprofit organizations to four causes.

1. The view that business techniques cannot be applied to the nonprofit organization. Most planning theory and practices have emerged from business experience. Its applicability to organizations without a profit motive is therefore suspect.

2. Day-to-day crises require the constant attention of the nonprofit executive and leave little remaining time for planning. This is a real problem, but it is far more important for an executive to have the planning framework of goals, objectives, and strategies as a basis for his or her decisions.

3. Attempts to adopt and implement other (corporate) organizations' planning models have failed to meet the nonprofits' expectations. Preoccupation with procedures and a mechanical adoption of some "best system" is an inappropriate emphasis. The focus needs to be on conceptualization and adaptation.

4. Action-oriented individuals, common among nonprofit organizations, whose pleasure stems from *doing* things, find the intellectual processes of strategic planning frustrating. Thinking into the future is not only difficult but evokes all those uncertainties one tries to avoid.

People also avoid planning because it requires a more intensive commitment, an ability to plan, and the resolution to implement the plan. It also takes a certain amount of paperwork.

To overcome these existing biases toward planning and to gain the cooperation of everyone in an organization, an executive director must first of all be alert to resistance. For the organization not presently involved in planning, new systems must be introduced slowly to minimize these powerful resistance factors.

Benefits of Planning

Organizations that do not plan incur "opportunity costs"—an economic term that refers to the value of those alternatives that are surrendered when a choice is made. For example, if an organization chooses to drop a program popular with its clients in favor of another program that can generate revenues, a decrease in client support may result. The potential loss of client support over the long term is an alternative that needs to be considered. The value of this loss is an opportunity cost.

Strategic planning integrates all an organization's "blocks."

Strategic planning minimizes any disparity between an organization's potential achievements and what it actually achieves. One result of good planning is that it identifies organizational weaknesses and replaces those weaknesses by identifying opportunities for success in other areas. Another benefit is that planning gives an organization's decision makers a chance to evaluate the risks of alternative strategies.[14] Boards that use strategic planning methods are able to more easily identify opportunity costs.

Planning is necessarily comprehensive because it integrates the various parts of an organization. It is the common bond between components of an organization and accordingly enhances the awareness of the interrelationships between those parts. "Good planning does not staple together the plans of the departments or divisions within an organization; rather, it weaves a fabric that should be stronger than a simple collection of individual plans. As such, it should provide a balanced approach to the organization's future in which the parts of the organization increasingly seek to fit their activities more effectively into the larger pattern portrayed by the overall plan and its underlying assumptions and premises."[15]

In summary, the benefits of planning are that it:

- not only provides direction, but also keeps everyone going on the same track
- gives a framework for decision making and limits randomly made decisions
- clarifies the organization's mission, goals and objectives, programs and services
- forces communication
- enhances the consistency of present strategies and decisions with the changing (future) environment
- offers a more coordinated effort
- helps an organization become "proactive" rather than reactive
- maximizes the cost-effective allocation of limited resources
- emphasizes alternatives and tradeoffs
- is results oriented
- provides for evaluation measures through action-stated objectives
- is useful in fund raising because its various components can be included in proposals
- helps attract community support—people respect an organization with a plan.

How-To's of Planning

The planning process needs to be highly structured because it is a rigorous exercise that demands a commitment from all levels of the organization. Who is involved, the environment and location where planning is to take place, the background information needed, and the expectations of those involved are all critical considerations. Such planning process strategies are the responsibility of the organization's top leadership and should never be delegated below the level of the executive director and chairperson or president of the board of directors.

The planning process involves several systematic steps as outlined below, but these steps may vary depending on an organization's previous planning experience.

1. The executive director and board chairperson or president should select the planning committee. Five to eight people is a comfortable working group, although larger organizations with more department heads to be represented may include 10 to 12 people.

The executive director and board head must sit on this committee and key management staff who report directly to the executive director may be included. The board's executive committee may be a part of this team, plus other board members with strong planning skills. Some organizations include an outside consultant or specialist to act as facilitator and guide to the process. Facilitators do not offer opinions on the planning content.

2. Elect a chairperson for the committee and a secretary who will record the planning process and outcomes; assign responsibility for arranging meeting times and places and for notifying committee members of meetings.

3. Try to find a meeting site away from the organization but avoid mountain cabins or other resort settings where there are too many distractions. Some have recommended a windowless room but that could be claustrophobic. Wherever you hold your sessions, it should be comfortable and roomy and offer enough wall space for hanging flip chart sheets. Avoid classroom-type seating arrangements.

Plan on spending one full day, if not two, on working out a first draft of your organization's plan. (An organization with limited or no previous planning experience will require more time.) Follow-up sessions may require half-days spaced one or two weeks apart. However, it is best not to drag out the planning process any longer than necessary to do a thorough job.

4. An agenda prepared by the executive director, board head, and planning committee chairperson should be sent to all committee members in advance. They need to know what is to be discussed and what they are expected to contribute.

5. An organization's experience in strategic planning or the existence of a plan that requires a review or update will dictate the amount of data collection and fact finding that must be done before the actual planning sessions begin. Usually the executive director and key staff are responsible for gathering the necessary background materials.

6. The key questions to be asked and subsequently addressed in a plan include: Who are the organization's constituents and who will they be in 5 to 10 years? What are the primary needs of these constituents now and in the future? What is the organization's mission and purpose? What assumptions can be made about the future? What are the organization's priorities today and what should they be in 5 and 10 years? What are the organization's strengths and weaknesses? What are the organization's key result areas—areas where ineffectiveness or failure would jeopardize the organization? (Key result areas may be, for example, program service, board performance, staff performance, financial management, or public relations.) What levels of performance—objectives—are required? What approaches or strategies should be employed to achieve organizational objectives? What funds are needed to support the plan? Who are to be the primary implementers?

All plans need to be linked to some time frame to facilitate measuring accomplishments. However, the time frame should be geared to the happening of events rather than inflexible deadlines.

7. Once a first draft of the plan is prepared, it is taken to the full board and other key staff for comment.

8. Follow-up committee sessions may require rewrites of the plan to accommodate other board and staff input or merely a final polishing.

9. The final plan goes to the full board of directors for approval.

10. The executive director may call a special staff meeting to communicate the results of the planning process and, of course, share the plan with all staff.

Members of the planning committee should decide which key constituents (e.g., funders, referral agencies, United Way) should be informed of the planning outcomes. (Two organizations' planning documents, with very different formats, are in the Appendix.)

One Agency's Planning Experience

Recently I was asked to assist a city's Division of Human Resources in writing its strategic plan. The planning task force chairperson was responsible for putting together the goals and objectives, projected outcomes, priorities, and financial recommendations that had emerged from each division agency. The accumulated data were in no particular order, and the comprehensiveness and clarity of the material submitted varied a great deal from agency to agency. In essence, there was a pile of data that had to be sorted and put into some kind of meaningful format. The chairperson felt she needed some assistance in formulating the mess.

The planning process of this two-year-old agency is of particular importance because it illustrates a strong commitment from staff. Planning in a private nonprofit agency involves the board of directors and staff, but as we see here, public agency planning lacks board of director involvement.

The division's planning process began in October 1983 and was conducted in four phases over a period of 11 months.

Phase 1—*Brainstorming:* The division manager called a three-day retreat of supervisory staff in October 1983. Participants were given an "overview action plan" beforehand to guide their discussion at the retreat. Their charge was to draft a statement of the division's mission and goals. By the end of the second day, this group had come up with nine broad goals, each of which contained sub-objectives and some of which included an action plan outline.

Program representatives, clerical through supervisory level, joined the retreat group on its third day to discuss and question the division goals the supervisors had outlined. Participants left the retreat with copies of the tentative goals to review on their own time.

Phase 2—*Review of Goals:* While the division's goals were being reviewed by staff, the division manager appointed a four-member task force to review and consolidate the work of the retreat.

Phase 3—*Analysis:* Incorporating staff comments, the task force prepared a draft plan. It took three meetings to do this. The task force circulated this draft among all division staff.

In late February 1984, four subcommittees that included all division staff were formed by the task force. Each subcommittee was assigned one or two of the goals with its objectives. They were to prepare action steps, consider implementation dates, project completion dates, assign responsibility for implementation, and consider required resources. An action plan format was provided to the subcommittees to facilitate and direct their work.

Phase 4—*Formulation:* The task force reviewed the committees' work and brainstormed various means for compressing their labors into a single document. The task force felt the final product should include an abstract, narrative, and implementation strategies.

The division manager appointed the task force chairperson to weave together the goals and objectives, projected outcomes, priorities, and financial recommendations. The chairperson was allowed to use other outside available resource persons, if desired, in writing this final product. A target date of August 15, 1984, was set for completion of the division's planning document.

The time required for this agency's planning process was far too long. Most organizations couldn't sustain an interest in a process that dragged on for nearly a year. Surprisingly, this agency was able to maintain the enthusiasm of all participants from start to finish. Perhaps it was because they were new at planning; perhaps it was because everyone was made to feel his or her ideas were important;

perhaps it was due to an enthusiastic leadership; or perhaps the wheels of public agencies are just expected to turn more slowly.

Implementation and Evaluation

Peter Drucker advises us that "the best plan is only a plan, that is, good intentions, unless it *degenerates into work.*"[16] One can have a good planning process and the resulting plan may also be excellent, but there must be a prescription for implementation. If a plan is to produce desired results, key people must be committed to work on specific objectives. This implies that there is someone available to implement tasks and activities, who has a time frame for achieving objectives, and who is accountable. The control or management of the plan is the responsibility of the executive director of an organization.

If objectives are written with action-oriented words, then they are measurable. If a plan's objectives are measurable, then a way to evaluate them is clearly stated. For example, if an organization's program objective is to reduce the rate of juvenile recidivism (rearrests) by a certain percentage within a given time frame, then an evaluation of this objective would involve determining the new rate of recidivism (compared to a baseline rate) at the end of that stated time frame. Just as it is worthless to create a plan that is never acted on, it is equally useless to have a plan that does not allow for evaluation. One must be able to gauge the results. The executive director is also responsible for the evaluation of the organization's plan, and it is the board's function to request progress reports.

Conclusion

In *Management of Public Sector and Nonprofit Organizations,* Curtis J. Tompkins says the number of nonprofit organizations participating in strategic planning in the 1980s will be significant. He attributes this prediction to four prime factors: his firsthand observations; a push from volunteer board members who are engaged in their own corporation's planning; increased professionalism among nonprofit managers who have been educated on the need to plan; and technical advances that facilitate the planning process and retrieval of information.

The survey of the boards of directors of Colorado's nonprofit organizations conducted in November 1984 showed that 77.4 percent of the respondents have an organizational plan and 26.8 percent of those plan for a four- to five-year period. In metropolitan areas with a population over one million, 62.6 percent of the nonprofit organizations have an organizational plan compared to 19 percent of the non-profits in small communities (population under 25,000); "big-city" nonprofits are much more inclined to plan. The survey also showed that only 23.3 percent of small organizations (by budget under $50,000) have a plan and that these organizations more frequently plan for only one year at a time.[17]

Despite the evidence that planning is increasingly appealing to a greater number of nonprofit organizations, there remain misgivings about the planning process itself. The steps outlined in this chapter can help to demystify the strategic planning process.

SUMMARY

Policies characteristically are those guides to whatever actions an organization must take to meets its goals and objectives over time. Major or philosophical policies, secondary policies addressing the fundamental programs of an organization, and functional policies regarding resource allocation are all a board's responsibility. In setting policies, a board needs to take into account the recommendations of staff, those of the organization's publics, and the broader general public. On the one hand, a board is responsible for creating policies, putting them in writing, and periodically reviewing them. On the other hand, staff is responsible for implementing policies set by the board.

Today's nonprofit organization should be engaged in strategic planning. Some important benefits of planning are that it gives focus and direction to an organization, limits random decision making, forces an organization into a more cost-effective mode, and helps bond the various components of an organization together. A board planning committee and the executive director should formulate the organization's plan. Staff implements plans, the executive director is responsible for evaluating plans, and it is the board's role to call for an evaluation report on a plan's effectiveness.

NOTES

1. Higginson (1966) as cited in George Steiner, *Top Management Planning.*

2. George Steiner, *Top Management Planning,* Chapter 10.

3. Ibid.

4. This table is adapted from Steiner's "Classification of Business Policy Areas" in *Top Management Planning,* Chapter 6. The major headings (I through VIII) are those areas covered by functional policies. The subheadings

are areas that come under the category of minor policies. A board should be concerned with the major areas.

5. Karl Mathiasen (source and date unknown).

6. Brian O'Connell, *Effective Leadership in Voluntary Organizations,* Chapter 25, p. 7. O'Connell takes this position a step further in stating, "Staff exists to help the volunteer do the work of the organization. The greatest sinner is often the president who far too often gives over responsibility to the executive director....Staff is hired to assist the volunteers to do their citizen jobs in fulfillment of the voluntary agency's mission."

7. William R. Conrad and William R. Glenn, *The Effective Voluntary Board of Directors,* Chapter 6.

8. Joseph Weber, "Managing the Board of Directors" (Pamphlet by the Greater New York Fund, 1975).

9. Peter F. Drucker, *Management: Tasks, Responsibilities, Practices,* p. 125.

10. Ibid.

11. Steiner, *Top Management Planning,* Chapter 1.

12. George Steiner, *Strategic Planning,* Part I.

13. Ibid.

14. Leslie E. Grayson and Curtis J. Tompkins, *Management of Public Sector and Nonprofit Organizations,* p. 140–48.

15. Ibid., p. 144.

16. Drucker, *Management: Tasks, Responsibilities, Practices,* p. 128.

17. Diane J. Duca, "Survey Report on Colorado's Nonprofit Boards of Directors" (Paper written for the University of Colorado/Denver, Graduate School of Public Affairs, Denver, May 1985).

Chapter 4
Recruiting and Sustaining Board Membership

RECRUITMENT OF NEW BOARD MEMBERS

Successful programs and organizations are often those with powerful people behind the scene. The advantages of a skilled management staff go without saying. However, it is an organization's board of directors, composed of people with financial resources or contacts and power, that can make a difference. Perhaps 20 years ago, when many newly organized agencies (particularly social services) were more like an extension of government, board composition and participation were less critical to an organization's survival. Today, success goes with those organizations whose board leadership is not only competent but also actively involved in the organization's affairs.

Two vital ingredients of a strong and powerful board are the selection of good people and their thorough education about the organization. While it is true that well-selected volunteers can be wasted if they are not properly motivated or educated, no amount of orientation can make an outstanding board from a group of poorly or inappropriately selected people.

Commitment, time, personal wealth or access to money, knowledge of the organization's field of endeavors, previous board experience, contacts, management expertise, leadership skills, and caring—these are all attributes that have been described as desirable traits of a board member. However, agreeing on what makes a good board member and choosing the board of directors for your nonprofit organization puts a great strain on anyone confronted with the task. You can't get too analytical about a formula that pretends to be a guide to effective trustee selection, as there is no standard formula that can replace the experience and good judgment such decisions require.

The Need for New Types of Board Members

An organization's need for different board expertise will change as the organization goes through various developmental cycles. An organization without full-time staff may need its board members to be hands-on managers. A new organization has a greater need for members' time, for experienced nonprofit board members, for organizational skills, for those with enough vision to see beyond the immediacy of start-up operations, for members with an extensive and wide range of community contacts, and for those with a deep commitment to the organization's cause. These needs never diminish but they are more apparent in an organization's embryonic stage.

An established institution embarking on a major physical plant expansion project may not have previously had a need for large grants; an organization expanding its program into new geographical locations will require contacts and knowledge of those new communities or neighborhoods; an agency facing major budget cuts in government support may need to develop new sources of financing or to curtail its programs. Each of these situations will demand a different level of board support and participation and may also require a different kind of board member. Short-term crises are the responsibility of an existing board, whereas planned changes in an organization's direction may involve recruiting new board members with different experiences and expertise. No one model of board composition can meet the changing needs of an organization. Sometimes it is difficult for an organization to recognize when membership changes are called for and to what extent changes need to be made. Making a clean sweep is a peril that should be avoided. The ideal situation is to enhance or change a board's membership without sacrificing the continuity and historical knowledge that old members bring to a situation.

Problems of Inappropriate Recruitment

Far too many nonprofit organizations pass out board memberships as a reward for those who have done a good deed for the organization; to friends of present members because they are nice folks (with little regard about what they have to offer the organization); and to anyone who says yes. Rather than searching out qualified nominees, it is easy to allow current board members to ask their friends to join the board. Of course, it is a plus to have congenial members, and it is fine if your board members' friends and colleagues have the talents your organization needs. Unfortunately, this type of recruitment can become inbred, and suddenly a board may contain people who all think the same way.

Sometimes, in an attempt to gain powerful and influential people, organizations may fail to create a board that is diverse in its representation of sex, race, religion, age, occupation, geographic locale, etc. Diversity for diversity's sake is not a worthy goal, but representatives from diverse groups bring breadth and greater depth of support to an organization.

Beware of the pitfalls in filling your board with (unwilling) specialists. For example, as a professional fund-raising consultant, I am not interested in sitting on a board's fund-raising committee. I request assignments on program, public relations, planning, or nominating committees—anything but more fund raising. It is a rare person who wants more of the same outside office hours. A colleague of mine who once had the responsibility of making appointments to various city commissions said he would not ask a doctor to serve on the Health and Hospitals Board for that very reason. Rather, he would appoint doctors to a commission such as Parks and Recreation, where they proved more willing to lend their energies and talents to a different type of activity.

Yet another kind of problem can arise with a board comprising reluctant or uninvolved experts. A foundation director once told me his foundation turned down an organization's grant request because its budget included large legal fees when the organization had three attorneys on its board. This foundation's trustees were of the opinion that the organization did not show wise use of its available resources. Unfortunately, the organization did not have a chance to explain its situation, and it probably was not even aware of the problem its board composition had created.

As a public charity or nonprofit agency your organization is subject to public scrutiny. If outside expertise is hired and is also present on your board of directors or staff, be prepared to counter with a rationale for this action. On the one hand, while your organization may have a perfectly logical and sound explanation, it may not appear so to those outside your organization. On the other hand, your organization may need to take a closer look at whether the talents and experiences represented on your board of directors are being used appropriately.

Organizations should not totally overlook recruiting particular skills or professionals for their boards of directors. All boards should have, for example, an attorney and an accountant, unless the organization is large enough to have these professionals on staff. The important point to remember is that professional expertise on a board is only valuable when the organization can freely call upon it. The pitfalls of a board filled with professionals unwilling to practice their expertise on your agency's behalf can be reduced with careful recruitment and screening procedures.

Clearly identifying what your organization needs from its board of directors is not an easy task. Recruiting to support the organization's true needs, taking time to cultivate prospective members, and detailing in advance what you expect of the full board, and the individual nominee in particular, are important steps to building an effective board. If these steps are followed in board recruitment, an organization is less likely to suffer the syndrome of disinterested or ill-suited experts.

Qualifications

The makings of a good board member begin with certain intangible personal characteristics to which I added some more tangible criteria. Personal qualifications have to do with how an individual behaves in a group setting. Some outstanding achievers may not be able to function in a democratic environment (which we presume a board to be), where all opinions are weighed equally, and decisions are made by the group. Tact and diplomacy and the ability to work with a diverse group of people are important. A degree of assertiveness is necessary in soliciting support from the community. You want people with integrity—people who when they say yes can be trusted to follow through. Likewise, you need those who can say no despite peer pressure or in the face of criticism.

Other traits of a good board member are more easily recognized. An interest in your organization's field is essential. It is not realistic to expect to convince someone to care about your organization unless he or she has a prior and genuine concern regarding the nature of your work or services. For example, someone may express an interest in your symphony's board of trustees because it is something he or she feels the need to support, or because it is a status-related position; yet, this person may not be a music lover and, perhaps, may never have attended a concert. Interest in a field would be evidenced by prior attendance or participation with your organization or a related one. You will be able to sell your organization over another if a potential board member has a bona fide interest in your field.

Time is obviously another factor of considerable importance. You have to take a person's word for willingness to give time. However, in order to assess the prospect's potential availability, look at whether the individual is in charge of his or her own time professionally and if he or she appears to be overly committed to other organizations. Avoid overcommitted people and those who would have difficulty taking off work to attend meetings. Steer clear of the individual already serving on four or five boards—time commitment could be a problem in these cases. However, there is always the exception.

A doctor friend of mine, in one year, served on 11 nonprofit boards, served as an officer for five of them, was active with all, and attended as many of their meetings as was humanly possible! I asked him about the inevitable time conflicts, and he said there are actually two major potential conflicts in serving on several boards—time and fund raising. "I'm an officer of enough organizations to have a say in setting meeting times. Where I don't have a say and a conflict occurs, I attend those meetings where I feel I'm most needed. Sometimes I attend two meetings in an evening. I'll look at the agendas and try to attend the most pertinent parts of each meeting. In fund raising, I try to work with different populations for different organizations and use different approaches." I have always heard that the best board members are the busiest and wondered if such busy people are simply oddities or part of a group of individuals with an extraordinary talent for organizing their time and who have a very big heart. My friend is both, but as he put it, "a bit of craziness is also helpful."

New members should bring to the board some skill or experience that will make them a contributing member.

An interest and willingness to do some particular job or to serve on some committee or in a leadership capacity, and the ability to do so, are essential qualifications for a board member. Each new member should bring to the board some skill or experience that will make him or her a contributing member. Members should also have a community point of view—an awareness of what is going on in the community, or at least in the neighborhood, in order to interpret how the organization fits into the broader scheme of things.

If some mythical board were made up of all millionaires, chief executives of *Fortune 500* companies, and the crème de la crème of a community's social set, it could probably still be improved. Power, money, and influence are a matter of potential for an organization only if those individuals use their strengths on behalf of the organization. So it would seem that even the best of boards might stand improvement until such time as all its members are giving to their full potential.

The Recruiting Process

Where one begins searching for good board members is the big question. Aside from any specific criteria an organization may have for its board's composition, the following are some general guidelines that can assist your search.

1. Try to get people who have demonstrated their ability to get things done. Pay attention to effective members of other boards of organizations similar to yours. However, be aware that those people might already be overcommitted. If someone does a good job for another organization there is no guarantee he or she will do the same for you, although the potential is there. Cultivate an interest in your cause among those proven "movers" and be prepared to wait until they have the time to give to your organization. Keep a list of future prospects and keep after them. A mover is worth waiting for.

One of my client organizations was very proud to have on its otherwise noninfluential board one member who was connected to a wealthy and distinguished old Denver family and who was also one of those movers. This lady had four fields of interest and served on four nonprofit boards representing those interests. Unfortunately, my client was number four in this person's ranking of interests. She limited her participation and use of her contacts to one specific task each year—that of the organization's annual fund-raising dinner. Nonetheless, her ability to get things done on behalf of the organization's annual dinner was worthwhile.

2. Look around for the bright young people in town and try to interest them in your organization before they become too busy. Read the business section of newspapers and note newly appointed execu-

tives from out of state. Notice companies bringing in management staff from out-of-state corporate headquarters. Be aware of new members of any leadership training programs that may be offered by your local chamber of commerce, downtown improvement association, or similar influential associations in your town. If your organization is affiliated with a national organization (for example, the Boys Club of Denver is a member of Boys Clubs of America), ask other affiliated organizations to alert you when one of their good board members moves to your city.

3. Look for men and women who are presently vice-presidents or middle management. Among these people will be future chief executives and policy setters. Read the business section of newspapers for promotion announcements.

4. Look at companies whose employees are known to be active in community affairs; companies where participation in the community is considered in an employee's evaluation. Also, many corporations restrict their corporate gifts to organizations in which their employees are involved. However, the potential financial support of some corporation is not sufficient reason to solicit employees for board membership. You should have a valid need for the talents they may have to offer. When you go to a corporate community affairs officer for assistance in identifying a prospective board member, be able to specify your organization's needs.

5. Look at the heads of successful small companies, but with a note of caution. If you solicit and recruit successful businesspersons just because they are that, you can't realistically expect the same levels of commitment and involvement they give to their own businesses for two reasons: First, they own their companies and do not feel that same sense of ownership with any other organization. Second, being a volunteer board member will most likely be an avocation. Substitute measures need to be developed for getting such businesspersons involved.

6. Consider using powerful and influential people to recruit power. There are probably many key people in your community who are interested in your organization's work but are too busy to serve on your board. Don't be afraid to go to these people, even if no one in your organization knows them personally, to ask for recommendations and recruitment assistance. They may offer to lend their name to help open doors, or better yet, they may agree to actually call on a colleague on your behalf. Or, they may say no. You won't know unless you ask. Aggressive recruiting pays off. Don't allow your organization's present and perhaps limited sphere of influence to limit your opportunity to get to the resources you need.

Several years ago, when I was executive director of the Girls Club of Denver, Inc., I had a board that talked about its desire for influential members but never did anything about it. It became my problem. One night as I was watching the news on TV, the station's president came on with a commentary. It occurred to me that this was a well-respected man with considerable influence in our city. The next day I decided to call him for an appointment to discuss our board's needs. After giving my most enthusiastic pitch about our agency, I sat back waiting for the expected "no," ready to continue with my real mission to secure referrals to other people of power. He said, "Yes, I'd be delighted to serve on your board." At that point, I mumbled something like "thanks" and fled. So, be prepared for the unexpected yes.

Before recruiting members for your board, it is wise to have your organizational house in order. To attract the high-caliber board members your organization desires, it is critical to have your organization's mission, goals, and objectives clearly stated; your program priorities defined; your budget in balance; and a strategic plan for achieving these things. It is pretty difficult to ask someone to support your cause when you are not really sure what that cause is. If your organization is in deep financial trouble, you may or may not be able to successfully recruit high-quality board members. Some may want to lend their leadership to such a situation as they enjoy a challenge—most others would not. Successful people want to be attached to successful organizations. Before you invite a prospective board member to observe one of your board meetings, consider what your meetings are like. Are they well organized, brief, and productive? Do they follow the agenda? Or, do members straggle in late, wander from the agenda, bicker over small points, and carry on for hours? Despite an interest in your organization, a prospect's interest can be dampened at an introductory board meeting if he or she is bored or witness to a disruptive or ineffective meeting.

The process of recruiting board members should not wait until a month before the organization's annual meeting. It takes time to cultivate desired prospects. Any worthy prospect will also need time to come to a decision about joining your organization's board of directors. Some kind of systematic recruitment procedures are necessary to effectively and efficiently fill board vacancies.

First, a nominating committee should pull together a profile of the board's current membership. In analyzing the board's composition, one would not only look at the demographic characteristics of board members (age, sex, ethnic group, education, income, etc.), but also at the skills members willingly apply and the areas in which they willingly give their time. For example, does the CPA help interpret the organization's financial statements? Are there members willing to work on employees' compensation packages? Such a profile should help to pinpoint strengths and weaknesses. If all the organization's present needs are adequately covered, then the committee should ask themselves if any new category should be considered in light of the organization's long-range plans. The important point is that there be some type of summary of organizational and board needs to guide the selection process.

Second, specific designations should be made regarding who is to be recruited to fill any gaps revealed by the analysis. Names may be drawn from the file of prospects that the organization maintains; recommendations should also come from current and past board members, from the organization's staff, perhaps from program volunteers, and from others in the community. Have at least two or three people in mind for any designation whenever possible, but place priorities on your prospects and go after the prospect who is most likely to say yes when the board position is offered.

Third, find out all you can about your prospects. If you are pulling names from a board prospect file, the prospect's background will be on file, and you will simply need an update. Talk to friends and colleagues of the prospect; talk to his or her employer, if applicable; talk to the board members or staff of another organization where that person has volunteered. Let these people know that you are considering the individual for board membership—they will appreciate the fact that your organization cares enough to carefully select prospective board candidates.

Fourth, evaluate designated prospects on the basis of their potential to contribute to the short- and long-term goals of your organization. List what you feel the prospect can do for your board of directors and what the organization and board might do for the prospective new member. This helps avoid tokenism as the selection of all board members should be validly linked to the needs of your organization and board. Consider also if the prospect has any conflicting business or voluntary affiliations. Another point for the nominating committee to look at in evaluating prospects is the individual's contribution to some desired board balance.

Fifth, put together a plan for cultivation and recruitment based on what you know about a prospect. Select the most appropriate person to approach the prospect, and if he or she is not a member of the nominating committee, a committee member should go along on the interview. Decide when and where to meet with the prospect and what information you'll discuss at your first encounter.

Sixth, plan a personal contact with the prospect. Your initial contact may be very informal—cocktails or a round of golf or tennis—where mention of your organization would be brief. You may invite the prospect to visit your agency to witness your program in action. The type of contact will depend on the prospect and the degree of cultivation the nominating committee feels is required. Most likely, you will meet with a prospect in his or her office, say that your organization is considering placing his or her name in nomination for board membership, and present basic information about your organization. If this is the case, then certain points should be covered during the interview:

- What the organization does (How the organization does it is a topic for board orientation);
- Whom the organization serves and where services are provided and offered;
- The role of the board volunteer;
- The role of staff;
- Realistic time requirements. (Include estimates not only for board and committee meetings but also for other board functions like training, special meetings, fund raising, etc. If you have in mind that this prospect will take on a leadership role, such as chairing a committee or being an officer of the board, then more time would be required of him or her. It is a real mistake to tell a prospect that membership on your board won't take much time.)

Your first contact is intended to be an overview—an opportunity to let the prospect consider board membership and an opportunity for you to assess his or her interest in your organization. Don't let this interview drag on. Thirty to forty-five minutes is ample time to tell your story and define your board's needs. If this interview runs longer, it should be because the prospect initiates many questions.

Depending on the responsiveness of the prospect, you may ask about his or her interest in becoming a nominee at this first meeting, or further cultivation may be indicated. All interested prospects should receive a kit of materials on your organization, which include current annual report, program brochures, board and staff rosters, budget, statement of purpose, goals and objectives, board members' job descriptions, list of board committees, and job descriptions for each committee. An invitation to tour the agency and attend a board or committee meeting should also be extended to the prospect.

The seventh step is to discuss with the prospect his or her committee interests. Be direct in explaining your expectations. After all, you are recruiting this prospect based on some gap you hope he or she will agree to fill. If you have somehow misjudged this person's interests despite your careful background research or if he or she expresses a reluctance to give time to the area where needed, it is wise to tell the prospect you'll hold his or her nomination until such time as there is an opening or need in the area or field of his or her interest. It does not benefit your organization to add a new board member who, for example, prefers working with your program committee when your finance committee is in dire need of a boost. However, if your program committee or some other committee relative to the prospect's interests has a valid need for additional expertise, that is a different matter. It is not easy to refuse an interested prospect especially when energies have been spent on cultivating him or her. You could avoid this awkward situation by discovering the prospect's committee interests earlier in the recruitment process, if appropriate. Use your best judgment, but remember that the strengthening of your board of directors and, ultimately, the success of your organization are at stake.

Finally, a letter thanking the prospect for his or her time and consideration should be sent even if the prospect declines. Thank you's should also be sent to all who have participated in the recruitment process, as well as to the person or persons who recommended the prospect.

Recruiting Examples

The Maricopa Camp Fire Council, Inc. (Phoenix, AZ), has established general criteria for board membership based on its desire to achieve a balance in three areas: term of office—(to accommodate members' rotating terms); geographic representation from all the counties served by the council; and profession or occupation. The nominating committee of five members includes council board members and one or two individuals who are members of the organization but are not on the board. The committee makes recommendations on prospective members, reviews past and present prospects, and then assesses each prospect based on the priority to achieve or maintain the prescribed board balance.

The nominating committee has devised several worksheets to help with this nominating and screening process. One worksheet maps out 16 occupational categories (banking, accounting, private business, insurance, etc.) and provides space for listing the present members per category and their remaining years of board service. For example, if no banking experience is represented on the board, or if there is a banker with a one-year term remaining, an effort may be made to recruit from that profession. Another worksheet is used by board members to recommend nominees and provide background information about each prospect. (See sample worksheet in Appendix.) The nominating committee makes the first contact with a prospective board member and usually makes the "sale." The prospect is given a *Board of Directors Position Description* and other information on Camp Fire. (See sample description in Appendix.) The agency's executive director says the nominating committee's recruitment procedures have changed the quality of the board for the better. She pointed out one problem that can occur when nonboard members are used in recruiting. A prospect who says yes to board membership is most often responding to the individual recruiter. If that recruiter does not sit on the board, there may be no one to encourage (on a personal level) the new person's participation in board activities.

The nominating committee of the Arizona Theater Company recommends an unlimited number of people to its Advisory Body.

Advisers meet with the organization's board of directors and have a vote, but in the event of a tie, their votes do not count. An individual's only route to the organization's board of directors is through the Advisory Body. This body not only provides training for board membership, but is also used to weed out (from prospective board membership) those with a minimum interest in the organization and those reluctant or unable to give the time the organization needs.

The executive director of a religious-oriented social service agency that provides emergency shelter for men and feeds the homeless has devised general guidelines to be used in the selection process of new members to its board of trustees. The following criteria were created at the request of the board. (At the time I interviewed the director, these criteria had not yet been ratified by the board.)

A board member should be:

1. A businessman in the community with a good and strong Christian commitment.

2. An active member of an evangelical church in the area. He should be able to receive a letter of recommendation from his pastor.

3. In a position to support the organization financially and should be informed that financial support is expected of all board members.

4. In a position of middle-level management or above, or own his own successful business. Whichever situation is his, he should be in a position where he deals with employees/personnel, larger budgets, operations, and is in a decision-making position.

5. Generally in charge of his own time or schedule. Not only does this allow him to be able to attend committee and other agency-related business, but also speaks of the level of the position he has in his company.

6. A man who can personally give substantial financial gifts or firsthand expertise in specific areas of need such as architecture, law, community relations, construction, etc., or, he should be a man with a reputation of being able to solicit and acquire these areas of help from other people in the community. Basically, he needs to be a well-known man with a strong reputation and ability to give or locate resources to further the agency's ministries. He needs to be a facilitator, not just an adviser.

Additionally, board members of this organization are recruited on the basis of their compatibility with the organization and its other members. The executive director feels there is no room on a nonprofit board for a devil's advocate. "We don't need that kind of bickering," he says.

When this motivated, young executive director accepted his position with the agency five years ago, he expressed the need to have a group of trustees who would actively help the organization, not just give their opinions. In the past, board members were recruited from the organization's volunteers because they were "good with the boys." The director felt that the agency's needs were changing and that a more professional board was needed; he accepted the directorship contingent upon radical changes in the board's structure and level of participation. The agency's board accepted the challenge of change, recruited new members, and has seen a stronger organization emerge with a budget and income that has doubled in three years.

WHY PEOPLE SAY YES

Before examining any techniques for motivating board members, the reasons why an individual joins a board need to be explored.

Altruism

People say yes to board membership for altruistic reasons. I've learned from interviewing many prominent chief executive officers that they want to give something back to the community in which they have prospered. Volunteerism for these individuals is a kind of payback, a statement of appreciation, a kind of *quid pro quo*. Similarly, there are indviduals who have a sincere concern about their community and want to do something for it. These people frequently were raised in a family where volunteerism was an integral part of their life; others just have a big heart.

The roots of volunteerism go back in time. People have come together to promote some common good for as long as there have been historical accounts of communal groups of people. Perhaps giving (of oneself) is, in part, instinctive. Western civilization's Judeo-Christian principle of "love one's neighbor" has surfaced in various social reforms since medieval times. Religious convictions cause many to give to their community. Many churches ask their members to tithe not only financial support but also their time in community services. Thus, people say yes for charitable reasons—because of their humanity to others.

Enlightened Self-Interest

An enlightened self-interest is another consideration. Some join nonprofit boards to learn about an organization or its mission—to explore the field as a career opportunity. Some wish to participate in a democratic process and to express their leadership in pursuit of an important social goal. To put one's expertise and experience to work in a charitable setting can be very rewarding and moves an individual upward toward the highest plateau of self-actualization.

Personal Involvement

Another reason that often results in a commitment to board service is an individual's personal involvement with an organization or cause. This is especially true in the field of health. If an individual or one of his or her family members has been well treated by a particular hospital, there is a feeling of gratitude that may lead to support of that institution. Parents of children with mental illness, juvenile diabetes, muscular dystrophy, and other illnesses or diseases will work hard for the agency that has helped them or for one that seeks a cure for their child's disease. People who have experienced cancer or heart disease in their family, for example, are more inclined to support organizations working in those fields. Some who recall pleasant childhood experiences at a particular camp or as a member of Boy Scouts or Girl Scouts may be willing to help those organizations in their adulthood. Likewise, alumni of colleges and universities or other private educational institutions will have a deeper commitment than those who have not had a personal involvement with the institution.

Ego-Centered

There are other quite different reasons for saying yes—egocentric ones such as fear, guilt, recognition, status, identification with a cause or specific organization, peer pressure, prestige or social climbing, and desire for business connections. External pressures, such as a corporate assignment or a requirement for managerial evaluation are other reasons. All of these can be every bit as motivating, although in a negative way, and a strong commitment to the organization will most likely be lacking.

Motives and Commitment

Obviously there are a multitude of reasons why people say yes to serving on a board of directors. Whether you consider these reasons as right or wrong, the key to keeping your board stimulated is to satisfy those personal needs of individual members. As this is easier said than done, learning and acknowledging the *why* is critical; it is the key to motivation.

If an individual joins your board of directors for altruistic, enlightened self-interest, charitable, or personal involvement reasons, then a personal climate already exists (within him or her) which is conducive to this member's becoming an actively involved and productive board member. For these individuals, it is important to offer specific and challenging assignments. These members want, and need, to be an integral part of the decision making for your organization; they need to see change or progress being made as a result of their efforts. To bore these members with envelope stuffing or some other menial and meaningless task where there is no demand on their skills and knowledge will result in resignations. Few people resign from a board because they are overworked or overly challenged. More often members quit because they are bored or frustrated by inactivity; they are not given the opportunity for personal growth and satisfaction.

If members join your board for some ego-centered reason, their membership may be static versus growth-facilitating.[1] These people are apt to stay at a minimum level of involvement. It becomes the job of the board president or chairperson to try to coax these individuals into a growth-facilitating position in order to gain their commitment.

Psychologists tell us that you can use small commitments in the form of minor achievements to manipulate an individual's self-esteem. Achieving one small success at a time and being recognized for that helps these people feel better about their participation. Feeling good about one's involvement with an organization is a first step toward commitment as it positively enhances one's self-image. "And once you've got a man's self-image where you want it, he should comply *naturally* with a whole range of requests that are consistent with this view of himself."[2]

Those who join boards because of external pressures may be motivated to immediate compliance but are unlikely to have any long-term commitment. "Social scientists have determined that we accept inner responsibility for a behavior when we think we have chosen to perform it in the absence of strong outside pressures....It [external pressure] may get us to perform a certain action, but it won't get us to accept inner responsibility for the act. Consequently, we won't feel committed to it [the act]."[3]

MOTIVATING YOUR BOARD

All nonprofit boards seem to experience their share of deadweights. If an organization finds that these deadweights seem to be more the rule than the exception, there is probably something seriously lacking in the way that organization recruits its board members. It is hoped that careful recruitment will significantly reduce the incidences of inactive board members. If, despite careful selection, you still find an inactive member or two, examine why that individual may have joined your board and employ some of the following principles of motivation to raise the member's level of commitment. If these and other incentives fail, forget it. Concentrate your energies on more responsive members.

It is tempting to exclude the total deadbeat from board functions and to save postage by not even sending mailings. This is the "ignore them and hope they go away" tactic, and it doesn't necessarily meet with success. More important, any negative treatment of any board member, no matter how worthy you feel they may be of such treatment, is bound to come back to haunt, and possibly tarnish, your organization's image. Treat your deadwood as you do other members and hope the remainder of his or her term passes quickly. Be grateful your deadwood is just that and not a disruptive member.

Frequent turnover, where you just can't hang onto good members, is another board problem. Here, too, the lessons of careful recruitment, along with the motivation principles and suggested incentives presented in this section can be applied to remedy the problem.

The Consistency Principle

Consistency in an individual's behavior is a highly regarded value in American society; it is said that consistent behavior offers a reasonable and productive orientation to the world around us. Psychologists have long pointed out the influence of the principle of consistency to direct human behavior, and theorists say the desire for consistency is a prime motivator of much of our behavior. Cialdini says the drive to be (and look) consistent is a strong and potent weapon of social influence. Once individuals make a difficult decision to take a stand on an issue, they are most willing to believe that decision is right and behave in a manner consistent with their stance. The key is commitment.

In applying this principle to a board setting, it is the role of the president or chairperson to extract a commitment from board members. Commitment strategies are designed to get members to take some action or make some statement that will move them to comply through the pressure of personal consistency. Successful salespersons often employ such tactics and certainly effective leaders do.

Ask an individual to assume a simple task or assignment and make sure that the assignment can be accomplished within a short period of time, for example, by the next board meeting. Assuming acceptance of an initial task, it is realistic to expect that the individual will also follow through with his or her next assignment because he or she wishes to be consistent. Assignments can become increasingly complex, span longer periods of time, and challenge the individual to assume increasing responsibilities. One may argue there are individuals who can be trusted to follow through on one occasion but not on another and, therefore, extracting a commitment from them is difficult if not impossible. This is true; this can happen. However, if you have done your homework on your prospects as prescribed earlier in this chapter, you will have made inquiries about a prospect's ability to follow through.

The Pleasure Principle

Freud's psychoanalytic theories are most well known for their concepts of motivation within the context of a biological and survival model.[4] Freud conceived of individuals striving to satisfy their personal needs in a world of limited and specialized resources (biological mode). For people's needs to be satisfied, certain behaviors are adopted that will lead to desired goals (survival model). Pleasure and happiness are among the primary goals. At the risk of oversimplification, ask what pleasures individuals derive from their membership on your board of directors. Even for those who do not have a strong commitment to your organization, there must be some pleasure in the association. Whatever those pleasures, they stem from the reason or reasons why those individuals joined the board in the first place.

One of my board members once told me that he enjoyed coming to our board meetings because he could relax; the pressures associated with his own company's meetings were not present. Another said she enjoyed the camaraderie. Others find pleasure in being a part of a group, in contributing to a community organization, in being needed. If an organization can sustain whatever pleasure an individual finds in board affiliation, members will be motivated to continue their involvement.

The Achievement Principle

John Atkinson presents us with a theory of achievement motivation which he sees as a result of conflict between approach and avoidance tendencies. "Associated with every achievement-related action is the possibility of success (with the consequent emotion of pride) and the possibility of failure (with the consequent emotion of shame). The strengths of these anticipated emotions determine whether an individual will approach or avoid achievement-oriented activi-

ties."[5] Achievement behavior is the result of an emotional battle
between a hope for success and a fear of failure. We can apply this to
board members in that they can be motivated to achieve (on behalf
of the organization) if their confidence in success is greater than their
fear of failure. Frederick Herzberg's extensive studies in the
workplace evidenced a similar theory. His studies showed that knowledge workers want to achieve and will work only if their situation
offers opportunities for personal and professional advancement. Otherwise, they simply go through the motions. Board directors are very
much akin to "knowledge workers" if not by occupation, then by
their role as a director. The point is that achievement is a motivator.
Board membership must offer opportunities for its members to
achieve something.

Incentives

A board president or chairperson does not have to be a psycholo-
gist to motivate his or her fellow board members, but recognizing
some principles of motivation—consistency, pleasure, achievement—
is helpful in effectively encouraging a member to take action, become
involved, and thereby strengthen his or her commitment. More easily
understood, and perhaps more frequently applied in motivating
individuals, are *incentives*. The difficulty lies in coming up with some
useful ones for the volunteer board member, as profit and monetary
incentives cannot be applied. What are appropriate rewards for board
members? What are some ways to express your appreciation for their
time and energies, for their successes, for their commitment?

Twenty-one ways to say thank you may be:

1. Have the board president or chairperson send personal
   thank you notes or letters.
2. Remember members' birthdays.
3. Ask a distinguished member to stand at the next board
   meeting and take a bow while everyone applauds.
4. Mention members' names and accomplishments or contributions in your agency's newsletter.
5. Keep a written record of members' contributions, achievements, hours given to board and committee meetings, number of gifts solicited or dollars raised for the organization,
   etc. Put this record of service in a little diary or journal and
   present it to the member at retirement from the board. (No,
   it's not too late at this point. Word of your organization's
   thoughtfulness will spread.)
6. Send a letter to employers thanking them for their support
   of your board members' community service work. Send

another thank you when a member's term expires and outline all the member has done for your organization.

7. Once a year, take out an ad in your local newspaper to list and publicly thank all your board members for their time and service.

8. Recognize board members at all your organization's events.

9. Ask your clients (if appropriate and heartfelt) to write notes to board members expressing the value of the services they've received through or from your organization. (This makes board members feel good about their affiliation.)

10. Give a little personal gift rather than, or in addition to, a plaque or certificate. It can relate to your organization's field or to an individual's personal interests or to volunteerism in general. (The retiring president of the Colorado Chapter of UNICEF was presented with a small bronze statue of a child with an inscription on its base thanking her for 24 years of service to UNICEF. One agency presented a gift of chocolate tennis balls to a board member with an avid interest in tennis. At Christmas, the Girls Club of Rapid City, Inc., presented its board members with an abacus inscribed: "(name), you really count!")

11. Submit newsworthy press releases on board members' contributions or achievements on behalf of your organization.

12. Scan your newspaper for mention of members or their companies. Cut out such articles and send it to the member (assuming it's a positive story); let members know that you're alert to events that affect them and that you care.

13. Praise members to their friends and colleagues.

14. Name a project members have worked on after them or after their companies. (In recognition of one board member's outstanding contributions for three consecutive years to the Girls Club of Rapid City's golf tournament, this annual fund raiser was renamed "The Highland Beverage Golf Tournament.")

15. Post a Board of Directors Honor Roll in the reception area or main entrance of your building.

16. Recognize members' personal triumphs or accomplishments: promotions, honors received, appointments, marriage, births, and so forth.

17. Congratulate members on accomplishments and milestones achieved by their family: a child's graduation, spouse's promotion, and so forth.

18. Nominate your board members for community service volunteer awards.

19. Reward members with a trip to your local organization's national, regional, or state conferences or training programs.

20. Let the employees in a member's office know he or she is appreciated. Drop in with a batch of homemade bread or something of this nature for everyone in the office.

21. Give members "recognition buttons" they can wear with pride. (You can order volunteer gifts or make your own.[6])

Treat all board members fairly and humanely. Board members are not objects to be used and discarded, to be shuffled from one task to another as it best suits the organization—that does not show appreciation. The axiom that "the business of boards is business" has taken on a different meaning to some organizations which feel this also means to be brisk and unfeeling. It is better said that "the business of nonprofit boards is people" who conduct themselves in a businesslike fashion.

Finally, honesty is another essential factor in retaining good board members. Let members know the facts—what is going on in the organization, good and bad. No one expects your organization to run smoothly all of the time, so keep the board informed of problem areas and potential problem areas. Members will feel better equipped to handle problems and crises and to make decisions about them if they have the facts.

SUMMARY

Board members should be recruited with care. It is as important to have experts on a board who complement an organization's needs as it is to avoid the problem of professional members who are reluctant to share their skills. As the needs of an organization change, so do its requirements for board membership. It is not easy to balance a board with diverse and representative members. There are many traits of a good board member but the best members are those who are interested in your organization's field, are willing to share their expertise and experience, and who have the time to do so.

In recruiting new members, look for those people who have a track record of accomplishments; look for those beginning to move up into positions of power. Consider asking others for recommendations. However, before adding any new members to your board, make sure your "organizational house" is in order. A systematic recruiting process helps to produce the kind of board members your organization needs.

The cultivation of prospective board members and the process of turning a prospect into a member requires an understanding of why people say yes to volunteering. People say yes for reasons of altruism, enlightened self-interest, personal involvement, and ego satisfaction. Why an individual joins a board is key to motivating him or her to take an active role in your organization and helps to deepen his or her commitment.

Carefully selecting the right people for your board is not enough—members must be motivated to contribute. The principle of personal consistency, the pleasure principle, and the achievement principle should be recognized as significant factors in motivating people. If these principles are applied along with various incentives and expressions of appreciation, boards of directors can avoid the problems of an inactive membership or frequent turnover of its members.

NOTES

1. William R. Conrad and William R. Glenn, *The Effective Voluntary Board of Directors,* p. 114.

2. Robert B. Cialdini, *Influence,* p. 81.

3. Ibid., p. 97.

4. Bernard Weiner, *Human Motivation,* p. 165–80.

5. Ibid., p. 191.

6. Volunteer recognition items are for sale through the California Hospital Association. Write for their brochure: CHA Volunteer Division, P.O. Box 1442, Sacramento, CA. 95807–1442.

Chapter 5
Orientation and Training of
Board Members

ORIENTATION OF NEW MEMBERS

Shortly after George accepted his appointment to the board of directors of the Denver Regional Transportation District, the board became embroiled in a bitter fight with management over a policy matter. George said to me, "You'd think a board that's been around for over 10 years would have some records, some written standards or even a board manual on policy issues for us to review and consider. Instead I found only great gaps in information." George's frustration stemmed from a lack of information. Many a new board member faces this same frustration.

Many organizations' boards have some kind of orientation for new members, just as many do not. Or, a new member may be given a large volume of dull data which he or she is supposed to read thoroughly in his or her spare time. (How many do you think actually go through such material?) Sometimes new members are asked to jump right in; their orientation consists of an introduction to other members at their first board meeting. They are expected to "learn as they go."

All board members should be given a formal and informal orientation before they ever attend a meeting of the board of directors (except for the board meeting they may have visited as a prospect). When there are only one or two new members coming on the board at a time, it is tempting to postpone the orientation until there are more participants. Yet, whether your board has one or 12 new members coming on at any one time, each and all are entitled to an immediate and thorough education about the organization and about the board and its procedures.

Purpose of Orientation

A frequent complaint by board members and about board members is that they do not understand the role they are to play. Even if a member has had experience with another nonprofit board, which may be helpful, he or she is not necessarily prepared to tackle your organization's situation. Not only do boards differ in their modus operandi but experience from one may have been limited or poor and thus may be nontransferable. Despite previous positive nonprofit board experience, new members still need an orientation to help integrate them into your agency's family. The closer individuals are aligned to your organization's goals, the greater their commitment will be over the long run. Chuck Haugen, senior community relations consultant for The Prudential Insurance Company in Newark, said, "Lots of people join a board and for the first year either speak without knowledge or they don't speak when they should. In both situations, the lack of board orientation is the problem. Members who have served on a board for a long time often unconsciously intimidate new members who lack the guts to point out that 'the emperor is not wearing any clothes.'"[1]

According to Haugen, the different backgrounds of board members can contribute to inappropriate board behaviors or a general lack of understanding about appropriate board functions. "Lots of businessmen get on nonprofit boards and tend to hang up their brains with their coats when they enter the board meeting. No one has told them the specific nature of their responsibilities, most don't know what to do—that they are supposed to bring their own experience to the board meeting. Some catch on to their job; others view themselves as super-supervisors and act as a jury to what is presented at board meetings. Grassroots members represent specific constituencies and often don't understand or appreciate the demands on the organization in its total environment; they tend to advocate their own constituent groups and this can be disruptive."[2] Thus an important purpose of orientation is role clarification.

The purpose of board orientation programs is twofold: (1) to give a new member specific information about the organization that is necessary for effective performance as a member of the board of directors and (2) to help the new member gain a working knowledge of the organization's goals and program services.

Orientation Procedures and Activities

The recruitment process is actually the initial stage of orientation. Prospects are introduced to the organization, to its goals and programs, and to what is expected of board members. Some organizations conduct orientation sessions for prospective board members, others hold such sessions for new members only. The following discussion centers on orientation once an individual joins the board. There are a range of activities that can be employed.

Bundling up all available information for mailing to the new board member, from bylaws to program schedules and brochures, is an approach that fails to recognize that there are actually two orientations required: orientation to the organization and orientation to the member's directorship. As in recruitment, a planned systematic approach to orientation is best.

1. Plan the orientation program.
   —During recruitment, prospects should have learned what is expected of them as a member of your organization's board of directors. Your board's *Responsibilities of Directors* should include a statement that participation in orientation is expected and mandatory. Therefore, it will not come as a surprise that one or two days (not necessarily consecutive) will be spent on orientation activities.
   —Too much written material too soon is overwhelming. Plan the distribution of materials in accordance with each orientation activity. For example, the time to hand out program brochures and information on the clients served would be during a tour of the agency's facility, which is scheduled to observe programs in action.
   —Use the background data gathered during recruitment to tailor presentations according to new members' personal and professional interests.
   —Consider assigning new members a sponsor—a more experienced board member who can help new ones learn the ropes.
2. Orient new members to the organization.
   —Schedule a meeting with the executive director. Assuming the new member has at least glanced at some of the written materials received during recruitment, this conference gives the newcomer an opportunity to ask specific questions about the organization's operations. For the executive director, meetings with new board members provide a chance to establish an early working relationship.
   —Plan a tour of the agency. If your organization has a campus facility, visit one building of every type. It's not necessary, for example, to see all classrooms; one will do. Even if your organization is not facility-based, a visit to the office(s) where the organization conducts business is desirable. When an organization has several program sites in its community, all of these sites should be visited. Board members will be called on to make decisions requiring knowledge about the organization's physical plant, so these agency visits are imperative.
   —Prepare a brief two- or three-page synopsis on key organizational demographics: number of clients/students/patients, program milestones, changes in purpose over the years, staff roster, trends, whatever is appropriate to supplement oral presentations.

—Arrange for new members to attend a staff meeting or briefing session. They should have the opportunity to meet other key personnel, learn about their respective areas of responsibility, and direct questions.

3. Orient members to the board.

—Have the board president make a welcoming call or visit to all new members.

—Prepare a biographical sketch on the full board and include terms of office, offices held, committee assignments, place of employment, position, other relevant information.

—Hold a social affair to initiate board social relationships on an informal basis.

—Schedule a meeting for all new board members with the executive committee and other committee chairpersons. This gives newcomers a chance to become acquainted with the board's leadership and with the activities of the committees. A discussion of board procedures, director's roles and responsibilities, and problems of the organization from the volunteers' point of view can give the new member a better perspective of the total organization.

—Give new members a board manual.

—Provide time for a debriefing among the new members and board president and the executive director. This is the new person's chance to have any remaining questions and concerns clarified. Debriefing sessions can also be evaluative. New members should be asked which parts of the orientation were most helpful, which were least helpful, and how future orientation might be improved.

—Make committee assignments and arrange for the committee chair and new member to meet and discuss the details of committee work.

—Pull together a small list of other relevant readings such as articles on boardsmanship.

Orienting new board members is making sure they become acquainted with all facets of the organization and the board. It is also introducing them to the possibilities of their service—to how they fit into the total organization and the impact they can have on it. Orientation may continue over several months or as long as necessary to give new members the support they need to do their job.

Orientation in Practice

When I was executive director of the Girls Club of Denver, Inc., we would select two of our girls to guide new board members around our facility. Our girls were not only enthusiastic guides, but they often (unintentionally) provided comic relief to our orientation sessions with their anecdotes. This activity not only gave board members a chance to meet the organization's clients but also helped to make members more sensitive to our clients' needs. At later board meetings when clients were discussed, members did not think of them as some group of nameless faces but as "Donna" or "Lizard." Since our organization served girls, we felt the introduction to some of our girls helped strengthen our board members' commitment. Meeting clients helps the board to know a real need exists.

One midwestern college has a trustee-in-residence program as part of its orientation. New trustees are asked to live on campus for two days and immerse themselves in campus life. They stay in a dorm, eat at the college dining hall, attend a class or two, meet with professors and students. They experience the institution. This first-hand familiarity with the college is an enormous help when they have to make policy decisions regarding faculty, students, campus life, curriculum, or the college's physical plant.

The Board Manual

A board manual is the most commonly used tool for educating new board members, but it is more than just an orientation tool. It should be the standard reference document for your organization's board of directors. As common as a manual may be, surprisingly few organizations give much thought to its content. What you include in your board manual will depend on the complexity of your organization. Your best guide is experience. What are the questions most often asked about your organization by new board members? Let your directors' concerns guide the content of your manual.

There are some basics that should be included in any board manual:

- articles of incorporation and bylaws with amendments
- organizational chart
- list of personnel and job descriptions of key personnel
- roster of board members including place of employment; position; home and business address and phone; name of spouse, where applicable
- description of board committees and their responsibilities, as well as staff and board committee assignments
- brief description of all current programs and their objectives, plus a clear definition of ongoing versus one-time-only programs or services
- policies of the board of directors
- information on the relationship of the organization (local or regional) to its national or parent corporation, if applicable. This

includes reporting requirements, funding support, services provided by the parent corporation, accountability requirements, etc.

● all sources of the organization's funding

● budget—planned and actual

● statement of cooperative agreements with other community agencies, e.g., United Way

● strategic plan summary

At the end of the manual you might include a personal planning section—a few blank pages where members can jot down issues or ideas they'd like to bring up for discussion in the future.

One organization prefaces its board manual with a statement on the importance of volunteerism. (See Figure 1.) Photocopies of letters of acclamation received by the agency and awards received for their services follow. Not only is this a nice touch but it is reassuring to new board members to learn they will be part of an organization that is held in high regard.

Figure 1. Sample Volunteer Statement

Welcome to Partners!

Did you know that nearly every significant social change in the last 150 years has come about as a result of the volunteer effort of people like you? Folks like Sojourner Truth, Samuel Howe, Albert Schweitzer, and Cesar Chavez have enriched our heritage as a nation willing to lighten the burden of our fellow man. Though our forefathers hardly thought of their neighborly actions as volunteering, they strengthened a tradition of volunteerism that has today become a way of life.

Partners has taken up the banner of citizen involvement, especially as it relates to children. Youth employment programs have been developed, alternative schools have sprung up across the country, youth counselors assist kids in learning coping skills that will enable them to tolerate sometimes intolerable situations. Still these remedies serve as no substitute for a community's concern for its young citizens.

Partners believes that communities can positively impact the problems that many youth encounter in their lives. By matching adults with kids on a one-to-one basis we see the development of a relationship which has the potential of increasing and creating many opportunities for youth.

Courtesy of Partners, Inc.
(Reprinted with permission from Partner's *Board Manual*.)

Partners' "Table of Contents" (Figure 2) illustrates the completeness of its board manual. Chapters are separated by tab dividers for easy reference and the manual is bound in a three-ring notebook. Board members can later add new and updated information in an organized fashion.

Figure 2. Sample Manual Contents

Table of Contents

I. Board/Council Members and Responsibilities
   A. List of Board Members
   B. List of Committee Members
   C. Description of Committees of the Board
   D. List of Advisory Board Members
   E. Decision-Making Process
   F. List of Council Members
   G. Calendar
II. Legal
   A. Bylaws
   B. Standing Rules
   C. Tax-Exempt Status Letter
   D. Articles of Incorporation
   E. Certificate of Incorporation
III. Program History
   A. Fact Sheet
   B. Range of Services
   C. Funding
   D. Program Evaluation and Procedures
   E. Juvenile Justice System
   F. Volunteer Program
      1. Job Descriptions
      2. Evaluation
IV. Personnel
   A. Organizational Chart
   B. Personnel Policies and Procedures
   C. Affirmative Action Plan
   D. Job Descriptions
   E. Performance Appraisal
V. Contracts and Financial Matters
   A. Budget
   B. List of Funders
   C. Most Recent Audit
   D. Contract Overview (if applicable)
   E. Financial Procedures
   F. Statement of Agreement
VI. Policy Statements
VII. Minutes and Current Issues
   A. Board Minutes
   B. Council Minutes
   C. Current Issues

Courtesy of Partners, Inc.
(Reprinted with permission from Partner's *Board Manual*.)

New board members should not just be handed their board manual. A part of an orientation session (preferably toward the end of their orientation to the board) should be spent going over parts of the manual. Features of the manual should be pointed out, with a word on how to use it as a reference.

BOARD TRAINING PROGRAMS

Ongoing Education

Orientation, even the best and most thorough, is not a sufficient education for today's nonprofit board of directors. To remain viable, boards need continual training in their roles and responsibilities. To keep pace with their everchanging environments, organizations must remain flexible, which implies a constant review and updating of their strategic plans. Planning and policy setting are major areas of responsibility for boards. To maintain their interest and strengthen their commitment, board members need self-renewal sessions. All of these reasons support the case for ongoing boardsmanship education. No coach would ever think to assemble a team of good players and put them into the "big game" without first holding practice sessions. Likewise, why bother putting together a good team of board members if you are not going to properly train them for their role in the organizational game?

A survey of Colorado's nonprofit boards of directors showed the majority of the respondents' boards reported no board training within the past 12 months. Of those 61 organizations (of 164 total respondents) that had some kind of board training, most (37.2 percent) reported an individual member attended a conference or workshop on behalf of the organization; 31.7 percent had a consultant or other organization make a presentation on some topic; 18.9 percent conducted their own board training program; and 6.1 percent (10 organizations) reported "other training."[3]

Any organization stands to lose if its board lacks a program of ongoing board development and education. Without opportunity for self-renewal as a group, your board can become stagnant. The infusion of new ideas to a group often comes from the brainstorming sessions conducted at workshops. The longer get-togethers afforded by retreats and workshops in an informal atmosphere help strengthen the group's cohesiveness in a way regular board meetings cannot. If losses in the area of group dynamics development do not concern you too much, perhaps the potential loss in the area of effective board performance does. So, if you are a part of that majority that has no ongoing program of board training, talk to your board president or fellow board members about initiating one.

When board members are first introduced to their responsibilities, board development and training must be included. Thus, the common excuse boards use to avoid training—that its members are unwilling or unable to give the extra time required—cannot be valid. Directors will respond to your request for their time if they not only believe their time will be put to good use but also have experienced that the time they do give to your organization is beneficial and appreciated. Also, if your board education programs, workshops, and retreats are meaningful, the directors will attend.

It is up to the board president to include boardsmanship education when planning the board's activities for the year. It is up to the board vice-president to plan specific educational opportunities for the board if he or she is charged with this responsibility as suggested in Chapter 2. The basis for all board educational programs should be the members' desire to improve themselves—individually and as a group. It is the responsibility of the board president to help instill and motivate members to this self-improvement mode, and the planned outcome of any board education program should be to improve the board's performance.

Eva Schindler-Rainman gives us nine assumptions about volunteers that can significantly influence their training:

1. Volunteers bring with them a wide variation of experiences, knowledge, and skills. *Implication:* Training methods that build on and use the volunteer's experience, knowledge, and skills will produce the best and most relevant kind of learning.

2. Volunteers, by and large, will come as self-directed, motivated, interested learners. *Implication:* Volunteers should help plan and conduct their own learning experiences as active participants rather than passive recipients.

3. Volunteers participate in training events because they want to learn to do their volunteer jobs. *Implication:* The training must be practical and relevant to the learner and must be related to life as they know it.

4. Many volunteers have been exposed to classroomlike learning situations that were not helpful, relevant, or exciting. *Implication:* The learning activities must take place in an informal, experiential atmosphere.

5. Volunteers have a number of important roles (as parents, workers, students, citizens) that compete for their time. *Implication:* Training should be planned to take into consideration the limited time available to most volunteers and to accept the legitimacy of their loyalties.

6. The world of voluntarism has not developed norms or procedures to support and reward participation in ongoing training programs. *Implication:* Training opportunities and

activities must be a rewarding and recognized aspect of organizational functioning.

7. Often the training format and content have been developed over the years and have not been revised or retailored for the particular participants at a particular time. *Implication:* Each training event, if possible, should be planned by trainers and some of the potential participants to meet the current needs of a particular group.

8. Training is often a one-time thing instead of an ongoing support opportunity for volunteers. *Implication:* Ongoing inservice training is necessary for volunteers, and the importance of follow-up should be communicated at the beginning of the learning experience.

9. Volunteer training is usually seen as an event sponsored by one organization, or for volunteers in one category, such as new, experienced, board, office workers, service personnel, etc. *Implication:* Training should be planned interorganizationally to utilize all the possible resources.[4]

Although Schindler-Rainman is referring to program-type volunteers, all her points are applicable to the board volunteer.

Retreats and Workshops

Before you conduct a board training program, you need to have in mind what you want to accomplish or you won't accomplish much of anything. Whenever appropriate, focus on the long term and avoid dealing with crises. Appropriate agendas may include restructuring the board or its committees, strategic planning, evaluation, future programs, bylaw revision, impact of institutional expansion or contraction, financial development, roles and responsibilities of board members, and board/staff relationships. Any area where the board feels its performance is inadequate, an endeavor that requires indepth or lengthy discussion, or any unknown area that requires a thorough education may become the subject for a board workshop.

Board members can become "workshopped to death"—there is a point of saturation. Conducting a training program in addition to regular board and committee meetings takes time as training programs must be carefully planned if they are to achieve some desired result. Therefore, calling for a workshop should be done with discretion. Not all new areas or performance problems need a special session. Many topics can be handled effectively by adding an hour onto a regularly scheduled board meeting; however, this technique should also be used with discretion.

The difference between workshops and retreats is largely semantic, although to some, retreats imply getting out of the city for more than one day. At a retreat, one may conduct various workshops. Whichever you choose to call your board training program, the time and place should be carefully considered. Stay away from holidays and choose a time when board members are not preoccupied with other pressing board business. Select a time of year when weather extremes are not expected to interfere with driving. Give members a choice of one or two dates to determine which offers maximum attendance—it would be rare to find a date when 100 percent of your board is free to attend.

Unlike strategic planning workshops where resort-type settings are undesirable, mountain cabins and seaside condos would be delightful for board retreats/workshops because social interaction is also a part of your agenda. Don't select a location that is more than an hour's drive unless your directors all agree about the time it may take to get to your chosen site.

I'm afraid Horace is having a hard time getting into the spirit of this retreat.

Define your training objectives in advance. Involve as many of the board as feasible in planning—it's their program. Take into account Schindler-Rainman's nine assumptions about volunteers. Budget for board retreats/workshops; there are possible transportation costs, lodging, meals, resource materials, photocopies, possible speaker's honorarium, and other associated costs. If your organization cannot afford these costs, it may solicit outside training funding from a foundation or corporation, or board members may share the expenses with the organization.

Consider using an outside facilitator, either a paid consultant or a volunteer from another organization. The leadership of the workshops may be co-chaired; select leaders who are able to maintain momentum. Assign someone to attend to the small details such as coffee breaks, meal arrangements, and support materials (flip charts, pens and pencils, paper, etc.) for the workshops themselves.

The agenda is very important and needs to be designed to keep the sessions focused and allow for ample breaks. Standard agenda rules are applicable. However, it is appropriate to specify that no official action will be taken, no resolution or motion passed.[5] Send out the agenda in advance along with a list of reading assignments. Assign someone, possibly a staff secretary, to record and summarize the workshops' discussions. A record of proceedings is important if follow-up action is to occur. Finally, don't forget evaluation. Ask participants what they understood the purpose of the retreat/workshop to be and if they felt that purpose was met. Ask them for their comments on procedures, most valuable and least valuable aspects, and recommendations for future programs. Preferably, an evaluation questionnaire would be mailed with a stamped return envelope a week or two after the program to allow time for the effects of training to sink in. The next regular board meeting may include a report on the evaluation responses. (See Appendix for sample workshop agendas.)

Board Training Resources

If you don't want to conduct board training yourselves or if your board is inexperienced, where might you turn for boardsmanship training? Once you locate an organization or consultant that specializes in this type of training, how do you know they are right for your board of directors?

First, where does one find training resources? A starting point is to look at the types of organizations most likely to provide training for nonprofit, volunteer boards of directors or to lead you to those who do. One obvious source is your local phone book's yellow pages. While you are not likely to find a heading for nonprofit board consultants or boardsmanship training, you will discover management consultants or management firms that offer board training. The kind of training organization or consultant you want may or may not be evident by its name. Look for key words such as technical assistance, nonprofit resources, community development, community services training, nonprofit support center. There are several hundred nonprofit management assistance organizations across the country that are dedicated to strengthening the nonprofit sector and that offer workshops or consultation. Not all offer boardsmanship training, but many do.[6]

Another source is colleges and universities and, in particular, community colleges. Take a look at schools of social work, business schools, schools of management or public affairs. Frequently, they either offer seminars for nonprofit organizations or have faculty who are skilled facilitators and trainers, or both. The Kellogg Foundation provides funding to a number of institutions of higher education and other educational organizations nationwide for "Lifelong Learning" which includes programs on strengthening volunteer programs, for preparing community leaders (board members) for their service responsibilities, and for other related volunteer programs. The foundation's program director for Lifelong Learning could help identify organizations and institutions in your area that are offering boardsmanship training.[7]

United Ways, community foundations, Junior Leagues, and state or local government agencies that fund your agency are also a source of referrals. VOLUNTEER: the National Center for Citizen Involvement is another good source for referrals nationwide.[8]

Most national, umbrella organizations (Boys Clubs of America, Girl Scouts U.S.A., National Association of Mental Health Agencies, etc.) offer inservice training programs for their affiliated agencies. Invariably, the subject of boards of directors is covered.

If your organization is not associated with a national organization, talk to another agency in your field in your community. Ask about the possibility of participating in their future board training activities. Of course, you are willing to pay for participation. Even if a national organization is not willing to open its inservice training to "outsiders," it may consider sharing, loaning, or hiring out its training experts. Seek another agency in your community that has used an outside consultant for board training and was satisfied. Talk to your friends who serve on other nonprofit boards; ask around.

The Right Trainer

Now, we come to the second question, "Are they the right trainer or firm for our organization?" Norton Kiritz, executive director of the Grantsmanship Center, once wrote about how to select a training program. He suggested eight points be considered:[9]

(1) define your needs
(2) distinguish between training programs and conferences
(3) distinguish between those sponsoring and those conducting the program
(4) ask questions about the training organization
(5) find out who your trainers will be
(6) what is a reasonable fee
(7) send the right person
(8) evaluate the training

Of these items, the first is the most critical. Once you successfully define your need, the other points are a routine matter of checking references. What is it about your board that needs improvement? Do you need to conduct better meetings? Do you need help in defining proper board and staff relationships or responsibilities? Does your board as a group lack certain skills such as planning or fund development? Maybe your board is just bored! Boardsmanship training is not a panacea to effective organizational management, but it sure can help.

A board must not only agree to work on a certain problem area but it must also want to do its job more effectively. There is no sense conducting boardsmanship training if there is no commitment on the part of board members to follow through on whatever new directions emerge from the exercise. Maybe some boards simply need an influx of new blood—boards can suffer from burnout.

Assuming that your board has identified a real need for training and all members agree to seek outside assistance in conducting a training program, the next step is to define your training expectations to prospective trainers. Select that trainer whose own expectations of results closely match those of your board.

Providing orientation and training experiences for new board members shortens the time it takes for them to become effective contributors to your organization. Inservice training and workshops and retreats can help to renew experienced board members' sense of purpose and commitment. Given that the conditions suggested in this chapter on conducting board development programs are carried out, your board can be strengthened, your organization wins, you win. As Richard T. Ingram says, "Some of the most rewarding experiences for trustees occur outside regular board meetings.[10]

SUMMARY

A program of formal and informal orientation should be given to all new members of a board of directors. Orientation must give members information about the organization and about their role as a member of the board. Planned orientations that provide an appropriate amount of written materials, an agency tour, introduction to staff, information on other board members, and details of the board's operations are best. A comprehensive board manual should supplement but never supplant a personalized orientation program.

Several assumptions about the value of volunteers contribute to well-planned board development programs. These include using the volunteer's experience, participation of volunteers in the planning and execution of the training, relevant and rewarding training, and respect for the volunteer's time.

Workshops and retreats are the most common format for board training. However, it is important to remember to have a purpose for all workshops and to carefully prepare the agenda. After a workshop, follow-up activities should be scheduled as well as an evaluation of the training. Several local or national resources are available to assist your organization with its board training. If a consultant or firm is to direct your board's training program, one with experience to match your group's needs is an important consideration in selecting the right person(s).

NOTES

1. Diane J. Duca, "Interview with Charles N. Haugen: Training Can Lead to Fewer Bored Boards," *The Board Letter,* Fall, 1984 (Denver, CO: Duca Associates), pp. 1–2.

2. Ibid.

3. Diane J. Duca, "Survey Report on Colorado's Nonprofit Boards of Directors" (Paper written for the University of Colorado/Denver, Graduate School of Public Affairs, Denver, May 1985).

4. Eva Schindler-Rainman, "Developing a Continuous Training Plan," in *The Nonprofit Organization Handbook,* ed. Tracy D. Connors, pp. 3–34.

5. New Jersey, Colorado, and other states have open meeting laws which may require "workshop" or "training sessions" for public nonprofit institutions to be open to the public. However, in Colorado (*Associated Students of the University of Colorado v. Regents of the University of Colorado,* 1975) the court interpreted the act (Colorado Sunshine Act, 1972) to exclude institutions of higher education because the act's provisions did not specifically cite "institutions of higher education." The act's provisions specified that boards and commissions of state agencies or authorities conduct meetings that are open to the public. An agenda that specifies no formal action(s) will be taken can preclude any problems, and it is wise to check with your state's attorney general office.

6. A list of organizations offering boardsmanship education programs or consultation is available from: Nonprofit Management Association, 1309 L St. NW, Washington, DC 20005, 202–638–3503.

7. W.K. Kellogg Foundation, 400 North Ave., Battle Creek, MI 49016, 616–968–1611.

8. VOLUNTEER, 111 North 19th St., Suite 500, Arlington, VA 22209, 703–276–0542.

9. Norton Kiritz, "Guidelines for the Selection of Training Programs," *The Grantsmanship Center News,* Nov–Dec. 1980 (Los Angeles: The Grantsmanship Center), pp. 43–45.

10. Richard T. Ingram, "Trustee Orientation and Development Programs" (A booklet by the Association of Governing Boards of Universities and Colleges, Washington, DC, 1981) p. 10.

Chapter 6
The Board's Fiscal
Responsibilities

FINANCIAL DEVELOPMENT

There is an old fund-raising story that tells of a wealthy old miser who, on his deathbed, called together his doctor, lawyer, and minister. He said to his friends, "They say you can't take it with you, but I'm going to try. I have three envelopes here with $60,000 cash in each. I want all of you to take an envelope and when they lower my casket into my grave, I want each of you to place your envelope on my casket." At the burial each of the men did as he had been instructed. But as they were on the way home, the minister confessed, "You know I really needed the money for the church's mission program, so I took out $20,000. The doctor said, "I, too, must confess. We're building a new clinic and I took out $40,000." The lawyer said, "I'm ashamed of both of you! I threw in a check for the full amount."

This story contains the faint implication that the business of fund raising is something of a con game. There seem to be many misconceptions about fund raising—what it is, how it's done, and who does it. It's envisioned to be an activity of the elite; people conjure up images of solicitations initiated over a game of golf at the local country club. Some feel fund raising is mainly peer pressure: one fellow twisting the arm of another. It is viewed as political clout: one businessman pledging his company's support to a project if a friend's company will, in turn, pledge support to his organization. Professional fund raisers are expected to appear as in a cartoon I once saw in an issue of the *Grantsmanship Center News*: clad in a three-piece vested suit with optional tie; exhibiting an ingratiating but determined smile, with a fast-draw handshake and a foot suitable for putting in doors; carrying, in one hand, press clippings touting previous projects and, in the other hand, a slide show of the organization's goals in living color!

Whatever the misconceptions about fund raising, boards have the ultimate responsibility for procuring their organization's essential financial resources; by law, no other body is responsible. Financing their organizations' operations is probably the greatest single matter of concern facing nonprofit boards. My survey of Colorado's nonprofit boards showed that the greatest amount of board time, 26.2 percent, is spent on financial issues. Boards devote an average of 17.8 percent of their time to administrative and general issues, 17.4 percent to program matters, 9.2 percent to other matters, 5.1 percent to personnel issues, and 1.4 percent to "unknown." One civic and welfare organization board reported that 50 percent of its time was spent on fund raising and another 30 percent on financial issues such as budgeting and fiscal control management.[1]

Because fund raising is so important and demanding, it is necessary, first, to be organized and have a clear sense of purpose. The following questions should be answered before your organization and its board embarks on a program of funds solicitation: What is fund raising to you, to your board members? What does it involve? What do you think your publics perceive your organization's proper fund-raising role to be?

Overcoming the Fear of Asking

Being alert to the attitudes your board members have regarding fund raising and solicitation activities is important because it can affect your style or methods of pursuing financial support for your organization. Therefore, during new member orientation, some time should be spent discussing with board members their feelings regarding fund raising and solicitation and their experiences in this area. Do they feel fund raising is a chore? Do they feel it is distasteful and something to avoid at all costs? Do they feel it's a staff responsibility? Do they recognize that it is a shared board and staff function? Do they feel they "can't," "don't know how," or "won't"? How one approaches fund-raising activities is a function of how one feels about it. Therefore, discovering the board's attitudes is a critical first step to their active participation in fund raising.

Suppose that despite your efforts to inform prospective members that they may or will be expected to solicit on your organization's behalf they still balk when it comes down to the actual asking. Often you will find volunteers have a very real fear of asking for money. To overcome such fear, several techniques can be employed: (1) Educate board members on the basics of fund raising. (2) Provide specific training geared to the personal interests of members. (3) Make fund-raising assignments based on past successes; for example, if members did well selling tickets to last year's benefit, ask them to do it again this year. (4) Make sure members know what they are raising money for and how donated funds will be used. A good background on the organization is essential—solicitors need to be well informed in order to handle questions that arise. (5) Role play or assign teams of experienced and inexperienced solicitors to make calls until the one with less experience feels comfortable in his or her asking role.

You need to accept the fact that some very good board members may never be effective solicitors. Some will flatly refuse to ask for money but will feel comfortable soliciting in-kind goods or services. This, too, is a valuable type of solicitation. Not every board member must be a fund raiser.

There may be those who are unwilling, for whatever reasons, to solicit anything. If your organization badly needs board assistance with fund raising and you recruit for that purpose and then find a reluctance to solicit, you may be faced with some hard choices. Do you go so far as to ask those board members to step down? Do you assign them other activities or tasks? Do you put pressure on those individuals to solicit despite their reluctance? Do you spend more time with them on fund-raising education in the hope that you can resolve their reluctance? Because of the individual organizational needs that exist, only your board of directors can answer these questions. Whatever decision is reached, any action you take, or decide not to take, will set a precedent for future situations. Also, bear in mind that the needs of your organization are everchanging, and the press of solicitation assistance may be less in the future.

Keep in mind that participation in fund-raising activities is not necessarily confined to direct solicitations. Board members can contribute to their organization's fund-raising efforts in many different ways (some of which may appeal more to a reluctant solicitor). Here are some examples:

- Give lists of names of prospects—individuals, corporations, foundations. (As a consultant, I would advise client organizations to begin by asking for board members' Christmas card lists.)
- If staff compile a list of targeted corporate and foundation prospects with notations on a corporation's chief officers and a foundation's trustees, board members could be asked to indicate whom they know.
- Call and arrange appointments with prospects they know. (It is not necessary for board members to be personally acquainted with a prospect—but it is desirable.) Or, staff may set appointments and ask those board members who have previously indicated their availability to make solicitation calls to accompany them.
- Use their influence; help open doors for development staff or the executive director.

- If staff make calls on prospects, board members may be asked to make follow-up calls, especially when they know the prospect. Or, board members may make follow-up calls or send written follow-up notes to those prospects they have visited.
- Sell tickets to friends, associates, and colleagues for the organization's fund-raising events.
- Assist in ranking prospects according to those most likely to give (call on these first) and by the amount prospects are most likely to give (categories or ranges of potential cash gifts).
- Host a luncheon, dinner, or other social gathering for prospects.
- Support the organization by attending its fund-raising events. (All board members should attend all events.)
- Add a personal note on letters of appeal.
- Present awards to donors.
- Give a presentation to a service club, association, or other organization.

Developing a Fund-Raising Philosophy

Once you have examined your board members' attitudes on fund raising, you need to establish some philosophy of fund development to guide your efforts. What is your board willing to do to help your organization raise funds? Again, attitudes must be considered. Do your board members have the attitude that "all's fair" in raising money for your worthy cause? Do they take a "no holds-barred" approach? Is there a prejudice for, or against, seeking government funds? Are your board members for or against soliciting big business or foundations? Do they have objections to earning funds either through service fees or some entrepreneurial endeavor? Strong feelings either pro or con regarding any funding source will dictate whether your organization solicits in that area.

I once asked a nonprofit technical assistance organization if it wanted to take over the publication of a resource newsletter I had been publishing through my consulting firm. I viewed the offer as a chance for the organization to add money to its coffers through subscription income and shared the newsletter's income and expense reports with the organization's executive director. It was also a natural tie to their organization's mission—they were in the business of training nonprofits in management and resource development. However, the response was "no" because their board did not want the organization to "earn" money. This board's philosophy of fund development was based on its view of the agency as a charitable organization, meaning all their services should be given.

Some individuals feel that if only they had lots of money it would change the course of their lives and make all "bad things" good. Some believe that money means power and use money to manipulate their relationships with other people. Fantasies and irrational feelings influence the way people think about money, and nonprofit organizations can also suffer from similar fantasies.

Money can contribute to illogical thinking. In a situation where a board encourages its staff to go for any and all available grants, the board's attitude may be to get the funds first and then figure out what to do with them. The goals and objectives of the organization may be placed second and not relate to the fund-raising effort. Boards should not focus entirely on the acquisition of funds but should also emphasize the direction, purpose, and goals of the organization.

A board's philosophy of fund development should be one that encourages planning and goal setting. It should be one that supports the organization's mission; it should be one of integrity. An organization's staff needs to know the board's philosophy if they are to implement fund-raising programs with the full support of their board of directors.

The art of solicitation has both philosophical and psychological dimensions, which when taken into consideration result in effectively tailored solicitation strategies. To be successful, each fund-raising appeal should differ, just as people are different and the reasons they give differ. Staff and volunteers must understand the psychologies— why people give—of philanthropic giving. (See Bibliography for readings on this subject.) Cultivating and soliciting funding prospects has been said to be a delicate art in human relations.

Board Giving

Before asking anyone else to contribute funds to their organization, a board should look to themselves. There is no question that nonprofit boards of directors should give to their organization, and they do. However, there's still a long way to go before we even approach 100 percent giving on the part of the trustees of nonprofit organizations.

In the survey of Colorado's nonprofit boards, 65 of the 164 respondents reported that over three-fourths of their board members make cash contributions. Of boards with a member donation rate of over 75 percent, youth and family services boards are most prevalent. The majority of hospital boards reported that less than 10 percent of their board members give cash contributions. There was no difference in the giving patterns of board members among organizations located in small communities versus metropolitan areas. Boards of all sizes either give generously (over 75 percent of a board) or they don't give at all (under 10 percent). No significant frequencies occurred in the middle ranges.[2]

Raising money is a basic nonprofit board responsibility. Comprehensive fund development programs with the board playing an active role are more essential then ever because there are more non-profits competing for a "pool of funds" whose supply is not increasing at the same rate as the demand. Board members' time and expertise are very valuable commodities, and we should never fail to appreciate that. But, organizations also need money. If board members are to be successful in their solicitation efforts, they must set an example by making their own personal contributions first. Not all board members are even modestly well-to-do and a contribution within one's means is all that is expected. It is ludicrous to ask and expect someone else to give if you have not. Besides, funding sources, particularly foundations, will frequently ask what percent of an organization's board members give.

Next on the agenda, we have board member pledges.

If your organization is one that has not previously asked board members to give (many board members don't give simply because they haven't been asked), and you suddenly decide to do so, don't expect an overwhelming response. If a member joins a board and isn't told that he or she is expected to make a cash contribution to the organization, he or she may or may not comply with a later request for giving. On the one hand, it is not fair to change the rules in the middle of the game. On the other hand, if you don't begin asking at some point, you'll never get those board gifts. The remedy is to make a point of requiring contributions from all new members.

Their example of giving can also have a positive effect on the reluctant ones.

It is the job of the board president to ask other members for their pledges or cash contributions. A general announcement may be made at a board meeting that the president will be calling on members for their contributions. The amount of an individual member's gift should remain confidential unless some member elects to announce the size of his or her contribution as a challenge or pacesetting technique associated with a major capital campaign.

Keeping Board Members Involved

An organization should have a number of different sources of funds. The less an organization depends on a single source or type of source, the better. Typically, a nonprofit may solicit and receive funds from foundations, corporations, individuals, government programs/agencies, service clubs, and other organizations (e.g., United Way, churches). An organization may also conduct special events or annual membership appeals, raffles, or bingo. The resource development committee usually defines and delegates those fund-raising tasks. Most organizations have some fund-raising personnel; however, a board should participate in all the organization's fund-raising activities. The extent of a board's involvement in each fund-raising area will depend on the strength of the organization's development staff, members' experiences and past successes in solicitation, and the degree of crisis (if any) associated with the raising of funds. Also, board members are more apt to maintain enthusiasm about fund raising if they have a choice of areas where they can participate.

Paul H. Schneiter and Donald T. Nelson, in *The Thirteen Most Common Fund-Raising Mistakes and How to Avoid Them,* talk about the important roles volunteers can play in raising money for a nonprofit organization. About one in five Americans give their time each year to some charitable organization, and many of those service hours are devoted to raising money. When volunteers have a significant role in a fund-raising campaign, there is a greater potential for success. Schneiter and Nelson give five conditions for the most productive use of volunteers in fund raising.

1. Volunteers work best if...they have only one assignment.
2. Volunteers will work best if...the requested service is limited to quick, easy, clearly delineated tasks that, upon completion, have high visibility.
3. Volunteers will work best if...not required to attend many formal meetings.
4. Volunteers will work best if...the requested service is limited to a relatively short time (18 months at most).

5. Volunteers will work best if...their contributions are publicly recognized.[3]

Board members are volunteers too and should be alert to the appropriate treatment of voluntary fund raisers. A "climate for success" is essential to any fund-raising program, and a board's resource development committee is responsible for helping to create that environment.

Profit-Making Enterprises

The corporate sector of our society does not have a corner on entrepreneurs; the nonprofit sector has long had its share. The Metropolitan Museum of Art has a successful mail-order catalogue business and so does the Smithsonian Institution. We're all familiar with the Sierra Club's calendars, Girl Scout cookies, and UNICEF's cards. These are just a few of the most well-known business ventures among nonprofit organizations. Then there are those hundreds of local thrift shops that are run by charitable groups, not to mention church bazaars, art fairs, etc. Enterprise in the nonprofit sector includes all those income-producing activities that are beyond the mission of an organization. It includes the ticket sales of symphonies and theater companies, museum-run gift shops and restaurants, university bookstores, private schools' tuition, subscription fees for publications, and more. Recently what has changed is the scale and nature of a nonprofit's business activities and the increasing number of organizations engaged in for-profit enterprises.

The nonprofit board of directors necessarily assumes an activist role in the business ventures and income-producing activities of an organization. Entering into enterprise is a major policy issue requiring board approval. Whether an organization considers enterprise will largely depend on its board's attitude. Conservative nonprofit boards of directors with cautious fiduciary attitudes will discourage an organization from joining the for-profit sector. They fear the prospect of failure and point to the great number of small businesses that are not successful; they claim the organization is not trained for business ventures. Other boards want to avoid having to work with the IRS in reporting "related" and "unrelated" income; some may use the scare of IRS penalties and potential loss of the organization's tax-exempt status as a deterrent.

It is up to a board to decide whether enterprise is a viable, alternative source of revenues for its organization. A board task force may be assigned to study the issue, work with the IRS on the matter of related or unrelated income, and make recommendations on the feasibility of specific business activities to the board and staff. The board as a whole must deal with the larger policy issue—is a business enterprise a real means to the organization's end? Does it support their mission?

BUDGETING AND FISCAL MANAGEMENT

Just as Congress grants budget authority to the federal government, a board of directors authorizes the financial obligations a nonprofit organization may incur. A budget is more than a set of dollar figures submitted for board approval; it is a fiscal policy tool. It says, in figures, what your organization's plan says in words; it defines a plan of action for meeting your organization's goals and managing its valuable and scarce resources. A budget is the fundamental tool for monitoring and controlling your organization's fiscal activities.

Budgeting is a process of allocation, and unless it is accompanied by a full understanding of the programs it supports, it can be a worthless exercise. The process of budgeting helps the board evaluate the impact of revenues and expenses on program expansion or contraction. Carefully prepared and properly used, budgets help keep the organization's plan on target.

The Budget Process

Putting together a budget that realistically covers all of an organization's needs and includes consideration of contingencies can be a lengthy process. It can also be tedious. However, organizations with a systematic budgeting process and a schedule of budgeting tasks find much of the tedium alleviated. The result is a budget which is a viable management tool. The following is an overview of the steps involved in systematically preparing a budget.

Step 1: A preliminary consideration is the selection of your organization's budgeting period. If your organization is new, you also need to establish a fiscal year. Sometimes it is most convenient to align your organization's year-end with that of your major source of funding; it simplifies accounting and reporting. Your budget period— that time of year when you begin the process—should avoid your organization's busiest program times. Staff should make recommendations to the board's finance committee regarding "down time," as they are most aware of their programs' peaks of activity. The finance committee establishes the budgeting period and is responsible for periodically reviewing its timeliness and duration. This committee should also reevaluate the appropriateness of the organization's fiscal year from time to time. The full board must approve any change in a fiscal year but does not need to approve the budgeting period.

Step 2: Planning and budgeting must occur simultaneously as each program area requires financing. The revenues and expenses relative to each program objective need to be projected. In this way, one can look at the alternative uses of funds and determine which programs are self-sufficient, which require fund-raising support, and which are, therefore, more cost-effective. Program staff are responsible for providing these initial projections in their respective areas. If your organization is embarking into new program areas, it will not have a history of revenues and expenses to draw upon. If that is the case, you need to talk to other organizations presently working in the field, to consultants, or to funding sources familiar with that type program. Staff and the board finance committee might share the responsibility for this fact-finding task.

Step 3: The allocation function of budgeting requires that program priorities be established. Your organization's plan and most current program evaluation are the two primary guides for setting priorities. The board finance and program services committees set these priorities based on the recommendations made by staff, and the full board approves them.

Organizations also need to have an alternative or contingency budget in the event revenues or expenditures are more or less than expected. Priorities tell where you might make budget cuts, which line item expenditures of which program would be reduced in the event of a revenue shortfall. This eliminates the need to indiscriminately cut all programs. Likewise, if a windfall occurs, it is just as important to avoid haphazard increases "across the board" and focus instead on boosting those programs that are a priority. The alternative budget requires full board approval also and should be kept on file.

Step 4: Once the organization's annual budget is made final, a cash flow analysis needs to be prepared. It is important for staff managers to know *when* what amount of their budget will actually be available to them. Knowing, for example, that revenues are projected to be lower in the months of July and August, certain expenditures in that interim can be deferred. The finance committee needs to be alert to consistent cash flow problem times. It might suggest to the resource development committee that some fund-raising activity be rescheduled or planned for those months when revenues are anticipated to be down. It is ideal to have a constant and level cash flow or to begin the fiscal year with a surplus of funds. However, the uncertainties associated with an organization's dependence on charitable contributions make this very difficult.

Step 5: Once the budget, alternative budget, and cash flow analysis have been approved by the board, monitoring and evaluation begin. The finance committee needs to ensure that there is a system of reporting that allows actual "results" to be compared with the budget.

A nonprofit board of directors should use the budget as a "benchmark," which can alert it to early signs that the organization may or may not meet its financial goals. Budgets must be planned to provide this kind of control and four elements must be present.

1. The budget must be well conceived and have been prepared or approved by the board of directors.
2. The budget must be broken down into periods corresponding to the periodic financial statements.
3. Financial statements must be prepared on a timely basis throughout the year and a comparison made to the budget, right on the statements.
4. The board must be prepared to take action where the comparison with the budget indicates a significant deviation.[4]

Budgeting Methods

If you take last year's budget and add 10 percent "across the board," or even if you meticulously add 7 percent to salaries, 10 percent to program costs, and 20 percent to utilities, that is incremental budgeting. It means you add (or subtract) a certain percent to last year's budget; line items are increased or decreased by increments. Most organizations use this method; it is easy. Incremental budgeting considers only one factor to cause the new budget to vary from the past year's—inflation. Although that is a real factor, it is not the only one or even the most important. There are several dangers in using incremental budgeting: you add to past mistakes, you assume a status quo and no programmatic changes are considered, and you assume all prior allocations were fair and equitable.

Program budgeting is a financial planning and analysis system based on the concepts of cost-accounting. The main criteria considered is the cost-effectiveness of a program, or how much it costs to "produce" an activity or program in relationship to the "good" it produces (clients served) and the revenues it generates. To determine the cost of a program, you must total the obvious expenses of salaries and materials, as well as the costs of promoting it, volunteer training in this area, the percent of utilities used and the percent of rent by the space the program occupies, etc. In assessing a program's worth, consider the number of clients served (numbers alone do not signify quality); the quality of program outcomes; the amount of income the program generates, if any; its public relations value; and even other less legitimate factors like its fundability and if it is a "favorite program" of the trustees. To cite an extreme example, if a program costs $50,000 a year, serves only 12 clients, requires two full-time staff, generates no income, and is unpopular with funders, it is not cost-effective. Program budgeting asks one to evaluate all programs and allocate funds to those which are most cost-effective—it forces one to establish priorities. With this method, a program must measure up to some standard, its worth is not assumed. The finance committee, program services committee, and their respective staffs work in tandem to set quality program standards and performance measures.

Zero-based budgeting makes no assumptions; therefore, it is ideal. It asks for a systematic review of all program alternatives. You begin with zero each year, as if your programs were all new. It forces a thorough examination of your programs and how they meet your organization's goals as they are presently defined. If a program is to be continued, it must be justified and have a priority ranking. Zero-based budgeting takes more time and paperwork than nonprofits can realistically give to their budgeting process. Therefore, some version of program budgeting is best for most nonprofits, especially if it incorporates the functional format described in the following section.

Budget Formats

The finance committee and board treasurer are responsible for deciding which budget format is appropriate for the organization's operating budget.* A budget format must not only reflect the various program activities of the organization, it must also be suitable for meeting the reporting requirements of the agency's major funding sources. There are many ways to format a budget, and an organization may experiment with combined forms. However, no standard format exists since budgeting is more a concept than a specific procedure. (See Appendix for a sample budget format suitable for adaptation by most types of organizations.)

A functional budget format is best as it allows for a breakdown, per line item, of the cost of each program area plus associated revenues per area. Typically, functional areas will include administration; fund raising or resource development; physical plant/building and grounds (when an agency operates out of an office, rent would be an administrative cost); and program, subdivided into major areas like education, counseling, or clinical services. When marketing and public relations activities consume a major portion of staff time or have particular significance to an organization (e.g., the Denver Childrens' Museum earns a major portion of its budget by marketing services and products that have related costs), they may be a separate functional category.

Specific expenditures like salaries, office supplies, rent, utilities, postage, transportation, and so forth are the line items of a budget and should always appear in horizontal columns. Functional cate-

---

*When something is referred to as a committee's responsibility, it is assumed there is staff input. Remember, all board committees should have key staff managers and/or the executive director as ex-officio members.

gories appear in the vertical columns of a budget. An easy method for determining functional budget categories is to create a vertical column for each department or each area employing a department head or director. You want to be thorough in representing your organization's functions, as this is essential to tracking the cost-effectiveness of programs. However, there is a point at which too many categories are broken out, and your budget becomes a nightmare of detail.

Organizations, except for the smallest, should have two operating budget formats. One should be the working budget of the organization, a highly detailed line item and functionally spread format. The other, for external purposes, should be a summary type budget used in brochures, reports, and funding proposals. The public does not need to know, for example, the salary of the janitor or even the executive director; a total of all salaries is sufficient. If a prospective funder requests more detail, it shows they are seriously interested in your organization and you can easily provide them with copies of your detailed working budget. You might even have a third budget format that would be a combination and compromise between these two formats.

The executive director determines which budget formats are appropriate for which of the organization's publics and under what circumstances. Assuming the staff and board have a good working relationship and that each knows what the other is doing, board approval on budget format is not necessary.

Fiscal Control and Other Matters

The nonprofit board is responsible for ensuring that the organization's budget is realistic, for ensuring that the organization has the funds it needs to operate basic programs, and for auditing the budget in order to make good decisions on committing the organization's funds.

The board treasurer is responsible for ensuring that there are good internal accounting controls, such as are listed below, and the board also needs to be aware of these.

- Personnel handling assets and records should be screened for competence and integrity.
- A system should be established requiring a proper signature or initials authorizing the purchase of goods and services and then approving the related payment.
- Only individuals with proper authority should be able to authorize such transactions, and the terms of the transaction should be checked for correspondence with those authorized.
- Access to assets should be limited to those with authorized custody or access.

- Periodic independent comparisons should be made between actual assets on hand and recorded accountability for such assets.

- Assigned and actual duties should not be incompatible from a security viewpoint. Different individuals should perform each of the following functions: authorization of a transaction, recording the transaction, custody of assets involved, comparison of actual assets on hand with accounts indicated by accounting records.[5]

Good organizational accounting and reporting procedures coupled with a properly prepared budget provide ample warning to a board that an organization may be headed for financial trouble. Unfortunately, there are still those boards that fail to recognize the symptoms or fail to take corrective action.

Nine years ago, as executive director of the Girls Club of Denver, Inc., I experienced just such a situation. The board treasurer and I presented to the board budget projections clearly showing that the organization's anticipated revenues would fall short of basic expenditures during the next six months and that within eight months we would be without operating funds altogether. Until that point, I had been the only fund raiser for the organization; the board had not assumed any financial development responsibilities. The organization's budget had tripled over the past five years, and I was aware I could no longer raise all the funds the organization needed without assistance from the board. (Our 15-member staff did not include a development officer.) I hoped the impending crisis would stir the board to take an active role in fund raising and "pleaded my case" backed with the financial projections. My board's response was, "You have always bailed us out in the past, surely you can do it again." The projections held true, and eight months later we were faced with the prospect of canceling our girls' summer program. The organization did receive a special foundation grant that would support its summer program, but by then I had been fired. Two executive directors and one year later, the agency closed for a lack of funds. (The need for a girls' club persisted, and two years ago, it reopened in the same neighborhood with a new board of directors.)

Other fiscal management matters that require a nonprofit board's attention deal with external controls. They may include the following:

Fidelity bonding—A board's finance committee determines if the organization should have insurance against employees' embezzlement or fraud. In most cases, it is simply a wise internal control. In other cases, funding sources, especially government agencies, may require proof of bonding insurance.

Loans—Nonprofits borrow money for working capital, to finance capital construction or equipment, or to mortgage property. All borrowing recommendations are made by the finance committee and require full board approval.

Accountability—Nonprofit organizations are accountable to a number of different publics, especially if they receive tax dollars. Contributors to a tax-exempt charitable organization have a right to know how their dollars are spent. Boards must be aware of to whom the organization is accountable and what reporting requirements will suffice. Organizations are no less accountable for their program services. The board is ultimately responsible for the organization's accountability.

Licenses—Some organizations, by the nature of their services, are required to be licensed by their city and state. Child care centers, hospitals, and health care centers require licensing, and educational institutions require accreditation; these are the most obvious examples. With licensing and accreditation, certain requirements must be met on a continuous basis. The board is responsible for ensuring the organization is in compliance.

Some cities and states require charitable organizations to have a solicitations permit. Usually such permits relate to soliciting the general public and are not required in order to solicit foundations and corporations nor do they apply to appeals to the organization's membership. A board needs to be aware of such regulations, and if the organization solicits funds in more than one state, the board must ensure compliance with a number of different solicitation laws.

IRS—Nonprofits are required to file a Form 990 with the IRS annually. Churches, church-affiliated organizations, secondary religious schools, and a few other specific types of nonprofit organizations are exempt. Most states also require annual filings.

Government-required benefits—If your organization has paid employees, it is required to withhold income taxes, and it may need to pay social security, unemployment taxes, workman's compensation, and federal unemployment insurance. A board must see that the organization complies with all applicable filings in a timely fashion.

Exemption status—A board must be aware of what circumstances, such as unreported business income, excessive lobbying, and violation of "public support" rules, might endanger the tax-exempt status of the organization and ensure that the organization does not jeopardize this status.

A nonprofit board of directors' role in fiscal affairs is extensive and, along with planning, this constitutes its most important responsibility. The board must see that the organization is solvent, maintains accurate and meaningful financial records, safeguards the organization's assets, anticipates financial problems, and complies with federal and state reporting requirements.

Either we've lost our tax-exempt status or we're bankrupt?

SUMMARY

Because there are misconceptions about what fund raising is and because many board volunteers are reluctant to solicit money, it is very important to educate board members on the basics of fund raising. Because some individuals may never feel comfortable with direct solicitations, there are other ways for them to contribute to an organization's resource development program.

Before embarking on any fund-raising effort, boards of directors need to examine their attitudes about raising money. Money is not an end in itself—accomplishing the organization's goals is the desired end. A philosophy of fund development that promotes planning and goal orientation should guide a board's resource development activities. Additionally, all board members should make cash contributions to their organization before they can, in good conscience, solicit from others.

When volunteers, specifically board volunteers, participate in solicitations on behalf of an organization, there is a greater potential for success. To keep members involved they need to be offered a choice of fund-raising roles, be given manageable assignments that lead to success, and be recognized for their assistance.

Profit-making enterprises are an alternative to charitable solicitations. Nonprofits have been engaged in successful income-producing ventures for many years. However, enterprising ventures are not appropriate for all organizations. A board should decide whether profit-making activities are a viable alternative source of income for the organization and if such activities further the organization's mission.

Budgeting and fiscal control are two other areas of a board's financial responsibilities. Planning and budgeting are inseparable because resources are allocated to an organization's priority programs through its budget. The budget planning process requires board participation and normally a special board committee manages the process.

Program budgeting in a functional format allows an organization to break down its expenditures and revenues by program area. This budget method makes it easier to tell which programs are more cost-effective than others. Sometimes an organization will combine or use different budget formats to meet the requests of its various publics.

A board is responsible for ensuring that its organization has good internal and external controls. A board needs to be aware of its agency's requirements for bonding and licensing, loans, required employee benefits, IRS filings, and tax-exempt status regulations.

NOTES

1. Diane J. Duca, "Survey Report on Colorado's Nonprofit Board of Directors" (Paper written for the University of Colorado/Denver, Graduate School of Public Affairs, Denver, May 1985).

2. Ibid.

3. Paul H. Schneiter and Donald T. Nelson, *The Thirteen Most Common Fund-Raising Mistakes and How to Avoid Them*, pp. 57–58.

4. Malvern J. Gross, Jr., *Financial and Accounting Guide for Nonprofit Organizations*, p. 294.

5. Arnold J. Olenick and Philip R. Olenick, *Making the Non-Profit Organization Work: A Financial, Legal & Tax Guide for Administrators*, p. 503.

Chapter 7
Holding Effective Board Meetings

by John E. Tropman and Diane J. Duca

> The following chapter was co-authored by John E. Tropman and Diane J. Duca. Tropman tells us one of the most simple and direct ways to improve meetings is to pay attention to agenda. Structured properly, the agenda can be a vital tool for effective meetings. The last section, dealing with the minutes, was written by Diane Duca.

Boards of directors as a group, and directors as individuals, cannot accomplish their tasks unless meetings, and the related or necessary processes to meeting development, are effective and efficient. Meetings must be meaningful, well planned, well run, and must produce results. A casual meeting that approximates a social gathering and does not deal with items at hand in a serious way will produce decisions of inferior quality and open the way for judicial review. Both board and committee meetings are a part of the overall management process and need to be well run.

Meetings need not be unpleasant for directors. Generally, the humor that people use to describe boards and committees refers to ineptitude and inability to accomplish objectives. "Boards," people say, "are forests of dead wood" or "Committees are groups that take minutes to waste hours." For more effective meetings, we need to understand why things go wrong.

DETERRENTS TO EFFECTIVE MEETINGS

America's character is not hospitable to group activity. Americans like to do things individually and it requires extra effort to participate in groups and in group decision-making activities. And,

Mr. Folby! We have "procedures" for expressing disagreement.

too, there are some hidden functions which add difficulty to board meetings—social expectations that transcend the particular situation.

Following are five reasons why board meetings can be ineffective.

Contrary to Values

First, boards and committees demand group interaction, which may be contrary to some American values. Zander observes:

> [We] are not all that interested in explaining or improving group life...individuals feel that the organization should help them; it is not the individual's prime job to help the organization. Basic values...foster the formation of groups that put the good of the individual before the good of the group. In Japan, in contrast, important values foster interdependence among persons, courtesy, obligation to others, listening, empathy, self-denial, and support of one's group[1]

Hidden Functions

Second, there are a number of hidden representation functions that boards and committees perform. For example, directors are expected to represent the diversity of the community and to provide a voice for all of those who cannot be heard in other ways. The pluralism inherent in these functions of representation can compete with goals of equality, justice, and unity. Trying to fill these different functions such as diversity, pluralism, and/or representation can create a number of difficult problems.

For example, functions of representation create difficulties because they are not defined in the mission statement of the board, although some bylaws state that the board is to be "representative." Hence, directors feel some sense of obligation to values that are vague and sometimes conflicting. Concern for those who will be affected by decisions may inhibit rapid and "businesslike" attention to items. There is no rule for the resolution of this kind of conflict, but it is important to be aware of this potential conflict.

Boards cannot play all roles, rectify all the injustice, and solve all the problems of inequality and still do the other things expected and required of them. It is best to bring hidden functions and expectations to light and to take some steps to deal with them. (Holding open discussions of representation, of the need for diversity, of the importance of different points of view is one of the best ways.) Attention to hidden and conflicting values recognizes their existence and importance and prevents the inevitable conflicts which surround such values from diverting the board or impeding decision-making activities.

Vague Decision Rules

Third, rules governing decision making are sometimes obscure. Policies and procedures should be clear and should be observed at meetings. This is especially true for nonprofit boards. Drucker points out:

> The basic...difference between a private service institution and a business is the way the service institution is paid. Businesses (other than monopolies) are paid for satisfying the customer....Service institutions are paid out of a budget allocation...from a general revenue stream not tied to what they are doing.[2]

Because money is a prominent decision concern and because profit is absent as a decision criterion, decision making is confusing and difficult for the nonprofit board.

Money is an important basis for decisions but so are other factors such as quality of service, client involvement, meeting new needs, and so on. John Naisbett, in his book *Megatrends,* asks the question, "What business are you in?" This question is not an easy one for the nonprofit board. Nonprofit organizations are likely to be in several businesses and the basis for making decisions will tend to vary from issue to issue. Clarification of the various decision bases is necessary for the board to understand the competing considerations that come into play during decision making.

It is also useful to specify rules for decision making—a vote, consensus, etc.—so that directors know how and when a decision is made. All too often decisions become implicit ("I assumed we had all agreed...") and some members are unaware that a decision has been made. It is important for the chair of the board, as well as other directors, to note that a decision has been made and to specify its content and nature.

Lack of Training

Fourth, individuals are usually not prepared for group roles—for group life in general or for board and committee life in particular. There is a simple lack of knowing what to do.

There are few publications, courses, skill sessions, and so on, related to general group processes. When they exist they seem to focus on the person-to-person aspects of group interaction rather than to emphasize the rules and roles of effective board membership. (It is the intention of this book to fill that void.)

In addition, too few boards prepare directors with board-specific information. Board preparation should include a discussion of the directors' job description, history of the agency or organization, a review of decision rules, etc. This small step helps train directors for their jobs.

Lack of Preparation

Fifth, some directors tend not to prepare well for meetings. For numerous reasons, including some of the points already mentioned, there's a casual approach of "let the chips fall where they may." Premeeting materials—minutes, agenda, supporting documents—may be inadequate or overadequate. (Overadequacy occurs when so much is sent to directors that they are overwhelmed and they don't read any of it. Information then becomes disinformation.) Directors may not regularly attend meetings and may not have read preparatory materials when they do attend. To counter this, material is often reviewed at the board meeting and this offends those who have prepared. Meetings then become one disappointment after another. For this reason, an investment in meeting preparation may be considered a waste of time by many.

These five reasons combine to create a self-fulfilling prophecy that almost ensures poor-quality board meetings. Since we don't believe in meetings; since they include a range of obscure and often hidden functions; since the decision rules that we use are unclear; and since we have neither the training nor take the time to prepare for meetings, they are likely to go badly. These assumptions are stimuli to inappropriate generalization. In other words, we come to believe that there is something inherent about meetings that makes them unpleasant.

Evidence of inept meetings only reinforces our original suppositions. This reinforcement, in turn, convinces directors that it would be a waste of time to spend their valuable energy and effort on improving meetings. Such a conclusion virtually ensures increased difficulty in the actual meeting. Hence, initial difficulty is exacerbated by the self-fulfilling prophecy. Once that mechanism is in operation, there is a downward spiral of meeting quality.

Also, in business, individuals on boards of directors are called directors. In human service organizations they are sometimes designated by the more neutral, less important term "member." Small as this difference appears, it conceals an important difference in expectations. If someone is called a director, he or she may begin to act like one. Therefore in this chapter the phrase "board member" has been eliminated and the word "director" substituted. Expectations create their own impetus for action or inaction.

This brief discussion of why things go wrong, with hints of how to right them, suggests that there is a recipe for improvement. The ingredients of this recipe, like all recipes, must be combined properly and applied promptly. One can't sprinkle a little bit here and there and expect things to come out in a good fashion. Boards of directors must have a systematic and planned approach to improve the quality of their meetings.

PRINCIPLES FOR EFFECTIVE MEETINGS

If board meetings are to be improved, new principles are needed to create a new kind of meeting structure. These principles form important bases for thinking about ways in which meetings can be improved.

The Personality Principle

Individuals often tell us that board meetings are bad because of "mental illness" on the part of individual directors. This is then illustrated with examples of abnormal behavior on the part of various directors. Often, directors are stereotyped by aspects of their personality—"Arthur Angry," "Tillie Talk-A-Lot," and "Sam Stall" are frequently found on boards of directors. However, it is more important to see deficiencies in procedures rather than in the character of individual directors and to look at the ways in which functions, procedures, and rules can be strengthened and improved. These "repairs" will make a substantial difference in meeting quality.

The Orchestra Principle

Board meetings should be like an orchestra performance. They should be the result of a process of development and preparation rather than the beginning. No competent orchestra would stroll onto the stage and begin to play without previous planning and preparation. Before the maestro raises the baton, selections about the pieces have been made, rehearsals have been held, and the proper soloists and accompanists have been procured.

An orchestra would look ridiculous performing a piano concerto with no pianist. It would be more absurd if the conductor said, "Ladies and gentlemen, please excuse me, the oboist has to leave early tonight. We know you'll understand. Unfortunately, the last piece on our program has an oboe passage in it. Therefore, we're going to ask the oboist to play those notes right now. And then, if you could kindly remember them when we get to the oboe section of the last piece, it would be a favor to us all. Thank you."

How often is this scene echoed in board meetings? The president says, "Members and directors, Sheila has to leave early. Therefore, we'd like to go directly to her business," regardless of the nature or complexity of that business or its position in the structure of the meeting. If directors would think of the meeting as an orchestra performance and demand the same quality and structure, they would be moving toward improved meetings.

The Report Principle

Reports have become the bane of many meetings. Most boards have numerous standing committees that are invited to report regularly whether or not they have any business. Thus, meetings have been transformed into oral newsletters, and the minutes become written newsletters.

All reports should be examined in advance for action, discussion, or information items and be scheduled in an appropriate place on the agenda. The Reports Principle contains two related and crucial elements. Unless there is specific business, no committee report is scheduled. Instead, an announcement of committee activity is attached to the meeting announcement.

Reports that require board action should be separated. Rather than having one treasurer's report that may contain items for decision, discussion, and information, those items are distributed to relevant places on the agenda. The treasurer, therefore, may appear three times on the agenda: once during the announcement stage; second, during a discussion stage; and third, during a decision stage.

This structure is no odder than having the oboist perform whenever oboe notes are required. No one would seriously recommend that each performer play all of the notes written for his or her instrument at one point. Yet agenda items are routinely grouped and scheduled only by content. Both the substantive link of agenda items and their action imperatives—decision, discussion, announcement—are important to the flow of a meeting.

The New Business Principle

New business is the enemy of many meetings. Frequently, presidents tell us, "We don't know what the directors want to talk about until they get there, do we?" Of course we don't, unless we ask. Indeed, this becomes one of the most important rules for effective meetings.

It is imperative to find out in advance what matters will require discussion in order to have present the information and persons germane to discussion. The discussion of new business is usually the most unprofitable part of a board meeting. Most participants are ignorant about new business matters, but ignorance does not deter participation. Lack of knowledge seems to increase the desire to say something regardless of how ridiculous it is.

The Reactive/Proactive Principle

Business is often introduced under pressure. The executive director or board president will indicate that an item requires immediate action. This makes reaching a quality decision difficult. Under pressure, clarity of thought and adequate information seem to be replaced by emotion and table pounding. As a result, a series of problematic decision-making steps may be taken. The retrospective analysis of decisions that have gone sour almost always indicates that a premature decision was made under pressure.

This kind of decision is reactive. Guidelines for action are already in place and have been established by external forces such as environment and outside funders. Within these guidelines, directors may have limited options, and it is the reaction to these limitations that causes pressure and frustration.

Instead of pressure responses, boards need to make proactive decisions. Boards must assume a decision-making style that anticipates future developments and tries to deal with them from an appropriate distance; a decision should not be made too far in advance because then the issue seems irrelevant and unreal; a decision should not be made too late because then pressure makes realistic or effective solutions difficult.

In the final analysis, what boards want are high-quality decisions. These do not just occur without effort. Often one observes outstanding or excellent performances which seem so flawless that they appear simple. Yet anyone who has played a violin concerto, sunk a 20-foot putt, or cast a fishing fly in exactly the right place understands that extensive practice goes into a flawless performance.

Likewise, board decisions need to be approached with care, not casualness. When care is taken, the resulting decision is likely to be of high quality and is likely to reflect the existence of a quality decision-making system. It is to such a system, its construction and operation, that we now turn.

RULES FOR EFFECTIVE MEETINGS

A board of directors needs to determine how to improve its meeting process—an exercise that would also apply to other meetings within both the organization and the community. The following rules are suggested for improving meetings, and all stress the importance of information, for without information it is hard to make good decisions. The cumulative emphasis of these rules is to follow up on items that need information, to focus on the information required, and to present information clearly and in a timely fashion so that the board can act on an issue and make quality decisions.

The Rule of Halves

The first rule is a simple agenda rule. It asserts that all items for an upcoming meeting must be in the hands of the agenda scheduler one-half of the time between meetings. Thus, for the monthly board meeting, the agenda items should be submitted at the two-week point. Agenda schedulers are usually the executive director and/or the board president. Frequently the executive will draft the agenda and then check it with the president of the board. This pattern works if the executive screens out items that can be handled by staff, breaks large items into manageable segments, groups small related items into a package, and assesses candidate items with respect to the availability of information. (There's little point in scheduling an item if information required for a decision is not available.) Sometimes the executive needs to check with others who might have items for consideration.

The Rule of Sixths

Once the agenda items have been assembled, they should be reviewed from the perspective of the Rule of Sixths. About one-sixth of the agenda items should be from the past—items that could be called "old business." About four-sixths of the agenda items should be contemporary—items that are current within a month or two (in the past or future). The final sixth should be "blue sky" items of anticipatory nature—items that look ahead 6 to 18 months. The final sixth can be the fun part of board meetings when directors have the opportunity to look ahead, to influence the future, and to structure their options. Here the principle of proactivity can be enforced.

Naturally, not every meeting will have such "blue sky" items but most will, and they allow a certain amount of psychological rehearsal. Executives and other agenda schedulers need to anticipate upcoming possibilities and take the board through a series of "what ifs." This permits the board to look ahead, and it forces meeting planners, executive directors, and board presidents to look ahead and construct scenarios. It is amazing how beneficial this technique is. Often an advanced discussion of a "what if" item permits the development of previously unconsidered alternatives and introduces concealed perspectives. In general, the quality of a proposal for future action will be improved.

Individual board presidents often tell us, "We don't have the time for what if-ing." Experience with boards and an analysis of board decisions teaches us that such statements are excuses.

There are, of course, emergency items that occur from time to time. But if the board's life is a series of emergencies, it is imperative that the board look at its decision-making system and seek ways to anticipate surprises and deal with them in advance.

The Rule of Three-Quarters

The Rule of Halves permits the Rule of Three-Quarters to operate. This rule states that at the three-quarters point between meetings, an agenda with appropriate attachments must be distributed. Executive directors and other agenda schedulers usually have to work very hard during the "third quarter" between meetings—that time between the halfway point (when agenda items are assembled) and the three-quarter point (when the fully developed agenda is sent out). During this time, necessary information is brought together, individual presenters are lined up, needed reports are copied, and so on. Following the Rule of Three-Quarters will get information to directors at just about the right time before a meeting—not too late to prevent them from reading it and not too early to invite them to put it aside.

Figure 1. How the Rule of Halves & the Rule of Three-Quarters Work

Week 1 - Secure agenda items
Week 2 - All candidate items for the agenda are due
Between week 2 & 3 - Rule of Halves—sort and sift agenda items; get the information and people needed
Week 3 - Rule of Three-Quarters—agenda and packet sent out
Week 4
Board Meeting

The Rule of Two-Thirds

The Rule of Two-Thirds divides a meeting into three parts. The first third is the start; the middle third is where the greatest amount of work is done; and the last third is the time for decompression. The two-thirds point is a good time for a break—something parallel to the "seventh-inning stretch."

The Rule of the Agenda Bell

The Rule of the Agenda Bell states that items should be outlined in ascending and descending order of difficulty, with the most difficult in the middle (according to the Rule of Two-Thirds, where the greatest amount of work is done) and items for discussion (again, by the Rule of Two-Thirds, the time for decompression) at the end of the meeting. Then, the free-floating nature of discussion will not disrupt decision making. If there is a seven-item agenda, the flow of the board meeting would look something like this:

1. Approval of the minutes of the previous meeting.
2. Brief noncontroversial announcements.
3. An item of modest difficulty to begin the decision-making process.
4. A moderately controversial item.
5. The item(s) of greatest difficulty. (This is the middle third of the agenda and occurs when most people have come, early leavers have not yet slipped out, and the energy to deal with complexities is at its high point.)

6. An item that needs discussion but does not require a decision and that helps relax the decision makers. This item serves as a break from the job of making decisions.

7. An easy item that ends the meeting on a note of agreement and bonds the group.

The agenda bell makes it possible to structure the meeting consonant with the time and flow of energy available for group decision making.

Figure 2. A Bell-Shaped Agenda Structure

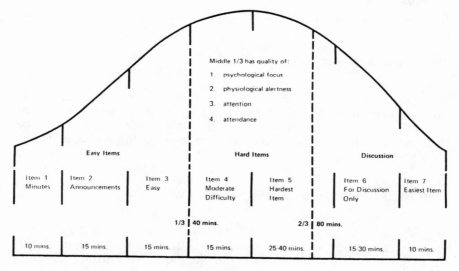

John E. Tropman, "The Agenda," p. 68 in *Effective Meetings, Improving Group Decision-Making.* Copyright © 1980 by Sage Publications, Inc. Reprinted by permission of Sage Publications, Inc.

The Rule of the Agenda

In making an agenda, special attention should be given to the language of the agenda. Items should be introduced with action words (approve, consider, discuss), not merely "The ABC Report." Each item should also receive one of the three possible item designations: information, decision, or discussion. If appropriate, a one-line description of the item should be included.

The Rule of Reports

The Rule of Reports assumes that most reports are too long and do not contain essential information. It argues for an executive summary in three parts: a declaration of the problem; a list of options for solution of the problem; and a statement of the solution recommended by the author of the report. This three-part executive summary is not only briefer than the report, but it also gives the group some tools with which to work. Since the recommended solution follows other options, decision makers can operate at their best; they can assess the positive aspects of previously unrecognized options, combine them with the recommendations offered, and bring about stronger and better decisions.

The Rule of Agenda Integrity

All items on the agenda should be discussed and items not on the agenda should not be discussed. If directors are going to study materials sent out prior to the meeting, that investment must pay off in discussion and decisions at the meeting. Should that not occur, directors will avoid preparation on the theory that it's not a good investment of time. As lack of preparation becomes evident, oral summaries of preparation materials may be presented at the meetings—a further waste of time for those who spent time reviewing the material.

New business items that may come up at the meeting are typically ones about which information is low and are poor candidates for discussion. If a new business category is necessary, it should be placed at the end of item six on the agenda and used to generate agenda items for the next meeting. New business items should not be discussed at the current meeting. As a courtesy to the directors, for the efficiency and effectiveness of the board's decision-making function, and out of concern for the integrity and purpose of the organization, the agenda must be followed.

The Rule of Temporal Integrity

The Rule of Temporal Integrity means "watch the clock." Begin on time, end on time, and follow a rough internal order of time using the agenda bell system. It is useful to post times next to the items on the agenda. Directors will then have a rough idea of the amount of time appropriate for a particular item. This is especially important for minor items that tend to balloon and take inordinate amounts of time. The sample agenda in Figure 3 uses this system. The Rule of the Agenda Bell begins with more modest items—minutes and announcements—so that if people are a bit late, a great deal is not lost. Starting on time is the best way to get people to come on time. One should always end on time even if the meeting was called to order a bit late.

Figure 3. Sample Agenda

Agenda
Better Board Association, Inc.

7:00–7:10   1) Minutes of Previous Meeting

7:10–7:30   2) Announcements
a) new meeting location
b) annual meeting dates
c) new staff member

7:30–7:45   3) Approve Grant Submission (*decision*)
A grant to the Better Boards Association for $5,000 is up for final approval. It involves training directors from other organizations on a pilot basis.

7:45–8:00   4) Approve Director Evaluation Design (*decision*)
The Evaluation Committee has designed an annual director evaluation form which will be used with each director. Final approval is needed. The form was previously distributed.)

8:00–8:30   5) Act on Fund-Raising Target for Next Year (*decision*)
The Development Committee recommends a commitment to a 20% increase in funds for the next fiscal year.

8:30–9:00   6) Agency Goals (*discussion*)
In preparation for the retreat, a preliminary discussion of agency goals is scheduled. Please refer to the goal options document distributed by the Goal Options Subcommittee.

9:00–9:01   7) Letter of Appreciation to "Sam's Service" (*decision*)
For free pop during our last meeting.

The Rule of Decision Audit/Decision Autopsy

It is important to evaluate meetings that are carefully planned and structured. Without evaluation, the feedback necessary to sustain quality decisions is not likely to be present. Therefore, both decision audits and decision autopsy are needed.

About six months should elapse between the time a decision is made and audited to allow for observation of how the decision has worked. Under the Rule of Minutes (see section on minutes at the end of this chapter), decisions are easily available and can be extracted and listed. After six months, three directors should be appointed to review and grade decisions, as follows:

- An *A decision* occurs when it is judged that all parties to the decision were winners. This is the "all win" decision. Everyone affected by the decision comes out ahead, although they did not necessarily have to come out equally ahead.

- A *B decision* is one in which there were some winners and some losers, but the balance of the outcome is positive.

- A *C decision* is one in which there are winners and losers but the winner/loser balance is about equal. The "B" decision might be called the "some win decision" and the "C" decision the "no win" decision. In this case, "no win" means that while there are no losses, there are no gains.

- A *D decision,* which might also be called a "nuclear war decision," is the "all lose" decision in which everyone is further behind after the decision than they were before.

The individual ratings of the decisions are then compared. Two patterns are sought. One pattern is agreement on the *A* or *D* level (these will be extracted for later autopsy). The other pattern is a divergence of grading, such as *A* given by one evaluator and a *C* by another. Dissimilar grades reveal disparity in the bases used to assess the decisions, and the discrepancy itself should become a matter for board consideration. For example, when there are differences in grades, it is important to use this difference to explore why there are (differences) and look at how these differences can affect decisions. It is a good way to explore value conflicts within the board.

The decision autopsy should follow the audit. A decision autopsy is simply the intensive examination of one pair of divergently graded decisions, an *A* and a *D*. Naturally, when the board does something right, as in an *A* decision, the directors should know what was done and how it can be repeated. Similarly, a bad decision should be examined to discover what went wrong and how it can be prevented. The potential defensiveness that a board will have toward reviewing a *D* decision will in part be blunted by discussion of the *A* decision.

Autopsies reveal a common pattern of difficulty. Among the most frequently occurring causes of bad decisions are the following: pressure; inadequate information; lack of board willingness to tolerate independence and differing viewpoints; and group thinking or premature and improper agreement on a restricted set of alternatives. These are the most prevalent causes and their prevalence does not make them less lethal. The rules discussed in this chapter and the perspectives offered elsewhere in this book can help to counteract these bad decisions.

No set of rules can guarantee perfect meetings, and experienced directors know this. It is also true that because of lack of training and lack of preparation, directors may approach board and committee meetings casually and with a relaxed sense of mission. While this approach is not entirely bad, it should be balanced by an understanding of the important range of activities for which directors are responsible as well as the potential legal liabilities for which the board may be held responsible. This realization should encourage the development of a systematic and planned approach to decision making.

MINUTES

It is not uncommon for the president to call for a volunteer to take the minutes of a board meeting. Since board minutes are the legal record of a nonprofit corporation, they should not be treated in an offhand manner, and the responsibility of minute taking should be assigned to a specific person. The purpose of recording the actions of an organization in minutes is to establish the legality of that action. Minutes are the concrete evidence of an activity; therefore, they must contain an accurate account of what was done at the meeting, not what was said. The secretary of the board is responsible for seeing that minutes are accurate.

To achieve that accuracy, there is a format for writing minutes that applies to both board and committee minutes. (See Figure 4.) Minutes should basically contain the following:

1. the name of the organization
2. the date, place, and kind of meeting (regular, special)
3. the time convened
4. the name of who presided
5. a list of who attended (note of a quorum is optional)
6. a notation of approval of the minutes of the previous meeting along with any corrections, and if corrected, how
7. a statement of the financial status of the organization briefly summarized, with a detailed report attached
8. a record of all motions that were made (except those withdrawn) and the disposition thereof, including motions made but not seconded, and those on which there was no action taken
9. a record of amendments to motions
10. a description of the program, if any
11. the time of adjournment
12. the signature and title of the person who wrote the minutes

(See Appendix for sample minutes using a paragraph heading style as well as one with a narrative format.)

Figure 4. Sample Minutes

MODEL MINUTES

_____(date)_____

The (special, regular, annual) meeting of ___(name)___ was called to order by the president (or vice president), _____, at (time, day, date) in the (place) with (number) active members and (number) guests present: (names of those attending) . (A quorum was present.) The minutes of the previous meeting, (date), were approved. (If corrections were made, add "as corrected.") The treasurer's financial statement reported a balance on hand (amount) . Copy of the financial statement is attached.

REPORTS — Reports were presented by (list officers, committee chairmen, and any others) and include important items reported. (DO NOT INCLUDE DISCUSSION UNLESS IT RESULTS IN ACTION.)

MOTION RE: — (All main motions and disposition thereof, with editorial entry in left margin, as shown. The format is: "It was moved by (name) and seconded that _____. Motion carried.")

BILLS — The following bills were allowed (if applicable), and the treasurer was instructed to pay them.

NEW BUSINESS — Under new business, it was moved by ___(name)___ that _____ _____. Motion carried. (The brief description of the content of the motion should appear in the left margin as above.) However, if a subject is presented and discussed and no one makes a motion, but everyone seems to agree that it is desirable, the president or the presiding officer may say, "If there is no objection, (activity) will be done," and the

GENERAL CONSENT TO DO: — Minutes will record it as follows: "By general consent it was decided to do (activity) .

PROGRAM — The Program Committee chairman, (name) , presented, (speaker's name) , who spoke on the subject _____. (If a panel, list members and may include degrees, titles, etc., which account for the choice of the program and participants.)

ANNOUNCE-MENTS — The president (or chairman) announced _____.

ADJOURN-MENT — There being no further business, the meeting adjourned at (time).

_____(Name and Title)*_____

*Person who took the minutes signs them.

The Rule of Minutes

According to John Tropman, minutes should be content minutes as opposed to process minutes, and they should be agenda relevant. Content minutes take each topic outlined on the agenda, provide a brief summary of the issue, record the various points of view, and then, in a different type or capital letters, state the decision. Tropman feels this style of minute taking is more comprehensive than other systems, especially those of the "process variety" which have endless streams of "he said/she said."

The Principle of Agenda Relevance is another consideration that Tropman considers critical. Here, he states, the numbering system in the minutes should be identical to that of the agenda, making it very easy for directors and other readers to find references to particular items. He says that using this system will prevent rehashing last month's business at this month's meeting.

Legalizing the Minutes

Just taking minutes does not finalize the legal record. The record is established after the minutes have been ratified by the board. The approval is complete after the minutes are read at a subsequent meeting and are corrected as necessary. Minutes should be transcribed as soon as possible after a meeting, and a copy should be sent to the presiding officer at once, even though that copy is not yet formally approved.

Mindell Stein, who was a registered parliamentarian in Colorado for over 40 years, said, "The original of the minutes should be kept in a bound book with the pages numbered. No page should ever be removed even if everything on it is erroneous. It should be marked to indicate it is unusable but must remain in the book. Corrections should be made in the margins, not in the body of the minutes and preferably in red ink. If there is an error which requires considerable space it should be made on the reverse side of the paper or attached to the page indicating its proper location."[3]

At times it may be impossible to obtain a quorum for a meeting. That necessitates some other method for approving minutes. Some organizations authorize approval by the executive committee with subsequent reports to the board. Stein offers an alternative method: "Another method is to allow the board membership to call attention to corrections. They note any corrections on a separate sheet of paper and return these to the secretary. The secretary compares any corrections with the notes made at the meeting, and if confirmed, incorporates these as corrections to the minutes."[4]

As a rule, approval of the minutes establishes their legal record and is final. However, minutes are susceptible to the procedure known as "amending something previously adopted," just as bylaws and constitutions are. If the existence of an error can be reasonably established, the minutes may be corrected even many years later.[5] In such a case, the procedure is similar to that required to amend an organization's bylaws.

A board should establish a rule regarding who, other than board members and the executive director, should regularly receive copies of minutes. States with "sunshine laws" pertaining to public charities may say minutes are a matter of public record but, in practice, they are treated as confidential material. In most cases, it is better for an executive director to orally summarize the significant outcomes of board and board committee meetings to other staff. This procedure minimizes misinterpretation on the part of staff and also allows them to ask the executive director questions.

The important characteristics of minutes are accuracy, understandability, and completeness. Too many words confuse a reader but as many words as are needed must be used to ensure correct interpretation of the organization's actions. Although "brevity is the soul of wit" and should be considered at all times, minutes should be taken meticulously. In conjunction with the bylaws and special rules of an organization, the minutes are the lifeblood of the group.

SUMMARY

To appreciate good meetings, one must first recognize the deterrents to effective ones. Board and committee meetings can be ineffective due to hidden functions, vague decision rules, a lack of preparation for group roles or group training on the part of directors, and a lack of preparation for meetings themselves. If meetings are to be improved, new principles need to be considered—personality principle, orchestra principle, report principle, new business principle, and the reactive/proactive principle.

John Tropman suggests several rules to follow for improving meetings: the Rule of Halves, the Rule of Sixths, the Rule of Three-Quarters, and the Rule of Two-Thirds. Because adequate information is essential to quality decision making, all of his rules emphasize the significance of information. These rules also underscore the importance of careful advance planning. The Agenda Bell and Rule of Agenda promote efficiency by ordering a method (precise scheduling) and by allowing discussion only on agenda items.

Bad decisions can occur when there is pressure on the decision makers, inadequate information, insufficient alternatives, or a lack of different points of view. Meetings can be evaluated for the types of decisions they produce. Several board members may be assigned this task of evaluating and rating the board's decisions.

Minute taking establishes the legality of the decisions made and the actions taken by a board. Therefore, minutes need to be accurate and follow a prescribed format. Tropman's Rule of Minutes says minutes need to focus on the content of a meeting and be relevant to the agenda. When minutes of a board meeting are ratified by the board, they become part of the legal record of the organization's proceedings.

NOTES

1. A. Zander, *Making Groups Effective*, p. xi.

2. Peter Drucker, "Managing the Public Service Institution," *Public Interest*, (33) (Fall 1973): 49.

3. Mindell Stein, "Board Minutes: Legal Record of an Organization," *The Board Letter*, no. 4 (Denver, CO: Duca Associates, 1981), p. 4.

4. Ibid.

5. *Roberts' Rules of Order, Newly Revised*, (Glenview, IL: Scott-Foresman, 1981), p. 394.

Chapter 8
The Board's Evaluation
Responsibilities

An important responsibility of board members is to appraise the performance of their organization. In order to do this, a questioning attitude is essential. Board members who ask questions are important to the vitality of an organization. Karl Mathiasen once said, "The board member who asks the dumb questions is one of the most valuable board members in creation! This is the person who looks at the issue under discussion without all the information, without all the facts, and says, 'But that doesn't make sense. Please explain it to me.' And that's when other people say, 'Well it does not make sense to me either, but I thought the rest of you all understood.'"[1]

Board members should not question every little detail of an organization's operations, but the complacent board that fails to question the rationale behind major decisions may be endangering the health of the organization. If a board has participated in setting an organization's goals, it cannot ignore how those goals are implemented. Members might ask the following questions:

- What is the purpose of this or that program?
- What should this or that program accomplish?
- What problem areas that are not presently served by the organization's programs need attention?
- Who does the organization want to serve tomorrow?
- How do the organization's clients benefit from the services provided?
- What does the organization offer that other similar agencies do not?
- Where are we failing? Where are we succeeding?
- If the organization did not exist, would it be founded—would there be a strong need for it?

These are program- and mission-related questions that board members should have had answered during their orientation. They are the kind of questions that should have been addressed during the board's planning process. After orientation, after planning, it is still the responsibility of all board members to keep on asking such questions if they are effectively to audit the organization. Members should also ask questions about their own performance and about the support they are giving to the organization. They should ask about the program evaluation process and procedures.

It's better to play it safe—if you don't understand, ask.

PROGRAM EVALUATION

The continued health of an organization depends on its having some form of periodic evaluation. The process of evaluation assists a nonprofit board in creating the organization's future programs. It can offer the opportunity for board and staff to vent their feelings and opinions. The most significant service an evaluation can perform is to identify aspects of a program where modifications are needed. In this regard, evaluation is important in bringing about organizational change. Boards need the kind of information evaluations offer to make decisions on continuing or dropping a program, to allocate resources to a program, and to judge the overall effectiveness of the organization and its programs in order to remain accountable.

Merely providing a service that helps resolve some social problem is no longer an acceptable justification of organizational worth. Documentation of that worth through the examination of an organization's progress toward resolving some problem is what evaluation is all about. The challenge for nonprofit boards of directors is to ensure that this happens.

Evaluation is a test of reality. When programs are in the planning stage, we perceive there will be certain outcomes, both in the way the program is implemented and in its results. Evaluation is a way to test our perceptions versus actuality. To do this, measure the degree to which predetermined objectives were met and compare these outcomes to a set of criteria. There are three main evaluation areas to be measured: (1) process, which is concerned with performance; (2) program, which is concerned with output; and (3) impact, which is concerned with the program's effect on the environment.

The evaluative question "how good is a program?" has been replaced with the more relative "how well does a program achieve its goals?" However, if the organization's goals aren't worth achieving, then it is of no interest if they are achieved. Proper evaluation needs to include some judgment on the value of the goals, on their feasibility, and on their appropriateness.

Both efficiency (process by which a program is accomplished) and effectiveness (impact of a program) are examined in evaluating a program by asking questions such as: How well is the program managed? What differences does it make and to whom? Are the costs of providing the service reasonable compared to the results achieved?

Evaluation is not intended to make judgments on the personnel carrying out the service program—that is a different issue—nor is it a magic answer to organizational problems; it can only reveal problem areas by identifying strengths and weaknesses. In itself, evaluation is not a decision maker but rather a means for decision makers to take action. And, there is no such thing as a perfect evaluation measure.

Problems of Evaluation

A board of directors needs to be sensitive to some of the issues regarding evaluation.

1. *No single criterion*—Corporations can judge merits of a product or service by a single criterion—profit. Nonprofit organizations do not have this measure, and to complicate the issue further, most nonprofit programs have multiple objectives. The more objectives there are associated with a program, the harder it is to come to any agreement on which of these is the most important.

2. *No comparable units*—One company can be compared to another company even if they sell different widgets because their profitability is a common unit of measure. In the nonprofit sector, one may be able to compare the effectiveness of one hospital with another hospital, but it is impossible to compare the effectiveness of a hospital with that of an institution of higher education. This presents a major problem in the allocation of funds among public services; how do we know which dollars are better spent if we cannot compare their effectiveness?

3. *Performance measures*—Since the primary goal of nonprofit organizations is to offer some kind of service, evaluation measures of efficiency and effectiveness are not based on financial statements. It is difficult for those businesspersons who sit on many nonprofit boards of directors to relegate the organization's financial statements to a secondary status.

4. *Costs and benefits*—The relationship between input and output in a nonprofit cannot be accurately measured. Would adding another professional service worker benefit the community by an amount that exceeds the added cost to the organization? How much money should be spent on trying to find a cure for children's diabetes? These kinds of issues are impossible to analyze in quantitative terms due to the lack of accurate means to estimate the benefits of incremental spending.

5. *Charitable funding*—Organizations that earn most of their revenues from service fees are subject to marketplace conditions in the same way a profit organization is, and they have few constraints on their organizational goals. Organizations that depend on contributions have less freedom of choice. Their goals and program offerings are not only constrained by the amount of donations received to support a program but also are constrained by funding source stipulations regarding clients served and types of services. This becomes an issue in evaluating programs and goals when there are inadequate funds to do what has been planned.

6. *Real life environment*—Evaluation deals with programs and people in their "real life environment." The program is the primary purpose of the organization, not the evaluation. Conflicts can occur between the demands of evaluation research and those of the pro-

gram; the latter has priority. Even though those who have been assigned the task of evaluation are responsible for providing the board of directors with information for decision making, their evaluation fact-finding activities must not interfere with the program.

7. *Control groups*—The use of pretest and posttest to discern change in a client's or student's behavior or knowledge as a result of participation in a program still does not accurately define a program's effectiveness. There are too many other external influences on an individual client or student to ascribe change to one program's intervention. Therefore, control groups are essential to quality program evaluation. The problem lies in finding equivalent control groups and in maintaining them.

8. *Expectations*—Many within an organization will disagree on what they feel an evaluation should do—on what questions it should answer. Board members may be more concerned with long-range planning issues. The executive director may be more concerned with operational issues, and program staff often have questions relative to the application of program methodology and its effectiveness. Unless these varied expectations are sorted out in advance, one can ignore the results of even the best evaluation by saying, "But that is not what we wanted to know."

There are many other problems associated with applying scientific evaluation techniques to social services programs. Boards need to be aware of these limitations.

The list of obstacles and pitfalls to program evaluation in the nonprofit sector is extensive. Board members need to understand the positive and negative sides of evaluation. Even if evaluation results are ignored, evaluation is a step in the right direction. It can give board members information that can diminish any uncertainties they may have about their organization's operations. It can help clarify the value of their decisions.

All organizations should undergo some periodic review, but not all program activities require an assessment of their outcome. A board must weigh the pros and cons of an evaluation where there is little money to allocate to the process and no readily available or qualified person to conduct the evaluation. A common sense approach is best.

Process of Program Evaluation

All organizations must build a team that combines individual efforts into one effort that contributes to a common goal. Organizational performance requires each program activity to be directed toward a mission. To judge the effectiveness of performance, there needs to be a systematic process for appraisal.

Phase 1. Some boundaries must be set to define the scope of the evaluation and how it will be focused. If a formative evaluation is called for, then the evaluation is conducted during the developing phase of the program so information can be used to modify a program in action. If a summative evaluation is requested, then the total impact of a program is looked at toward the end of the program to decide whether to continue or expand it. Expectations at all levels of the organization need to be determined—what questions are anticipated to be answered by the evaluation. This is the evaluation planning stage.

Decisions must be made about who will be responsible for the program evaluation. It is most appropriate to place the overall responsibility at the level where decisions regarding the evaluation's results are made. Program directors should not be asked to judge the value of their own programs, although they need to participate in the process. The executive director, then, is the one responsible for evaluation implementation as he or she reports directly to the board with recommended changes.

Unless the cost of evaluation has been budgeted, the board may be asked to appropriate funds. The cost of program evaluation will depend on its estimated duration and on costs incurred by the use of staff time and consultants, the purchase of measurement instruments, the use of clerical time in preparing evaluation reports, the printing of the evaluation report, and other related costs.

Phase 2. This next stage involves the preparation of a program statement. Meetings are held with program staff and evaluators to determine and define which goals and objectives of which programs need the closest scrutiny. The program statement is intended to be a guide for the evaluation process because it records the goals of a program as well as their expected outcomes and operational procedures or methodology. This stage would not be necessary if the organization's plan contains, as it should, specific objectives accompanied by a program rationale and measurable expected outcomes.

Phase 3. This is the implementation stage where data are collected (summative evaluation) or, if data have been collected all along (formative evaluation), summarized. If evaluation instruments are to be used, they are employed here. Various evaluation techniques such as questionnaires, interviews, case studies, comparison groups, and posttests would be administered.

Phase 4. The evaluation data are analyzed in terms of usefulness for program improvement. An evaluation report should be prepared, tailored to the audience for which it is intended, and based on what is credible information to that public.

For all program evaluations, a board will want three questions answered: (1) How important is the program service? (2) Is the program well managed? (3) Is the program cost-effective? To ensure that some action is taken as a result of the evaluation and to ensure results, keep everyone (board and staff) informed of the evaluation's progress from the beginning. When everyone is a part of the process, there should be no surprises; when everyone is a part of the process, all have a feeling of ownership in the process.

Evaluations can be conducted on a total program, on one facet of a particular program, on the entire organization, or on one aspect of the organization other than its program, such as financial development, public relations and marketing, or volunteer involvement. A community services audit is a special type of evaluation that helps the board of directors learn how the organization is perceived by key people in the community. It gives insights into how the organization fits into the total scheme of community services.[2] This audit should be conducted by someone who is familiar with the organization but not a part of it. Boards may find that a community services audit is most helpful when coupled with a feasibility study to determine public image and potential fundability before embarking on a major fund-raising campaign.

EVALUATION OF AN EXECUTIVE DIRECTOR

Nonprofit boards of directors are well aware of their responsibility for hiring the organization's executive director and are equally aware that as the executive's employer, they have the sole power to fire him or her. However, somewhere between this hiring and firing authority also comes the responsibility for evaluating the executive director's performance, and this is a responsibility all too often overlooked.

Appraisal of an executive director should begin shortly after he or she is hired, at the moment the director puts together objectives for the year. (All nonprofit executives or administrators should write some type of annual work plan on behalf of the organization. This plan may or may not employ a management-by-objectives approach or some other course of action, but it should address the organization's plan, describe the executive's main areas of responsibility as defined in the job description, list action steps to be taken toward specified objectives, and indicate expected measurable outcomes.) The board president and the executive should review the plan and then bring it to the board for a vote of consensus to show that the board agrees this is how they expect the executive director to spend his or her time. It is important for the board and executive director to align their priorities each year.

The evaluation of the organization's chief executive is usually done annually and is often conducted by the board's personnel committee. Some boards establish an appraisal task force for the evaluation and include a professional colleague of the director on this committee. Some organizations may, under special circumstances, find it necessary to evaluate the executive every six months; and other circumstances may lead a board to make their appraisal less frequently than once a year. Variances that occur in the frequency of an executive's performance appraisal will usually be related to whether the organization is in some kind of crisis.

The Evaluation Process

The process is fairly simple but systematic. The board committee assigned the evaluation asks the executive director to write up an assessment of how well he or she has achieved the work plan. Deviations from this plan, along with explanations, should be provided by the executive. The committee should review this assessment with the original work plan. Other board members should be asked for their comments.

The executive director then meets with the committee to discuss both his or her and the board's comments. This is not to be a judgment session but a sharing of planned versus actual performance. It is an opportunity for both parties to identify weak areas and come to agreement on ways to improve. Both parties should have a chance to point to special achievements.

The committee next writes up a written and formal report with recommendations, if applicable. The committee's report is shared and may be commented on by both committee members and the executive; both parties sign the report. The board must approve the evaluation report before it is placed in the executive's permanent personnel file.

The evaluation process outlined above is one approach. A board may find that some other process works better in its organizational setting; a small organization may find these procedures too formal; a hospital, for example, may feel a full peer review is most appropriate. In any event, there are certain key points that all boards of directors should consider in exercising their responsibility to evaluate the executive director.

- Define the purpose of your evaluation. Hopefully, it will be based on a desire to improve your executive's performance, recognize accomplishments, and encourage personal growth on the job. It must be constructive.
- Review the executive director's job description. A job description often becomes outdated without anyone noticing, especially when the executive has been with the organization a number of years. The position description may include responsibilities that have since been delegated to other or new staff positions; it may inappropriately include some responsibilities that belong to the board (especially in the area of resource development); it may not clearly delineate any specific respon-

sibilities and be terribly vague. The executive director's evaluation time is an ideal time to bring his or her job description up to date and in line with the present organization's realities.

- Confidentiality of the executive director's evaluation is not, as some would feel, an issue. Every aspect of the evaluation and its proceedings should be shared with the executive. Those who make judgments on another's performance need to be held accountable.

- Consider carefully your sources of information. It is up to the board committee conducting the evaluation to decide how far afield it needs to go in gathering feedback on the executive's performance. Some committees involve the organization's top staff managers, others do not ask any staff for information, and some ask all board members. The decision not to use staff is usually based on the concern over possible "retribution" in the staff's evaluation by the executive or on the concern that petty personal issues may interfere with an objective appraisal. Another option is to solicit opinions from others in the community, perhaps a professional colleague with whom the executive has worked closely, or perhaps a major referral or funding source. Who is asked to participate will depend on the purpose of the evaluation and on the information the board committee decides will be most useful to them in making their appraisal.

- If the executive director has been hired on a contractual basis or has, at least, a letter of agreement, the contract or agreement should also spell out the basis for evaluation. The responsible board committee should ensure that the evaluation follows any prior prescribed performance standard measures.

- Decide on an evaluation format. The committee might use some type of checklist that simply indicates if the executive has behaved in certain ways or done certain things. A rating system may be employed where the various participants indicate, on a given scale, how well the executive has performed in specified areas. A narrative format can be used whereby comments are collected and summarized with an addendum for identified strengths and weaknesses. This latter method is open-ended in that evaluators are not guided in any way as to their comments. Or, a combination of all three formats may be useful.

- All evaluations should relate to the degree in which performance and activities advance the organization's goals. The executive's evaluation is no exception. This linkage to organizational goals should appear in the executive director's job description and again in the work plan.

- Include remedial steps or some action plan to provide follow-up on the evaluation with a time frame. If the evaluation were to indicate a need for some specific changes, there should be some deadline for that happening. Any plan for improvement must be mutually agreed on by the executive director and the board. If an evaluation is to make a difference, this aspect must be taken into account.

There are probably additional areas that concern many boards—these are just some basics. The important point to remember is that to make the evaluation of the executive director meaningful, it must be fair and objective.

EVALUATION OF A BOARD

Just as nonprofit boards of directors need to assume responsibility for the evaluation of the organization and its executive director, they also need to take their own pulse. The challenges facing nonprofit boards today require imaginative leadership and the ability to thoughtfully examine basic organizational issues like quality and costs. Board leadership is a time-consuming responsibility that should not be taken lightly. A board needs to know if it has the capabilities essential to this type leadership and, if not, what it could do to acquire them. Self-assessments can produce some answers.

A self-assessment of the board as an entity and as individual members should be conducted periodically, at least every two years. The kind of assessment needed is one that helps bring about positive and practical changes in the board as a group and in individual members' performances.

Principles of Self-Assessment

There are a number of principles underlying any self-assessment evaluation that apply equally to organizations and individuals. The first is that public, not private or confidential, assessments are most likely to produce change. An initial step in a "change process" is to identify where you are at the present and where you would like to be. The basic ingredients of self-assessment include a description of the present and a prescription for the future. Sharing this openly enables changes to be made with less trauma because those involved in the process have a share in the "ownership of change," having participated in making change occur.

Second, assessment involves gathering valid data about what is happening and what should be happening, including one's perspectives about these. It is a process of determining truths about oneself and the organization and of making those truths public.

Third, a good self-assessment leads to action and the capability of dealing with uncovered truths. Not all board members have the same capacity to deal with truths about themselves and the organization; this capacity must be developed.

Finally, there is the principle that people are better able to deal with the truth when they take part in discovering it rather than being told by someone else. Thus, a main goal of personal and organizational revitalization is to enhance one's capacity to discern truths and act on them.

Dean Schooler, a fellow consultant and instructor at the University of Colorado/Boulder, takes a different view about principles relative to self-assessment. He suggests that there is a set of preferences and assumptions underlying board activities. He calls these "the preoccupations of boards." "Whether or not a particular preoccupation or concern is healthy or pathological will depend on the individual board and board member. Indeed, depending upon the situation, an individual concern may be either productive or unhealthy for a board or organization. In many cases, a given board tendency will harbor both advantages and disadvantages....Inventorying preoccupations can be an opportunity to bring subsurface assumptions to a greater level of awareness and to assess their consequences for the organization."[3]

The following statements may be a real concern for some boards depending on whether they represent a "healthy or pathological preoccupation."

- Willingness to work with less than complete attendance or chronic absenteeism.

- Delegation of fund raising to professionals, outside consultants, and development staff.

- Desire to work solely with manager or chief executive officer and have little contact with others in the organization.

- Satisfaction with obvious indicators of success or failure (indicators expressed in numbers or dollar values that can make evaluation easier.)

- Preference for glancing at agendas and materials prior to meetings and doing "homework" during board sessions.

- Perception that board membership primarily involves a symbolic act of community service and involvement, rather than a tangible commitment of time, personality and effort (cf., one membership competing, sometimes, with multiple board and organizational memberships).

- Assumption that election to a board of directors reaffirms one's qualifications and that minimal new or additional learning is required for governing the organization.

- View of the board's role as primarily to protect and insulate the organization.

- Perception of the role of the board as more a legal than a social or political process.
- Assumption that larger boards make better boards.
- Preference not to rotate chairmanships but instead have one person remain in a formal role over a long period of time.
- Assumption that staff will follow through on board directives without later board monitoring and review of the implementation process.[4]

Using this partial checklist (Schooler's full list of concerns includes 28 points) or some similar inventory can provide an impetus to self-evaluation—it is a starting point for discussion. But, unless it leads to a formal and structured self-study, the use of an inventory may not produce constructive results. It is the exercise of a formal board self-evaluation that produces an improvement in board morale and commitment.

The Self-Assessment Process

A successful board self-evaluation has prerequisites that should be taken into account before initiating it. First, and most important to the "ownership" of evaluation, the assessment should be internally motivated. If some outside agency or individual pushes for a board evaluation, the positive aspects of its results are lessened and individual members may resent the time and effort spent.

Second, the educational value as well as the performance appraisal value need to be understood. It should also be understood that the value of an evaluation lies in its benefit both to the organization and to individual board members.

Third, the leadership for any board's self-evaluation needs to come from the board itself. There should be board involvement in planning and implementing the process, in reviewing the results, and in taking follow-up action.

A final prerequisite to consider is that there are multiple desirable outcomes. A board should decide in advance what it hopes the end result will be. One major outcome may be the increased board morale and commitment mentioned earlier. Another may be planned self-improvements. In all cases, a byproduct should be some type of written report and summation that can be shared with all members of the board, the executive director, and perhaps certain elect constituencies or publics.

The entire board should participate in making an assessment. In Chapter 2 it was suggested that the board vice-president take on the responsibility for board development, which would include board self-evaluation. If your board does not feel that is an appropriate role for the vice-president, the president can assign a task force. Or, if your board has a standing committee for board development, this is obviously within its purview.

In any case, several board members should be assigned to plan the evaluation process and make recommendations on procedures and techniques to the full board. The board should approve the assessment tools and techniques to be employed and agree on how they will be implemented. Board members may fill out some type of questionnaire, confidentially and on their own time; some time may be set aside at a regular board meeting for this purpose, or, depending on the complexity of the self-evaluation and its desired outcome, a special workshop may be held. The evaluation task force or committee tallies the responses and assumes responsibility for preparing a report.

Some nonprofit boards of directors may wish to have their executive director participate in the process and complete an assessment. Other organizations' boards may invite their advisory bodies and other constituency groups that have a stake in the board's effective performance to become involved. The full board should agree on whether to invite a broader participation—it is risky and can be threatening.

In preparing the report of responses, particular attention should be given to markedly divergent opinions; areas that appear to be confusing to respondents; notable differences in responses from new versus experienced members; and notable differences in the opinions of the board's leadership and those of other members and the executive director or other participating constituencies. Areas requiring further study should be highlighted. The committee or task force should also venture recommendations for change, but it is up to the full board to take action. Board members and other participants need some time to study the evaluation report and its recommendations before a meeting to discuss it is scheduled.

Rating Effectiveness

James G. Paltridge, in an article written for the Pacific Management Group and presented at the 1981 National Society for Fund-Raising Executives Conference, suggests 17 areas that should be rated in order to determine a nonprofit board's effectiveness.

1. goals defined, reviewed
2. goals known, understood
3. long-term planning
4. board powers, responsibilities
5. board organization
6. bylaws
7. board membership composition
8. board-executive relations
9. organizational structure

10. information reports
11. board meeting preparation
12. group dynamics
13. new member selection
14. orientation, education
15. role in community
16. resource development
17. conflict of interest

The United Way of Greater St. Louis produced *Management Evaluation Manual* (1977) to help United Way agencies evaluate their effectiveness in four management areas: basic criteria for nonprofit social service organizations, planning, personnel practices, and fiscal control. The *Manual* posed a series of questions in each of those areas that, for the most part, required a simple "yes" or "no" or "nonapplicable" response. Each of the four sections included specific questions pertinent to the board of directors. Some of the sections regarding board effectiveness included series of questions in the following areas: board representation and balance, selection process, meetings, functions, areas of board control, and board's role in fiscal control.

Francis Pray, a former vice-president of the Council for Financial Aid to Education and a development consultant, devised a "report card approach" (see Appendix) to evaluation that could be used to rate the effectiveness of college trustees. Pray's systematic rating procedure required trustees to make an honest and objective appraisal of their board service. Although directed at college trustees, the "report card" can be easily adapted to other nonprofit agencies. Points are scored in each of the following areas:

1. suitability as a trustee
2. general preparation as a trustee
3. specific preparation for action as trustee
4. ambassadorship
5. participation in the development program of the college
6. committee activity
7. attendance
8. performance as chairperson of the board or chairperson of committees
9. special service

Other criteria that have been used in rating a board's effectiveness focus on posing first-person questions such as "Am *I* a good board member?" The National Information Bureau, Inc., suggests that there are attitudes that are the basis for a quality board member. The good board member:

1. is dedicated to helping others and modest in the light of his responsibilities as a Board member.
2. approaches his responsibilities in the spirit of a trustee on behalf of contributors, their intended beneficiaries, and the public at large.
3. stands up for his convictions, even at the cost of misunderstanding or disapproval in his business or social life.
4. backs up other Board members and staff, rising to their defense when they are unjustly criticized or attacked.
5. treats staff as a partner in a high calling, while maintaining overall supervision and control.
6. avoids being overawed by others on the Board, whether they be executive staff; tycoons of business, labor or society; professionals in social work, education, medicine, etc.
7. welcomes information and the best available advice, but reserves the right to arrive at decisions on the basis of his own judgment.
8. respects the right of other Board members and of staff to disagree with him and to have a fair hearing of their points of view.
9. accepts as routine that decisions must be made by majority vote and will at times go against him.
10. criticizes, when necessary, in a constructive way, and if possible by suggesting an alternative course.
11. recognizes that his time and energy are limited and that overcommitment may prove self-defeating.
12. endeavors to keep disagreements and controversies impersonal, and to promote unity.
13. maintains loyalty to his agency, within a higher loyalty to the welfare of the community and humanity as a whole.[5]

Hiring Consultants

Consultants are useless in a board evaluation unless a board wants to evaluate its effectiveness and comes to the decision itself to hire outside assistance. Using a consultant to motivate a board to conduct a self-evaluation is inappropriate since board members must be self-motivated to appraise their own performance. Outside assistance, when called for, does not have to be a paid professional; it can be a volunteer board member from another nonprofit organization who can share a personal evaluation experience. It can be a former board member from your organization; a staff person from another community agency that specializes in working with volunteer groups; or a local community college professor who is knowledgeable about group processes, evaluation, or organizational development.

If a board decides to use outside assistance in its self-evaluation, it needs to be quite clear about what this person is expected to contribute to the process. It is not a consultant's role to make judgments; rather, a consultant brings knowledge of the different ways boards function and specific experience in nonprofit board evaluation.

A consultant can assist a board's evaluation committee or task force in selecting an appropriate self-evaluation tool or technique. The consultant may devise a method of evaluation for those areas in which the board wants to appraise its performance. He or she can act as facilitator if the board opts to conduct an evaluation workshop. Consultants can also be helpful in appraising the value of the evaluation process, in helping a board to understand the application of what they have learned about themselves as a group and as individuals. A consultant never supplants the full board's participation in a self-evaluation.

SUMMARY

Whatever type of evaluation is being undertaken—program, personnel, or board self-study—the purpose is to increase skills and knowledge in order to effectively work toward an organization's stated mission and goals. Boards of directors need information on the value of a program in order to make good decisions. Three types of evaluations—process, program, and impact—can give boards information on the cost-effectiveness of an organization's services, its management efficiency, and its impact. Because boards are responsible for ensuring that program evaluations take place, they need to be aware of the various problems and the resistance to evaluation that may occur. A systematic evaluation process that begins with a clear definition of the questions to be answered and ends with an analytical written report contributes to the effective performance of the organization.

A board's responsibility in the area of personnel does not end with the hiring of an executive; it needs to evaluate him or her. The result of this evaluation will be constructive if it is focused on ways to help the executive improve his or her performance and recognizes his or her achievements.

A board that constantly asks questions enriches its performance as a viable governing body. A self-assessment of the board as a group and of its individual members should be undertaken at least every two years. Principles of self-assessment should be applied to the evaluation process and the board needs to examine the preferences and assumptions that underlie its activities. The process of board self-evaluation should be initiated by the board itself, and it should also provide leadership in the process. Other groups, such as advisory boards, may be asked to participate, and the organization's executive director is often called on for his or her input. While any number of criteria may be used to rate board effectiveness, a series of assessment questions relating to a board's composition, organization, functions, and control are common. An alternative to self-assessment can be to hire a consultant. However, a decision to use the services of an expert from outside the organization must eminate from the board. Positive responses to the questions raised, whether through self-assessment or from a consultant, usually indicate that the organization is successful.

NOTES

1. Karl Mathiasen, "Confessions of a Board Member" (A booklet by The Alban Institute, Inc., Washington, DC, 1976), pp. 4–6.

2. Timothy S. Brady, "The Community Services Audit," *Voluntary Action Leadership* (Fall 1981): 29–31.

3. Dean Schooler, "The Preoccupations of Boards—Healthy or Pathological," *Voluntary Action Leadership.* (Spring 1980): 29–30.

4. Ibid.

5. National Information Bureau, Inc., "The Volunteer Board Member in Philanthropy" (New York, 1975), pp. 19–20.

Chapter 9
Building Working Relationships

BOARD/EXECUTIVE RELATIONS

I once had a board president who called our agency three or four mornings a week at 8:00 a.m. to see if I was in the office; she never did call at 10:00 p.m. to learn that I was still at my desk. A colleague of mine reported that she had a board member who would appear weekly at her agency during program hours to look over the shoulder of her program director. These behaviors are inappropriate for board members, but it is not unusual for nonprofit board members to be confused about where their responsibilities stop and those of staff begin or vice versa.

Board/staff relationships refer to the relationship between the board of directors and the organization's executive director or administrator, since staff below this level usually have limited direct contact with board members and a lesser influence with the board. Additionally, most of the literature in the field and the few surveys that have been conducted on nonprofit boards point specifically to the interaction between the executive and the board president as the most important factor in board/staff relationships. The personal support of the organization's executive for the board president is critical to successfully establishing the president's leadership role. Conversely, a board president who trusts the competency of the organization's executive will seek the support of other directors for the executive's initiatives. The key to an appropriate balance between board and staff is a positive relationship between these two leaders based on trust and honesty.

A Dynamic Interaction

Board and staff have previously been called a "team" and re-ferred to as "partners." Articles and books written on nonprofit organization management often conclude that a board/staff relationship is a partnership, one that depends on mutual trust and fails when there is a lack of understanding or communication about the roles and responsibilities of each partner. However, it is important not to interpret partnership as a passive relationship. Because there is a delicate balance between the functions of any board and an executive, a constant state of tension exists. Conrad and Glenn call this "dynamic tension" and are careful to point out that this is quite different from a constant state of conflict, which is undermining to the health of an organization. Dynamic tension is manageable conflict and can be healthy for an organization. Tension inevitably occurs when a balance of power is being sought or is shifting. The saying that an organization has either a strong executive or a strong board of directors doesn't have to be true; both can be strong.

The trend toward professionalism among nonprofit organizations has, in part, led to staff-oriented organizations. Boards of staff-dominated organizations sit back and let the executive and the staff do all the work; they excuse themselves from involvement on the basis that staff are more knowledgeable. These become known as "yes-boards" with the primary activity of "rubber-stamping"; they have lost their board/staff balance. The balance can tilt the other way too—an organization can be board-oriented. In this case, a board composed of powerful members refuses to share responsibility with the executive, insists on making all decisions including operational ones, and dominates the organization. Here the entire staff's effectiveness is undermined, which can result in loss of purpose. In both instances, board and executive fail to recognize their mutual need for each other, and there is no trust in their relationship.

In a recent PONPO (Program on Non-Profit Organizations) paper, Melissa Middleton examines several factors that can influence the dynamic interaction between a nonprofit board and an executive director. One is the difference in the socioeconomic status between the organization's executive and board members. In many social service agencies, the executive is in a "middle-range status profession" while board members are recruited from professional and business "elites." In this case, the executive may feel awed, overwhelmed, or impotent, and it is unlikely that the executive will dominate the board. With many small grass roots organizations, it is unusual for powerful and wealthy trustees to be attracted to the board and executive dominance is more common.[1]

Related to the factor of socioeconomic status is whether the executive is viewed by board members as a professional. In organizations where the executive has been promoted from within the organization, the executive is likely to feel grateful to the board for his or her job success and be more accepting of board domination. More frequently, the executive has professional status and the board does not, or board members represent different professions. The executive with professional identification is likely to dominate a board. Similarly, the professional executive, even with a board of other professionals and elites, is likely to dominate when he or she is most knowledgeable about technologies important to the institution. Given this element of professional status, an executive is inclined not to trust lay decision makers in setting goals and policies for the organization.[2]

Another factor is the life cycle stage of an organization. Chapter 4 discussed how the organization's stage of development influences the recruitment of board members; it also effects board/executive relationships. A board is more likely to dominate at the organization's start-up stage because the legitimacy and resources, or access to resources, that board members bring to the organization are so critical at this point. In an organization's midlife cycle, an identity crisis involving consolidation, merger, or major expansion can push the board into a role of dominance, as once again board members' resources and influence in the community are crucial.

If trust and need are the cornerstones of dynamic interaction between the board and executive, then the executive must understand that board members volunteer to help, not to interfere. Volunteer board members need to understand that their reputation (in affiliation with the organization) is dependent on how well the executive manages the agency. If this mutual need is understood and if the board and executive understand their roles, a mutual confidence develops that leads to trust.

Maintaining a Balance

If trust exists, the freedom to disagree also exists. Both the executive and the board have the right to differ, and both must recognize the other's need for information. Growth in a board/executive relationship follows an extensive dialogue and examination of responsibilities.

An executive should remember that board members bring to the board special talents, influences and contacts, and expertise that the organization could not otherwise buy. Board members contribute their collective wisdom and objective points of view to decision-making situations, which enable them to bring about change. A wise executive is sensitive to the potential of the board and expresses his or her thanks often.

Board members should appreciate an executive's expertise and knowledge of the organization, for without access to that information, they could not make good decisions. The executive is also the link to all other levels of the organization's staff and, therefore, the main means for implementing board policies. A wise board supports the executive it hired (unless given substantive cause not to).

Effective board/executive relationships begin and end with good communication. A board cannot even fulfill its most basic role—that of hiring an executive—unless it is knowledgeable about the organization and its needs and problems. This information is supplied by an executive director (assuming, of course, the organization is not hiring its first). Both a board and an executive should expect the other to respond promptly to requests for information, to return phone calls, to be accessible, and to meet scheduled deadlines. The information an executive shares regarding programs should be concise and figure-oriented, as this best satisfies the businesspersons who sit on many nonprofit boards of directors. Board committee chairpersons who request documentation from other staff should be sensitive to the overtime that task may require and should check first with the individual's supervisor or the executive director. Information sharing from both parties must be timely and relevant to decision making.

Finally, the responsibilities of the organization's leadership—its board president and executive director—are rarely as neatly defined as a set of bylaws or job descriptions may suggest. In exercising their respective leadership roles, the president and executive must recognize when to defer to the other for a final decision.

There are so many types of nonprofits that it is impossible to prescribe exactly how much attention should be paid to board/staff relations. Too much emphasis risks diverting attention from the constituents, who are the reason for an organization's existence. Too little emphasis risks casual concern on the part of board members and subsequent loss of support. Finding that delicate balance is difficult but worthwhile for the effectiveness it can bring to your organization.

Hiring an Executive

The board's job is to hire the executive director in a responsible manner. Using good personnel practices in this process is important. Boards need to be knowledgeable of Equal Employment Opportunity and Affirmative Action regulations in their role as employer in order to avoid potential lawsuits.

An organization's personnel policies should state procedures for hiring the executive director, which a board can use as a guide. Policies may state, for example, who is responsible—a board personnel committee or a specially assigned search committee. Policies may dictate recruitment procedures such as a first posting within the organization, general advertising, and/or announcements to similar organizations in the field. Written guidelines expedite the hiring process.

We can see that you're good with people, but can you run an organization?

A new emphasis for a nonprofit executive to have skills formerly associated only with for-profit organizations (e.g., marketing, accountability, entrepreneurialism) has emerged with added importance on the "leadership qualities" of management. As a result, the role of the board in hiring the executive director has become more complicated and demanding. Part of the problem lies in establishing criteria to measure the necessary qualities in an applicant—for example, what tests might a board committee use to accurately measure the management style of the applicant or to determine what management style, or combination of styles, best fits the needs of the organization. Larger organizations will have a personnel director to assist the board in determining measures useful in the hiring process. The work and educational experiences of a candidate coupled with personal interviews have traditionally been used as a guide in making hiring decisions. "In-basket" exercises (simulated situations) are also a frequently used assessment tool. However, the validity of responses in simulated situations is questionable. Whether the candidate will carry over judgments or decisions from a contrived problem situation to real life is unclear.[3]

There is no easy way for a board to select an executive director, and there are no shortcuts in this important decision-making process. Once a board committee has narrowed the field of candidates down to two or three individuals, these finalists may be asked to meet with the full board. A straw vote may be taken by the full board, which could help influence the decision of the committee responsible for hiring. It is usually the committee who makes the final selection, but the full board must ratify that decision. In the final analysis, it is that candidate who seems to be most compatible with the working style of the board president who will be offered the position.

MAXIMIZING PARTICIPATION

The process by which an organization is managed successfully cannot be limited only to its management. The process must also include the role and function performed by the board of directors. In this way, and only this way, will the total management foundation be developed. The enormous economic, financial, social, legal, regulatory, international, and other pressures which exist today have greatly complicated the environment in which institutions must function. They have forced multiple and changing demands upon organizations which hope to survive and prosper....The combined pressures have emphasized the need to have a framework which will allow these and other requirements to be achieved.[4]

This framework includes, of course, a board that functions efficiently. The more involved a board of directors, the more efficient it can be, and this efficiency results in an increased accountability on the part of the organization's staff. An involved board is one that has found ways to maximize the participation of its membership. We've already addressed several of those factors that contribute to a board's participation and enhance its commitment: committee assignments, expressing appreciation, conducting effective meetings, ongoing education. There are a few additional factors that merit mention.

Terms of Office

Nonprofit organizations' bylaws include the terms of office for its board membership; three or four years are most common. In addition, bylaws typically say a board member may serve more than one term; some limit the number of terms, some do not. A case can be made for limited terms. Boards can become fatigued and less effective without even realizing it when they lack an infusion of new faces and new ideas. Limiting terms of office is one way for a board to cull inactive members. And too, the same old board year after year limits an organization's sphere of influence in the community and its opportunities to develop new connections. These problems show us the value of new members.

Without prior knowledge and experience with an organization, new members can legitimately feel free to ask those "dumb" but probing questions about policies and purposes. New board members are fresh, they bring enthusiasm and energy to the board. They are often the ones most willing to take on assignments that older members may consider tedious and no longer a challenge. It is also assumed that new board members bring with them new skills, experience, knowledge, and contacts that the board may have previously lacked.

The value of the experienced board member lies with the understanding and knowledge of the organization that comes with tenure. Experienced board members are spokespersons for the organization because of their experience. Karl Mathiasen calls board members with four to six years tenure—those completing a second term of office—a board's "senior citizens." Their greatest contribution is their memory and history with the organization. "Their value is in knowing what the organization has been doing, what it has tried in the past, some of the successes and failures encountered, and the organization's relationships with other groups and people in the same or similar fields. The experience and wisdom accumulated in the last years of service on the board give them balance and judgment about new ventures. They can recall for both the board and staff the original purposes and goals of projects and programs which may now have shifted direction and changed in their rationale. Normally, the principal officers of the organization are drawn from this group. This seems wise not only because they have developed a familiarity with the organization's work, but also because the board itself has had an opportunity to judge each member's effectiveness in handling committee assignments and assuming responsibility for major board activities."[5]

There must be a point of diminishing return associated with long-term volunteerism. It is not realistic or even imaginable for a board member who has been with one organization 8 to 10 years or more to maintain that initial level of energetic commitment. After about 8 or 10 years on a board, individuals become too familiar with the organization and can become annoyed hearing the same old problems come up over and over again. It is difficult for senior members to attack organizational problems with vigor, much less creativity; many times they have lost their enthusiasm and are apt to become nonsupportive of activities proposed by either board or staff.

An unfortunate situation is the reluctance of an organization to test the indispensability of a good board president or other leader. It is not easy to find good volunteer leadership. Therefore, when an organization does find that individual who is able to lead and inspire board and staff, it is natural to feel an impending loss to the organization at his or her leaving. If you are that "indispensable leader" and truly a leader, you would be among the first to acknowledge that the organization will manage without you. A truly effective leader will have established good management practices at the board level and attracted other people with leadership qualities to the board during his or her tenure. Not only will the organization be well prepared to do without you, but it will probably also benefit from the change as it gains confidence in its abilities.

To ensure that your organization does not incur the problems of "too senior" a board member, rotation terms should be addressed in the organization's bylaws. For example, after two three-year terms, a board member must resign. Some bylaws specify a year off the board after two terms but allow renomination to the board after that year. This rule accommodates both the individual who in four to eight years has earned a rest and the organization that likes and needs to keep good people involved. Other organizations specify a year off after every term of office. This type of frequent rotation is excellent for purging a board of inactive members but places a bit of a strain on an organization's need for continuity. Terms of office and the process of rotations need to be as carefully planned as the recruitment process in order to achieve a desirable balance of tenures.

Organizations without rotating terms of office have other techniques to move people around within the organization. The use of an honorary board is fairly common. Senior board members who maintain an interest in the organization but are no longer active may be made honorary board members. This means they are publicly affiliated with the organization but have no authority; they do not attend board meetings and do not have a vote. An organization will publish its list of honorary board members alongside its board roster. Honorary status should be used with discretion and reserved for those who have truly been outstanding contributors to the organization or for those who are prominent members of your community and whose continued affiliation with your organization is beneficial. Normally you do not make someone an honorary board member unless he or she has served on your organization's board of directors. In this way, an honorary board differs from an advisory board.

In the late 1960s, Mrs. Lewis Rumford II wrote about a concept called "planned rotation." This is the notion that volunteer board members become experts in serving on boards in a particular field. She suggested that board members could be more valuable to a community and to the organizations they served if they developed a "concentrated knowledge" of a field of interest, rather than serving on a number of boards in various fields like medical centers, colleges, and arts organizations. "With planned rotation, a member who has mastered his basic homework may move from a private child welfare agency to a public welfare committee and then back again to another private agency board, with his community understanding and sensitiveness to his board role hopefully deepening each time."[6]

Idea Sharing and Discussion

Two other important components of a board's participation are idea sharing, which leads to problem solving, and discussions, which lead to good decisions. Both are vital to maintaining a board's interest. The best ideas and most focused discussions emerge from groups of people who are concerned about the needs of their fellow group members. This concern requires a certain degree of cohesiveness developed over time, which for a nonprofit board may be difficult to develop because of a rotating membership.

Four basic elements should be present for boards and committees to work together as a team: (1) The group should have a *raison d'etre,* a purpose, a reason for working together. For a nonprofit board, this requirement is a given. (2) Members of a group should be interdependent, reliant on one another's skills and experiences in order to accomplish certain work objectives. Most nonprofit boards are interdependent since they are handpicked for the variety of abilities and backgrounds they bring to the organization. However, boards don't always recognize their interdependence. (3) Members of a group need to be committed to the notion that working as a group is in their, and the organization's, best interest. They need to understand that their effectiveness in a board setting depends on principles of democracy. (4) A group needs to be accountable to some larger entity. Nonprofit boards are accountable to a number of publics: the organization, community, funding and referral sources, constituents, and others.

Even when these four elements of group cohesiveness are present, they must also be in balance. An effective board needs to focus on getting things done and on the way things get done and to place both in proper perspective. This process of finding the balance that results in group cohesiveness is known as "team building."

At times, any group may have difficulty generating ideas whether their efforts are directed toward planning, goal setting, problem solving, decision making, or other matters. It can be just as difficult for a group to verbalize thoughts as it is for a writer to overcome "writer's block." A primary requirement for an open exchange of ideas is a nonconstraining atmosphere. If board members have previously taken time out to get to know each other at a social occasion and on an informal basis, then friendly relationships have a chance to develop. A relaxed atmosphere where people are comfortable with each other greatly facilitates a flow of creative ideas. When a group does get stalled, there are techniques useful for generating ideas, for expanding a discussion, and for maximizing group participation.

- Brainstorming. This most commonly used technique for generating ideas is often abused because people don't follow the rules. In true brainstorming, all ideas mentioned are listed (on a flip chart) exactly as they are said; the recorder does not paraphrase. Ideas are not discussed when they are given, nor are they judged. It is permissible to build on someone else's idea and crazy ideas are acceptable. A time limit should be set and at the end of that time, the group looks at the list and selects four to six ideas for discussion.
- Paper Passing. This is similar to brainstorming in that no restrictions are placed on an individual's response. A primary difference is that group members respond to some particular statement confidentially. The facilitator reads a specific problem or statement to the group and asks each individual to come up with four to six responses on separate pieces of paper. The idea jogger may be phrased like "How can we..." or "The best way to...is...." After a set time period, the participants' papers are collected and sorted into piles according to the ideas' feasibility, category, frequency of response, or other selected sorting criteria. The group then chooses which "pile of ideas" it wants to discuss.
- Round Robin. One of the oldest techniques for encouraging maximum group participation, the group leader simply goes around the table asking each member's viewpoint on some stated question, problem, or issue. While this technique is intended to coax quieter members to participate, it doesn't always work because a frequent response may be, "I agree with what has already been said," or "I pass." Round robin still puts some folks on the spot where paper passing does not.
- Grandmother's Review. An old adage in fund raising suggests that one should have one's grant proposal read by his or her grandmother; if she understands the request, then the funding prospect will too. A variation on this theme is to take your organization's problem, or whatever it is that needs a fresh idea, to someone outside and far removed from your organization. The less someone knows of your situation, the more creative his or her ideas might be. This is based on the notion that it is always easier to solve someone's else's problem than your own. An adaptation of this is to ask board members of

other organizations in your field for their ideas based on their experience in a similar situation (assuming confidentiality is not a concern).

Discussion won't be productive unless a group's participants listen to the ideas and opinions of others, pay attention to those who have special expertise in the area under discussion, and generally recognize that the contribution of every member is valid. A group also needs to heed the personal feelings of its members. Any working group, such as a board of directors, should feel free to express its feelings. No group can afford to lose a participant because he or she feels an aversion to the matter under discussion. Unhappy members not only draw attention from the main issue but also can hamper the productivity of the full group. When a group is able to listen and share information freely, the result is better decision making because maximum information is generated and brought to bear on the issue.

HUMAN RELATIONS ASPECTS OF BOARD MANAGEMENT

Managing Conflict

The very nature of nonprofit organizations and the diverse people the organization brings together makes some conflict inevitable. All boards at some time are forced to deal with the problem of dissidents. They may range from one who "nitpicks," to the "devil's advocate," to the "maverick" troublemaker. The first is usually harmless and the latter can be outright destructive to the entire organization. It is important to be able to distinguish between an occasional dissident and one whose chronic discordant behavior may signify a real emotional problem on that individual's part.

Diversity and dissent can be productive in a board setting because they stimulate discussion and problem solving. A member who expresses disagreement can force others to clarify their position and rationale and this, in turn, leads to a broader understanding of the question at hand. A nitpicker, for example, may simply be trying to make a point for change and his or her persistence may eventually effect that. Dissidents also keep a board from becoming complacent; members are forced to reexamine their thinking. In other instances, the occasional dissident can help to forge support for an issue by consolidating other members' opinions.

Unfortunately, disagreements can deteriorate into a conflict between individual board members or with the executive director when differences of opinion on an issue are taken personally. Members representing a constituency that feels it is not receiving due attention from the organization may become dissidents. Some mavericks may be self-acclaimed spokespersons for a certain faction of members. Whatever the reason for discordant behavior, it is important first to try to determine its roots. The board's leadership plays a major role in helping to keep conflict impersonal and disagreement healthy.

To avoid or diffuse conflict, the board president might do the following:

- Ask for different opinions on an issue even when there appears to be total agreement. This gives permission to the individual who may be suppressing disagreement to bring his or her concerns out in the open.

- Disassociate ideas from the individual who offered it. Rather than saying, "What is your reaction to Sue's ideas?" the president might ask, "What do you think of the suggestion to...?" This avoids potential disagreements with a person.

- Protect minority opinions. A person who voices a different or unpopular idea may become discouraged from future participation if his or her idea is ignored or ridiculed. The president can protect minority viewpoints by first recognizing them and then calling for their clarification.

- Insist on keeping to a well-planned agenda. This dissuades those who like to nitpick.

- Take a firm stance when personal attacks are made during a board meeting. Say "Let's concern ourselves with (or pay attention to) the problem, not each other."

- Adhere to the rule for effective meetings and the principles for maximum participation. In an environment where people feel free to express themselves and have a format for doing so, dissidents have no role.

One extreme way to handle conflict in a group setting is to totally ignore it. The other extreme is to lay aside the agenda and talk through every disagreement. The first extreme is very frustrating and can breed additional dissidents because those who are not disruptive will recognize what is going on and may eventually take sides with the dissident on principle. The second extreme will bore people, prohibit the conduct of business, and eventually discourage member participation. Either extreme is obviously unhealthy to the group process and to the organization. Group leaders must learn to manage conflict in a way that facilitates the group process and does not interfere with the business of the group.

Conflict that is potentially harmful to an organization may be treated differently by various groups. Some nonprofit leaders suggest

1. Let them (dissidents) have enough rope and they will hang themselves.

2. Recognize that many dissidents are hungry for recognition. Give them an assignment or position that will satisfy such an appetite.

3. Bide your time—many rebels eventually become a part of the organization's establishment.

4. If possible, don't let a dissident catch your other board members by surprise. If you see trouble coming, quietly let some of the key members know it in advance of the meeting.[7]

When an executive director is involved in conflict with a board dissident, it is usually more effective to let the board (the dissident's peers) "deal" with the dissident. Some executives may confer with a board dissident in private to try and reach an understanding, or at least a truce. At the very worst, an executive may need to round up supporters among the board and counterattack. An executive director, more often than not, has the respect of the board, and if he or she should personally be attacked by a "maverick," the board will support the director. Any professional executive should have enough self-confidence to get through most conflict situations with a "grin and bear it" attitude.

The Importance of Leadership

The management style of a board changes with its leadership. Leadership refers to the board president, since this is the person who has the greatest authority and exerts the most influence on the board of directors. Leadership is situational—one who is a leader under a certain set of conditions or circumstances might not be given that same recognition under different situations. The type of leader elected to the board presidency will reflect where an organization is in its life cycle or in relation to current pressing problems. A board leader will be chosen on the basis of having the best skills to manage the organization's affairs at the present time. An organization facing severe financial problems is more likely to seek out a board president with a "get tough" style of leadership. An organization in its midlife cycle which is reexamining its future directions may be more inclined to elect a thinker or a "change agent" type of leader as president of its board of directors.

One important reason for organizational planning is that it helps to identify future personnel requirements (staff) and the type of (volunteer) leadership needed. When recruiting board members, it is wise to keep an eye on your organization's future leadership needs in order to have on the board an experienced member with the skills most relative to meeting the challenges the organization will experience as it grows and changes.

It is easier to analyze what makes one style of leadership more effective under certain circumstances than it is to select a good leader. A board needs to recognize that a leader's authority does not emanate from the individual but rather from the position he or she holds. A board should also be aware that there are certain situational aspects that need to be considered when making leadership choices.

The nature of the task situation is one aspect. The more predictable an organization's situation and the more stable it is in the present, the more predictable its performance will be. In this situation, a leader who has tendencies toward tight control and standardized procedures and possesses a conservative outlook will be able to maintain the organization's course. The opposite is true when the organization's course is uncertain. In this situation, leadership needs to manage the unpredictable, so a leader will need to be flexible, a risk-taker, and a delegater. Under conditions of stress, a leader with a great concern for people is apt to be more effective. This type can minimize the organization's crisis by paying particular attention to the personal needs of the membership. If the board and staff, despite their frustrations with the organization's crisis, are able to maintain a high morale due to their leader's sensitivity, they will be able to work more effectively to resolve the organization's problems.[8]

A second aspect is a leader's expertise. When a board president is clearly an expert and knows more about the organization and the nature of its business than any other member, a leadership style of unilateral control on his or her part is appropriate.

> People hate to be asked their opinion when the person asking already knows the answer, especially if the opinion is less expert and cannot change the asker's conclusions. Occasionally, a leader may wish to give an assignment to someone less skilled in order to help develop that person, but in that case, the object is growth, not necessarily the best product. In general a good rule of thumb is, "if you know the answer and what you plan to do, do not ask a subordinate's opinion. If you ask you risk creating feelings of being manipulated, which decreases trust, and, in turn, accuracy of communications upward. This does not rule out the potential value of allowing subordinates to ask questions in order to understand what is intended or to express their concerns about your planned action. Such airing of concerns can allay their doubts and build their belief in your decisions in ways that will facilitate its implementation.[9]

Third, participatory leadership, involving all members of the group/board, is best when the decisions to be made by the board are not routine; there is little time pressure; and other members are competent (can work on their own) and motivated. Leaders always have to struggle with the push-pull of involving other members of the group and the need to get the job done. True participatory leadership requires more time and is sometimes abandoned for the sake of expediency.

A fourth aspect, and one related to participation, has to do with the attitudes and personal needs of other members. If the board in general is composed of committed individuals who enjoy working on the challenges presented by a nonprofit organization, then a leader who exercises little control is appropriate. Conversely, if board members do not collectively have a degree of independence or need for autonomy, a leader should be able to exercise tight control and specify expectations and performance criteria.

Changing circumstances produce different demands on an organization's leadership, and the appropriate leadership style for an organization also changes. Leadership styles and the conditions of leadership are not always easily defined or recognizable. A board's responsibility is to assess, to the best of its ability, when a change in leadership style is indicated. To perform effectively, a board must recognize when things are going wrong with the organization and realize that it must assume responsibility for initiating change.

SUMMARY

An effective board is one that has managed to develop and maintain a balanced board/executive director relationship. Boards are out of balance when a strong executive director and his or her staff dominate the organization or when a powerful board refuses to share responsibility with staff. A difference in socioeconomic status between a board and its executive director, the recognized professionalism of the executive director, and the life cycle of the organization are factors that can negatively influence the dynamic interaction between a board and its staff. Good board/staff relationships are built on trust, communication, and clearly defined roles.

The success of an organization is related not only to the quality of board/executive management but also to the extent of board member participation. To make the best use of board volunteers and to avoid directors' burnout, there needs to be rotating terms of board membership and officers. Board participation and commitment is stimulated by a continual infusion of new perspectives and ideas, which occurs, in part, by bringing on new members. Idea sharing and discussion are also important to maintaining a higher level of board participation.

The successful nonprofit board is able to manage conflict and recognizes that some conflict can be stimulating and productive. It is the board president's job to learn how to manage dissidents and to recognize which conflict situations may be harmful to the organization. Thus, it is important to select as board president one who has the leadership qualities and expertise to meet the needs of the board, its membership, and the organization.

NOTES

1. Melissa Middleton, *The Place and Power of Non-Profit Boards of Directors,* Ponpo Working Paper No. 78 (New Haven, CT: Yale University, Program on Non-Profit Organizations, 1983), pp. 33–41.

2. Ibid.

3. Anne Nickerson, "The Board's Job Is to Hire the Executive Director in a Responsible Manner," *The Board Letter,* no. 13 (Denver, CO: Duca Associates, 1984), pp. 3–4.

4. James G. Lagges, "The Board of Directors: Boon or Bane for Stockholders and Management?" *Business Horizons* (March/April 1982): 50.

5. Karl Mathiasen, "The Board of Directors," (source and date unknown).

6. Mrs. Lewis Rumford II, "The Board Member and the Executive: How They Serve the Agency and Community," *Child Welfare,* 47 (3) (March 1968): 171–74.

7. "How to Get along with the Dissidents on Your Board," in *The Nonprofit Organization Handbook,* ed. Tracy D. Connors, pp. 2–58.

8. Allen R. Cohen, Stephen L. Fink, Herman Gadon, and Robin D. Willits, *Effective Behavior in Organizations,* pp. 272–79.

9. Ibid., p. 278.

Appendices
Sample Documents

University of Utah National Advisory Council Bylaws

ARTICLE I
NAME AND DURATION

Section 1.1 — Official Name. The official name of the organization referred to in these bylaws is the University of Utah National Advisory Council (N.A.C.).

Section 1.2 — Duration. The existence of the N.A.C. shall be perpetual, except that it may be terminated by a majority decision of its members or the executive committee, as hereinafter constituted.

ARTICLE II
REFERENCES AND DEFINITIONS

Section 2.1 — National Advisory Council. The expressions, "National Advisory Council," "Council" or "N.A.C.," as used herein, shall all mean and refer to the University of Utah National Advisory Council.

Section 2.2 — Additional References or Definitions. As used herein, the following expressions shall have the meanings ascribed to them:
A. "President" shall mean the President of the University of Utah;
B. "Administration" shall mean the official leadership and management officers of the University;
C. "Chairman" shall mean the incumbent chairman of the N.A.C.;
D. "University" shall mean the University of Utah; and
E. "Member" or "members" shall mean and refer to an active member or active members of the N.A.C., unless the context requires otherwise.

ARTICLE III
OBJECTS AND PURPOSES

Section 3.1 — In General. The general objects and purposes of the N.A.C. and its members are as follows:
A. To conceive and implement ideas and influence, thereby creating channels of involvement between the University and the mainstream of contemporary life;
B. To advise and assist the administration and Institutional Council of the University;
C. To respond to the needs of the University as consultants, information sources and evaluators;

D. To contribute to a clear sense of University purpose and direction; and
E. To aid the University in connection with its financial and fiscal matters
   and needs, such as rendering assistance in obtaining funds and gifts from
   the private sector, including individuals, business organizations and foundations; and by way of specification but not in limitation to assist and support the University of Utah's Permanent Endowment Fund.

Section 3.2 — Specific Functions of the N.A.C. Specifically, it is contem-
plated that the N.A.C. will accomplish the following:
A. Advise and work with the administration and assist the Institutional Council
   of the University concerning all aspects of its objectives and programs;
B. Conceive, formulate and implement projects for the advancement of the
   University, which are specifically assigned or entrusted to it by the administration and the Institutional Council of the University;
C. Assist in improving the relationship between the University and its constituencies both within and outside the state of Utah;
D. Work with the administration and the Institutional Council of the University in developing and establishing University policy for raising funds and
   implementing the programs necessary for the development and maintenance of the University's resources; and
E. Provide counsel to the University for the investment of contributed funds,
   whenever specifically requested by the administration.

Section 3.3 — Additional Functions. The N.A.C. will provide liaison between
the University and its alumni and friends. The N.A.C. will also provide ways
and means to give recognition to deserving individuals who assist the University. The N.A.C. will provide the University with guidance and advice in its
various academic, administrative and service activities, and seek to implement
ideas and knowledge affecting the University and leaders of the non-Univer-
sity community, thereby establishing a permanent two-way process of communication for the benefit of both sectors.

ARTICLE IV
ACTIVE MEMBERS OF THE N.A.C.

Section 4.1 — Number. The number of active members of the N.A.C. shall
not be less than twenty (20) nor more than forty (40).

Section 4.2 — Characteristics and Attributes of Active Members. All
active members of the N.A.C. shall possess such attributes of character and
integrity as are established by the executive committee and the incumbent
active members of the Council. Active members will be persons who have
demonstrated successful patterns of achievement and living, and whose backgrounds, expertise, personalities and abilities will enhance the accomplishment of the objects and purposes of the N.A.C., as stated above.

Section 4.3 — Eligibility. Generally, active members will be chosen from
the alumni of the University, but prior attendance at the University shall not
be deemed a prerequisite to be an active member.

**Section 4.4 — Nomination of Active Members and the Nominating Com-
mittee.** Prospective active members of the N.A.C. shall be those persons
who are nominated as candidates for membership by the nominating committee. The nominating committee shall consist of the President, the chairman and the vice chairman. At least 30 days prior to the time any person
is proposed for membership at any fall meeting of the N.A.C., the three mem-

bers of the nominating committee shall meet or communicate by telephone and decide upon the names of candidates for membership to be presented to the N.A.C. at the meeting immediately following such determinations of the nominating committee. The decision of two or more members of the nominating committee as to proposed candidates shall be controlling. Any active member of the N.A.C. may at any time propose a person for consideration by the nominating committee as a candidate by addressing to the President or the chairman a written communication suggesting such name and containing essential information and background relating to said person in sufficient quantity and detail so as to inform the nominating committee as to the qualifications of such person for membership in the N.A.C.

Section 4.5 — Voting on Candidates. At any fall meeting of the N.A.C., the chairman will inform the active members concerning the desirability of filling vacancies in the membership and submit the report of the nominating committee, including the names of any and all candidates proposed for membership by the nominating committee. Forthwith following such report, the active members shall vote upon the names of said candidates and a person shall be approved and installed as an active member if he or she receives a favorable vote of the majority of the active members present at a meeting wherein a quorum is present.

Section 4.6 — Terms of Office of Active Members. All active members shall be elected to serve for a two-year term of office. At the expiration of that term, the membership may vote to reelect such active member for another two-year term, but only if the active member's name has been submitted as a candidate for election to membership by the nominating committee, as provided in Section 4.4 above. Active membership in the N.A.C. shall not exceed five consecutive 2-year terms.

Section 4.7 — Resignation. Any active member may at any time resign as an active member of the N.A.C. by submitting a written resignation to the chairman. Such resignation shall become effective when the chairman receives such written resignation.

Section 4.8 — Removal of an Active Member. Any active member of the N.A.C. may be removed, with or without cause, by a majority vote of the N.A.C. at a meeting at which a quorum is present, provided that no action will be taken to remove an active member unless such action has been previously recommended to the N.A.C. by a majority vote of the nominating committee.

Section 4.9 — Removal for Non-Attendance. Any member of the N.A.C. who misses three or more consecutive semiannual meetings of the Council shall be placed in an inactive status and shall be named an emeritus member of the Council.

Section 4.10 — President as an Active Member. The President of the University shall automatically be an active member of the N.A.C. and shall be accorded all of the rights and privileges of an active member, including the right to vote.

Section 4.11 — Executive Director of Development and Vice President for University Relations. The executive director of the Development Office and the vice president for university relations of the University shall be ex officio members of the N.A.C. and shall be invited to attend all meetings of the N.A.C., but shall not have the right to vote as active members thereof.

ARTICLE V
MEMBERS EMERITUS

Section 5.1 — Members Emeritus. Members emeritus will consist of all people who have been active members of the N.A.C., but whose membership has terminated by reason of resignation or expiration of term as an active member, provided that any active member who has been removed pursuant to Section 4.8 above shall not become a member emeritus.

Section 5.2 — Active List of Members Emeritus. The executive director will keep an active list of the members emeritus.

Section 5.3 — Communications with Members Emeritus. The N.A.C. will attempt to maintain continuing communication with all of its members emeritus. At the discretion of the President, the chairman or the executive director, copies of communications and reports transmitted by the N.A.C. to active members may also be sent to members emeritus.

Section 5.4 — Assistance by Members Emeritus. From time to time the N.A.C. may call upon or seek the assistance of members emeritus, either individually or collectively, to accomplish the objectives and purposes of the N.A.C.

ARTICLE VI
MEETINGS OF ACTIVE MEMBERS AND PROCEDURES

Section 6.1 — Regular Meetings. Regular meetings of the active members of the N.A.C. shall be held semiannually in the spring and fall of each year. The hours, date and place for such meetings shall be as determined by the chairman of the N.A.C., acting with the approval of the President. The chairman or secretary shall give written notice of said meetings mailed at least 30 days prior to the holding of such meetings.

Section 6.2 — Special Meetings. Special meetings of the active members may be called at any time by the President or the chairman by giving the active members at least 10 days written notice mailed in advance of the proposed meeting.

Section 6.3 — Quorum of Active Members at Meetings. A quorum of the active members at meetings shall consist of at least 50% of the then membership of the N.A.C., present in person at such meeting. An active member shall not be permitted to give his proxy to another active member or any other person.

Section 6.4 — Voting Upon Membership and Other Items of Business. Each active member shall have one (1) vote at all meetings, exercisable only if the active member is personally present at the meeting. Assuming a quorum of active members is present at a duly constituted and held meeting, all items of business, including approval and installation of a candidate for membership, will be determined by the majority vote of the active members present at the meeting. In other words, if a majority of those active members present vote in favor of a resolution or an item of business, including the election of an active member, the vote will be effective and controlling.

ARTICLE VII
OFFICERS

Section 7.1 — List of Officers. The N.A.C. shall have the following officers: a chairman, a vice chairman, an executive director, a secretary and an assistant secretary. The N.A.C. may also appoint such additional officers and assistant officers as are necessary or desirable, in the opinion of its members.

Section 7.2 — Election of Officers. At the regular fall meeting of the N.A.C., in calendar years having an even last digit, the active members of the N.A.C. shall elect from among their number a chairman and a vice chairman to serve for a two-year term of office. The executive committee may but need not submit a report at such meeting containing its recommendations of the names of persons to be considered as candidates for said positions. Candidates receiving the highest number of votes of the members present shall be deemed elected. In the event of a vacancy in said offices occurring for any reason, including death, incapacity or resignation, the President will appoint a successor to serve the unexpired term.

Section 7.3 — Terms of Office. The terms of each elective or appointive office of the Council shall be for two years. An officer may serve for a second or third term, but no elective or appointive officer shall serve for more than three consecutive terms.

Section 7.4 — Removal. Any appointive or elective officer may be removed at any meeting of the Council, either with or without cause, by a majority vote of the active members of the N.A.C. present at such meeting, provided that no action will be taken to remove an officer unless such action has been recommended by the executive committee to the N.A.C.

Section 7.5 — Executive Director and Secretary. The director of development of the University shall automatically be the executive director and secretary of the N.A.C. The N.A.C. members shall not have the right to remove from office the executive director and secretary.

Section 7.6 — Duties of Council Chairman. The Council chairman shall be responsible for the administration and performance of the objects and purposes of the N.A.C., and working with the President and executive committee will supervise the organization and affairs of the Council. The chairman shall preside at all meetings of the Council. The chairman shall be a member of all committees with full voting privileges thereon. The chairman shall be considered the chief executive officer of the Council, and shall from time to time make recommendations to the Council for the purposes of promoting its usefulness and effectiveness to the University. The chairman shall be responsible for planning, implementing and supervising the meetings of the N.A.C. and its programs.

Section 7.7 — Duties of Vice Chairman. In the absence of the chairman, the vice chairman shall perform the duties and functions of the chairman and serve in his or her place. The vice chairman shall have other duties as may be assigned to him or her by the N.A.C.

Section 7.8 — Duties of Executive Director. The executive director shall be responsible for assisting the Council, its officers, the executive committee and the other Council committees in carrying out various projects in the service of the University.

Section 7.9 — Duties of the Secretary. The secretary shall perform the customary duties of such office, keeping records of the meetings of the Council, the executive committee and the Council committees. His duties shall include giving notice of meetings of the Council and notice of meetings of the executive committee. He shall also be responsible for keeping the membership roll and performing such other duties as may be assigned to him.

Section 7.10 — Nomination of Officers. The nominating committee will nominate candidates from the active members at large to fill vacancies and/or expired terms of office. Candidates' names must be submitted to the secretary who in turn will notify all active members of the nominations at least 30 days prior to the meeting at which the nominees will be voted upon by the Council.

ARTICLE VIII
THE EXECUTIVE COMMITTEE

Section 8.1 — Composition of the Executive Committee. The executive committee shall consist of the following persons: the President, the chairman, the vice chairman, the executive director and secretary, and the vice president for university relations. The President shall preside at all meetings of the executive committee.

Section 8.2 — Authority of the Executive Committee. The executive committee shall have the powers and authority contained in the bylaws or delegated to it by the Council. The executive committee shall also have the authority to exercise all the powers of the Council when the Council is not in session.

Section 8.3 — Quorum. A majority of the members of the executive committee shall constitute a quorum for the transaction of business.

Section 8.4 — Agenda for Meetings. The executive committee, working with the chairman, will assist in formulating the agenda for the regular and special meetings of the N.A.C.

ARTICLE IX
OTHER COMMITTEES

Section 9.1 — General Provisions. Except as the same may be expressly provided to the contrary, the executive committee shall have the authority to establish and set policies and procedures for all committees of the N.A.C.

Section 9.2 — Committees and their Membership. Committees may be appointed by either the executive committee or the N.A.C. Whenever an appointment is made, the appointive authority, i.e., either the executive committee or the Council itself, will direct and supervise the activities of the committee it appoints, including the selection of members, receiving reports and discharging the committee.

Section 9.3 — Terms. Ordinarily, the terms of membership on committees shall be for two (2) years unless otherwise specified by the appointive authority.

Section 9.4 — Quorums of Committees. A majority of the members of a committee shall be a quorum for the transaction of business.

Section 9.5 — Responsibility of Committees. Each committee shall be responsible to the N.A.C. for the proper conduct of its function and its duties shall be carried out in collaboration with the executive director of the Council and appropriate University staff members.

ARTICLE X
RECORDS

Section 10.1 — Maintenance of Records. The Council shall maintain a central file at the Development Office of the University which is deemed the N.A.C. headquarters office. All such records shall be available at all times to the active members and officers of the N.A.C. and to its authorized agents.

Section 10.2 — Minutes. The secretary will be the custodian of the minute book of the N.A.C., and the same will be kept at the Development Office of the University.

ARTICLE XI
FINANCIAL MATTERS

Section 11.1 — General Statement. In view of the fact that the purpose of the N.A.C. is essentially advisory, it is not contemplated that the N.A.C. will engage in any financial transactions or affairs, and no officer, member or representative of the N.A.C. shall have the power or authority to expend any funds, commit for the expenditure of any funds, borrow any monies, incur any indebtednesses, or otherwise engage in any financial affairs or transactions on behalf of the N.A.C., its members or the University.

Section 11.2 — Bank Account. It is not contemplated that the N.A.C. will have any bank account, and no authority is granted, express or implied, for the establishment of any such bank account or authority with respect thereto. Should the N.A.C. have occasion at any time to be involved in any financial transaction or affair, such as a luncheon, dinner, etc., the financial arrangements, involvements and transactions pertaining thereto shall be conducted solely and exclusively by the University acting through its officers or by the executive committee of the N.A.C.

Section 11.3 — Traveling Expenses. It is contemplated that each member of the N.A.C. shall pay and discharge his own traveling expenses, including traveling fare, room cost, meals, tips, etc., incurred in connection with attendance of meetings, or otherwise, and neither the N.A.C. nor the University, nor others, shall be under any duty or obligation to reimburse or pay said member for such expenses.

Section 11.4 — Miscellaneous Provisions. Because of the fore-going provisions, it is not contemplated that any officer or member of the N.A.C. shall have any authority to execute any instruments on behalf of the N.A.C. or the University, such as checks, drafts, contracts, etc.

ARTICLE XII
AMENDMENTS

Section 12.1 — Amendments of Bylaws. Amendments or supplements to these bylaws may be made at any time by a majority vote of the membership of the Council, provided that notice of the proposal to amend or supplement the bylaws must have been given in the notice of such meeting in order for such an amendment or supplement to be considered and acted upon as a matter of business at such meeting.

Bylaw Section on Committees

ARTICLE VI

COMMITTEES

Section 1. *Standing Committees.* The following named committees shall be the permanent standing committees, with the executive director being an *ex officio* member of all board committees:

    A. *Executive Committee.* The executive committee shall consist of five members: the chairman, vice-chairman, secretary, and treasurer and one additional member of the board of directors. The chairman of other committees, individually or together, shall be invited to meet with the executive committee when deemed advisable and each chairman shall have the privilege of meeting with the executive committee when he requests. The powers and duties shall be delegated to the executive committee by the board of directors to which the executive committee shall be responsible.

    B. *Public Relations and Promotion Committee.* The board of directors shall each year appoint upon nomination by the executive committee a public relations and promotion committee of not fewer than three nor more than seven members. It shall interpret the Counseling Service's program to the community via all media, prepare press releases, pictures, and other promotional material, and conduct open houses, luncheons and other promotional events. The committee will coordinate and work closely with the executive director.

    C. *Grievance Committee.* The grievance committee shall consist of three members, with one member from the executive committee and two appointed by the board of directors. It shall review grievances brought to its attention which have not been satisfactorily settled with the executive director. The committee shall meet and will render a decision within 15 calendar days after the date of receipt of the grievance.

Courtesy of the Interfaith Counseling Service, Inc., Scottsdale, AZ. Reprinted by permission.

Section 2. *Special Committees.* The board of directors, or the chairman, shall, at appropriate times, designate special committees (personnel, nominating, budget, long-range planning, etc.) as it or he may deem advisable, shall fix the duties of such committees, and appoint and remove their personnel.

Section 3. *Minutes and Records of Committees.* A record shall be kept of the proceedings and determinations of all standing committees and the reports of all special committees. The minutes of the meetings of any standing committees shall be preserved in the same manner as the minutes of meetings of the board of directors. Notice of all committee meetings, standing or special, may be given orally or in writing by the chairman of the committee or the secretary of the corporation.

Board Member Job Description

MARICOPA COUNCIL CAMP FIRE BOARD OF DIRECTOR POSITION DESCRIPTION

Purpose of Position:

Together with other members of the Board is legally and morally responsible for all activities of the agency. The Board is solely responsible for determining agency policy, approving the annual budget and determining the goals of the agency.

Minimum Job Requirements:

A demonstrated interest in the agency's service goals. Specific experience and/or knowledge in at least one element: administration, finance, personnel, program development, evaluation, public relations or communications. Representative of some aspect or segment of the population in the community. Available time.

Key Responsibilities:

Policy Administration

Establishes and/or continues the legal or corporate existence of the agency. Ensures that agency meets legal requirements for the conduct of the agency business and affairs. Responsible for adopting bylaws and ensuring that the agency operates within them. Acts on proposed revisions to the bylaws. Adopts policies which determine

Courtesy of Maricopa Camp Fire Inc., Phoenix AZ. Reprinted by permission.

the purposes, governing principles, functions and activities and courses of action of the agency. Assumes ultimate responsibility for internal policies which govern the agency.

Evaluation

Regularly evaluates and reviews the agency's operations and maintains standards of performance. Monitors the activities of the agency, including: reviewing reports of appropriate committees; confirming, modifying, or rejecting proposals; counseling and providing good judgment on plans of committees or the Executive; and considering, debating and deciding issues.

Public and Community Relations

Gives sponsorship and prestige to the agency and inspires confidence in its services. Understands and interprets the work of the agency to the community. Relates the services of the agency to the work of other agencies and focuses on social reform and progress in the community as a whole.

Personnel

Selects, employs and evaluates the Executive Director. Approves policies which govern the administration of personnel. Participates in recruitment, selection and development of board members, where primary responsibility for this activity is assigned to a nominating committee.

Finance

Approves and monitors the corporate finances of the agency. Creates a financial climate for fulfilling the agency purpose. Sees that sufficient funds are available for the agency to meet its objectives. Authorizes and approves the annual audit. Responsible for all expenditures dealing with the facility, its improvements or purchase of additional land or buildings.

Nominating Committee Form for Board Recommendations

MARIOCOPA COUNCIL CAMP FIRE
1515 E. Osborn
Phoenix, Arizona

TO THE NOMINATING COMMITTEE:

I hereby propose for the *Board of Directors Standing Committee* of Camp Fire, _____ who has my full and unqualified endorsement.

_____ Proposer

Type or Print Name in Full _____

Marital Status _____

Husband or Wife's Name _____

Under 20 ____ 20–35 ____ 35–50 ____ over 50 ____

Residence Address _____

How Long at this Address _____

Telephone _____

Business Address _____

Telephone _____

Nature of Business and with Whom Connected _____

_____

How Long a Resident of Arizona _____

Memberships in Camp Fire and Other Organizations, Past and Present
(Please give address)

Name	Street	City	State

Known by the following Board Members of Camp Fire

_____

_____

_____

_____

_____

Brief Biography _____

_____

_____

_____

_____

Signature of Sponsor _____

Date _____

Mailing Instructions for Bulletins:_____
  Home Address _____
  Business Address _____

If Person is accepted would you want to be involved in contacting
that person? Yes _____ No _____

Planning Documents

The following statements from The Denver Area Council of Boy Scouts and the Interfaith Counseling Service illustrate two ways to prepare long-term goals.

Cover Letter and "Update, Long Range Plan": 1985–1990.

May 1985

To the Leadership, Friends and Investors in the Denver Area Council, Boy Scouts of America:

The Denver Area Council is building a fine tradition of in-depth planning that has led to the establishment of strategies that have had considerable impact upon the organization.

The enclosed represents a summary of current recommendations that are presented from this, the third edition of the Long Range Plan that has been updated every two years.

I'm grateful to the following subcommittee chairmen for their leadership and determination to pull all of this information together and participate in this important endeavor.

Bruce W. Hulbert - Membership Study
P.K. Ware - Quality Unit Study
Glen L. Ryland - Program Utilization of Facilities and Property
Lloyd C. Whittall, Jr. - Staff Organization and Utilization
Richard F. Walker - Volunteer Organization and Utilization
Joseph R. Lincoln - Finance Study

When our President asked me to take on this responsibility, I gladly agreed to do so because I believe so much in what the Council is doing for young people, and I believe whatever we plan, project and recommend will have a substantial, positive impact on the Boy Scout program in our Council.

Most sincerely,

Bob

Robert K. Timothy
Chairman
Long Range Plan Update Committee

MEMBERSHIP STUDY

CHAIRMAN: BRUCE HULBERT

The number of Scouting age youth in the area served by the Denver Area Council, Boy Scouts of America is expected to increase by approximately 3½ percent (4,783 market increase) during the next five year period from 1985–1989.

The committee recommends that the Council target an increase in membership of 12 percent during the same time period. The recommended goals are outlined on the attached Membership Study Worksheet, Page 6. The growth in membership is specifically recommended in the following areas.

1. CUB SCOUTS +5.8 percent growth (+790) = 1 percent increase in market share.
   Our demographic projection indicates a 4.5 percent (1,346) increase in the Cub Scout (includes Tiger Cubs) market during the target period. 5.8 percent growth absorbs the population trend and increases the market share served by the Council, from 34 percent to 35 percent.
2. BOY SCOUTS +23 percent increase (+1,463) = 4 percent increase in market share.
   Our projection indicates a stable Boy Scout market during this target period. The 23 percent increase in Boy Scout membership would position the Denver Area Council to serve the same market share (23%) as the current national average.
   The current market penetration served by the Council is low as compared to similar market shares served by like size Councils as well as the National Boy Scout market

density. This gain in Boy Scout market share is the most significant challenge to the Council.

3. <u>EXPLORERS +16.3 percent increase (1,009) = 1½ percent increase in market share.</u>

   The Explorer age market will grow 3 percent (2,344) during the next five years. The 16.3 percent increase represents 1½ percent increase in the market share and is consistent with recent growth patterns in the Exploring program.

   The Exploring program, serving high school aged youth, has shown the strongest increases over the past two years. Maintenance of the momentum gained during the past two years should help the Council achieve the above growth.

4. <u>TOTAL COUNCIL MEMBERSHIP +12 percent increase (+3,262) increase = 1.3 percent increase in market share.</u>

   The Membership Study Committee recommends an 8 percent increase in the number of Scouting units serving the Council area. The growth is outlined on the attached Unit Study Worksheet (Page 6). This growth is consistent with the established pattern set forth in the 1983 Long Range Plan with one exception. (The exception is the acceleration of growth in the number of Boy Scout Troops [10 percent]). This growth supports the anticipated increase in Boy Scout membership by making this program more accessible to the market.

Issues and Recommendations

1. <u>Increase the level of service in Denver and Adams Counties.</u>

   Denver and Adams Counties represent the lowest percent of market share served in the entire Denver metro area. Our demographic study revealed that these counties have the greatest percent change in ethnic population and contain the greatest percent of families *"at risk"* which similar United Way studies indicate that these communities will have the greatest demands for children's services.

   The Council recently responded to this need by employing three full-time staff members to serve Denver County and maintained two full-time staff members to serve Adams County. This concentration of manpower resources has stabilized our position of service in these counties, but are far from reaching the level of performance realized by the remainder of the Council.

2. <u>Addition of professional manpower resources to serve the Centennial District (Aurora).</u>

   The area served by the Centennial District is expected to grow by 8.5 percent during the next five years. Selection of an additional executive staff member was recommended in the 1983 Long Range Plan and our study confirmed the need for this additional position.

The committee also noted the potential for significant growth in the Douglas County area. The committee recommends that the Council be aware of future developments in this area for consideration of additional manpower resources.

3. <u>Lower the entry age for the programs of Scouting to (at least five or six years of age).</u>

Competing programs for the Scouting market (sports, Indian Guides, etc.) are available to boys well before the entry level of the Tiger Cub program (7 years of age). The Scouting program is only available to our market after they have had the opportunity to participate in alternate programs. It is concerning that the Scouting program ask a boy and his family to wait to join, potentially after the boy has entered another group or activity and built a relationship of friends and interest in other areas.

4. <u>Emphasize marketing the Scouting program as a youth and family development program, with special attention given to service to single parent families.</u>

The Boy Scouts of America desires to be perceived by adults as a program that they can effectively use to provide a positive set of values for their children.

The single largest change to the Scouting market is the family structure, in which our market lives. Scouting is currently not perceived by the single parent as a family development program but as "just another activity."

Initial changes to our Council programs, which have made our program more available to single parents have been met with positive results. Continued marketing of the "Youth and Family" development programs and availability of the Scouting programs must be emphasized to all families.

It is recommended that marketing "the means" by which a single parent could participate in the Scouting program, coupled with relaxing the high level of structure now required in Scouting units would enable more boys of single parent and families with special needs to participate.

5. <u>Increase the level of service to the Hispanic Community.</u>

The fastest growing population in the Denver metro area is the Hispanic American population. The Hispanic American population also represents the lowest market share served by the Denver Area Council. A conscience effort must be made by the Denver Area Council to serve the Hispanic American population if the Council is to maintain and increase its share of the market served and realistically offer its services to all communities within its boundaries.

The Council's concentration of professional manpower resources in Denver and Adams Counties has contributed to this effort and the "In-School Scouting" program has caused traditional Scouting units to form in Hispanic neighborhoods previously unserved by the Council.

Also, increased communication leading to understanding of the purpose of the Scouting programs and the opportunity for involvement by Hispanic organizations, leadership and youth must be emphasized.

6. Use the Exploring program to encourage high school students to complete their education.

Our study of school figures noted packets of significant high school dropout rates, (two areas in excess of 20%).

The Exploring program serves high school aged youth through corporate sponsored career interest programs and career awareness programs.

The committee recommends a concentration of corporate sponsored career interest Explorer Posts in targeted "high dropout" rate areas. The attraction of the Explorer program has been successful because it shows the student more about the student's own career choice. Placement of these programs in specific service areas will enable the Explorer Post leadership to emphasize the need for continued education while the members participate in their career program.

7. Continue the Quality Program thrust which has lead to retention of membership.

The Denver Area Council has realized growth during the past three years from two sources.

1. Reaching further into the community with its service, through programs like "School Night for Scouting" which made the programs of Scouting more visible and accessible and "In-School Scouting" which takes the Scouting program into previously unserved areas.

2. Increasing the retention of its membership through the "Quality Unit" thrust. The two major factors influencing the tenure of the Council's membership are:

    A. The Quality of the program the member and his family receive.

    B. The accessibility of the Scouting unit to the member.

Growth in units as outlined in the Membership Study Worksheet agrees with this premise and the committee strongly recommends continued "Quality Program Thrust" which further contributes to Council growth. Retention rates are to be compared on an annual basis, by program.

8. Develop a data base of available market, by program, by district to measure the success of the Council's localized service.

    The Membership Study Committee has compiled a data base that can be shared with district leadership for the purpose of goal setting and achieving levels of market service, by program. Page seven of this report is a map of the Council showing district boundaries and page eight shows the total data base, by district, which can be broken out by program on a year to year basis.

SOURCE DATA

Colorado Department of Education—Jo Ann Keith

- Enrollment projections—School Finance Unit—December 17, 1984
- Colorado Non-Public Schools—Fall 1984

Denver Public Schools—Ruth Kari

- Review 1983 Method of Demographics Study
- Colorado Non-Public Schools—Fall 1984—Methods

Mile High United Way—Cecilia Broder

- Health and Human Services Needs of the Denver Metropolitan Community—August 1984

Colorado State Demographer's Office

- Population Projections—January 1985

The demographic figures studied for this report to the Long Range Planning Committee served to validate the trends and growth anticipated in the 1983 Long Range Plan. The trends were further validated by outside sources which gathered consistent numbers.

QUALITY UNITS

CHAIRMAN: P.K. WARE

The sole reason for the existence of the Denver Area Council, Boy Scouts of America, is so that youth of Scouting age will have the opportunity to participate in a "QUALITY" program of citizenship training, character development, physical fitness, and leadership development.

The only way an individual can participate in the programs of Scouting is by registered membership in a Scouting unit. The continued emphasis of this Council is to provide the highest "QUALITY" Scouting program possible within a unit setting. The Council is successful only when it produces a platform on which an increased percent of units conduct successful program for their membership.

The only proper avenue available to, a local Council, to extend the "QUALITY PROGRAM OF SCOUTING" to its membership is through its Scouting units. Therefore, the Council must work to strengthen the quality of program presented by its units.

Choices

1. Set high standards that all units are encouraged to strive for, but only select units achieve

OR

2. Set minimum standards of performance that all units are *expected* to achieve.

Recommendation

It is recommended that:

1. The Long Range goal of the Denver Area Council will be to have 75% of its units earning "THE NATIONAL QUALITY UNIT AWARD" by 1989.
2. The Council and district primary performance criteria be based upon the percent of units achieving minimum standards set forth in the "NATIONAL QUALITY UNIT AWARD" program.
3. The Council and districts challenge will be to provide service and programs enabling all units to meet the "NATIONAL QUALITY UNIT AWARD."
4. The Council Commissioner Staff be charged with the responsibility of administering the "NATIONAL QUALITY UNIT AWARD" program by reviewing this criteria on an annual basis to ensure that it is consistent with the Council Long Range Plan. Then annually set objectives to accomplish the Council Long Range "QUALITY UNIT AWARD" standard objective of 75%.

FACILITY UTILIZATION TO MEET OUR PROGRAM NEEDS

CHAIRMAN: GLEN L. RYLAND

In addition to our Francis S. Van Derbur Scout Service Center, our Council owns two program related facilities as well as being involved in negotiations to acquire an in-city property.

JOHNSON PARK
PEACEFUL VALLEY SCOUT RANCH
CAMP TAHOSA

Each of the above properties needs to be examined in light of current needs and determinations made as to their most productive and efficient usage in terms of program.

Because of political/bureaucratic delays in freeing Johnson Park for the Denver Area Council, this facility is ignored in these findings and will be treated when conditions change.

Summary Background

Camp Tahosa

Camp Tahosa was acquired by the Denver Area Council in 1936 and was its primary summer camp for 45 years. It was shut down after the 1981 season because of the high cost of running duplicate camping programs at both Tahosa and Peaceful Valley, the burden of required maintenance costs and environmental damage due to overuse. In 1983, after volunteer efforts and funding, the camp was made available for limited short term camping. There continues to be a strong undercurrent for retention and some use of this facility.

Peaceful Valley Scout Ranch

Peaceful Valley Scout Ranch was acquired in 1961 as a result of a Capital Campaign. It has been used as a summer camp since 1964 and as the *only* Denver Area Council summer camp since 1982. The developed area is only a fraction of the total acreage of the camp and this limited area has been named Camp Cris Dobbins as a result of a substantial endowment gift. There are other areas within the Peaceful Valley boundaries suitable for camp development including a section in excess of 600 acres on the west side of County Road 25.

Findings and Recommendations

Peaceful Valley Scout Ranch

The planned combination dining and activities building at *CAMP CRIS DOBBINS* is essential and must continue to be the highest priority, capital and endowment objective in the near term. Camp Cris Dobbins should be restricted to summer camp operations to avoid overuse and "overexposure" to our users. Some minor off-season exceptions may be granted for training and special events.

An alternative camp at Peaceful Valley offers great potential for absorbing increased summer camp utilization when the capacity of Camp Cris Dobbins is reached in 1988 at about 2,500 campers. Establishing an alternative camp would allow a camping program different from that of the heavily structured one at Camp Cris Dobbins. This would permit more of a cafeteria or menu plan wherein the units would select the alternative site and program and participate in a commissary feeding operation. The units would develop their own programs as well as choosing various activities at Camp Cris Dobbins such as the lake, horses, rifle and archery. Locations suitable for such alternative camping exist, particularly on the mesa to the north of the lake area. Water wells appear to be sufficient for this growth.

As treated in the prior issue of the Long Range Plan, there is still a need for a "no frills" family camping area devoted primarily to the families of volunteer unit leaders. It is believed that this would be a positive factor in retention of qualified leaders, whose families do not always appreciate the Scouts taking a week of the leaders' vacation away from the family. There were two areas considered for this, and the recommendation of the committee presently points to a wooded area in a hollow north of Camp Cris Dobbins. There would be sufficient proximity for use of the lake and other facilities when Scouts were not there.

West side of County Road 25 is believed to offer great potential for development primarily for off-season unit camping (September 1st to May 31st) and district events such as camporees. Accessibility is vastly superior in winter to the basic Peaceful Valley area east of the highway. It is recommended that the usable area be divided into three subareas which could support multiple events as well as providing for site rotation for unit camping. Latrines, a shelter placement in each subarea and a water distribution plan to use available water will be required.

Camp Tahosa

Camp Tahosa holds great potential for enhancing the outdoor experience without competing directly with Peaceful Valley. The approach recommended is to utilize Camp Tahosa to offer an "elite" program experience, as well as "off-season" (September 1st to May 31st) unit short term camping. We would make available three refurbished lodges (without lights or heat other than the fireplace). The old dining hall would *not* be used for feeding, but would be utilized as an activities' building. The "elite" program for Tahosa would be emphasized for summer camping as well as throughout the year. The concepts of a super ropes' course, (constructed and maintained by volunteers) as well as high adventure programs featuring low impact camping will be offered. Further, a cold weather "survival" type training program (for both youth and leaders) can be offered and Sandy Bridges (developer of such a program at the National High Adventure Base in Ely, Minnesota) is willing to guide the start-up at Tahosa. This approach would address several of the needs of the Scouting program:

> Retention of Webelos Leaders
> Life Scout "Dropouts"
> Troop Leader Development
> Improved Unit Program
> Marketing
> Overall Generation of Enthusiasm

We believe that the Tahosa program could effectively use the out-of-doors as an effective tool in teaching leadership, personal strength, decision making, safety and teamwork. Sufficient water is available to support such recommendations and such use may actually be beneficial in enhancing our water rights.

Caveats

Specific capacity limits need to be set early and adhered to at Camp Cris Dobbins to avoid serious environmental damage.

Specific locations identified for various functions should not be inflexibly selected now to permit decision making to adjust to changing realities as time passes.

The implementation of greater facility utilization and the types of programs visualized will likely result in capital requirements as well as a greater need for more trained staff and budgetary pressures.

Any program considerations must be financially self-supporting.

STAFF ORGANIZATION AND UTILIZATION

CHAIRMAN: LLOYD C. WHITTALL, JR.

Staff Organization and Utilization Committee Amended Charter:

To Determine:

A. Are processes in place to administer the organization today and are those processes of the proper depth to allow for substantial growth during the planning period?
B. Do the structures in place actually serve the constituents and maximize the potential of the market?
C. How do the assignments of the Denver Area Councils Human Resources compare with other successful councils in maximizing the resource allocation?

In preparation of this report

A. I visited with:
   William R. Kephart - Scout Executive
   A. Ely Brewer - Director of Field Service
   Charlie Arbogast - Senior District Executive
   Norton Rainey - Director of Development
   Ray Boyd - Director Exploring Service
   Paul Needham - Program Director
   Bob Hanawalt - Region Field Executive BSA
B. I reviewed many documents pertaining to the various practices and procedures focusing on personnel development and generic office and financial administration.
C. I associated what I heard and read, seeking answers to two basic questions:
   1. Are the policies and procedures in place to manage the line functions of the Denver Area Council to maximize the potential of the Council?
   2. Are the scouting professionals committed to those procedures, using those procedures, and are the results meeting or exceeding market potential?

Significant Findings:

A. A Professional Management System is in place. Hiring; Training; Financial Management; Compensation; Management Development; Goal Setting; all are in place.
B. There is evidence that these systems have helped to produce the proper results.
   The measurement would be the "Index of Growth," comparing this Council to national averages, **and** ongoing

community support measured by dollars contributed and
the depth of voluntary community leadership.

C. The most significant finding is that with the four Levels of
Management I interviewed, the consistency of purpose was most
evident. Our leadership is "singing from the same hymnal."

This consistency can not be underestimated and must
continue to be leveraged throughout all levels of the Council, both in professional and voluntary leadership.
With that, our potential has no bounds.

D. The budgetary system is properly tied to program activity goals
and objectives. Procedures are in place to alter both budget
and program in the best interest of the Council upon concur-
rence by the Executive Committee. Dispensation of budgeted
dollars for programs can be easily attained but with proper
financial accountability.

Concerns:

1. The financial stability of this Council is in evidence by other
reports. Tremendous progress has been made here. Personnel
stability has greatly improved over the last three years. Concern, however, exists regarding career advancement and diversity of job assignments creating skills which would enhance an
executive's ability and position for advancement. Salaries paid
to Council executives are at or above Boy Scouts of America
standards. The use of the Council's financial stability for continuity of development of the middle management employee
body, i.e., team leaders, would allow flexibility in salary treatment thus maintaining the continuity of personnel and program which has greatly enhanced this Council's effectiveness.

2. The growth potential of this Council, as exhibited in my full
report, indicates a need for additional executive personnel to be
planned in the 1986 environment. In the areas of Field Executives, two additions should be made and a program director's
assistant should be added as well. These additions in a planned
environment can only enhance the future of the Council.

A Final Comment:

I found the Denver Area Council comprised of a group of professional managers, dedicated to a common purpose. The Council is admin-
istratively sound and poised to continue development of the Denver
market.

I look forward to continued success.

GOVERNING BODY ORGANIZATION AND UTILIZATION

CHAIRMAN: RICHARD F. WALKER

Background

Any successful organization must have a clearly defined governing structure. It is also important that this structure be reviewed periodically to ensure that it is functioning efficiently in carrying out the mission of the organization. There has been some confusion regarding the functions of the Executive Committee versus the Executive Board of our Council. There also seems to be a growing trend for non-profit boards to modernize their structure, since in the past they have been slower to respond to change than corporate businesses. Our Council utilizes the busiest people in town and their time is the lifeblood of our organization. We must be sure that this valuable asset is utilized in a careful and efficient manner.

The By-Laws of the Council have not been reviewed and updated for sometime. Therefore, it makes sense to do this along with changes in structure.

It is within this framework that we have conducted a review of the governing body and organization of the Council and make the following recommendations to be implemented as part of the 1985 Update of the Long Range Plan:

Recommendations

1. Establish a Board of Trustees as the governing body of the Council.
2. Keep the present Executive Board to carry out the responsibilities delegated to it by the Board of Trustees.
3. Retain the present Advisory Council to provide guidance and advice to the Executive Board.
4. Amend the By-Laws of the Council to provide for the above structural changes and for such other matters as are required to bring them up-to-date.

Discussion

Board of Trustees

- Members of the Board would be:
  Chairman of the Executive Board
  President of the Council (serve as Chairman of Board of
    Trustees)
  Treasurer
  Council Commissioner
  Scout Executive/Secretary
  All Vice Presidents
  Past Chairman of the Executive Board
  Legal Counsel
  Others as elected
- Board would have final approval on purchase or sale of assets of Council.
- Scout Executive as C.E.O. of organization would report to the Board.
- Board would set general policy regarding program and budget and would ensure that such programs and budget approved by the Executive Board conform to these policies.

Executive Board

- Members would consist of active Scout volunteers from all segments of our community.
- All members of Board of Trustees would be members of the Executive Board.
- Responsible for approving program plan and operating budget as long as they conform to the general policies of the Board of Trustees regarding these functions.
- Membership limited to 100.
- Sensitive and responsive to community needs.
- Serve as a leadership resource pool for committee work of the Council.
- Meet at least quarterly to review program and budget.

Advisory Council

- Members would consist of friends of Scouting.
- Former volunteer leaders of Scouting.
- Provide a pool of talent from various segments of the Council to carry out specific tasks on an individual basis.

FINANCE

CHAIRMAN: JOSEPH R. LINCOLN

It is the intent of this study to articulate those factors that have been instrumental in this organization's establishment of a highly successful development program over the past four years. These positive and motivational factors will continue to be driving forces that will result in future success. We want to communicate squarely and without apology our fund raising philosophy that moves contrary to many of the trends of today.

The volunteer organization is faced with the same challenges of a profit making organization. However, the unique blend of a professional staff and volunteers necessitates effective execution to meet the broader challenge of funding.

- Executive Board members have three purposes: to make policy, to raise money and to give financially.
- A well-conceived development program evolves around two basic factors in the equation—a strong case and leadership. The Boy Scouts are fortunate to have a strong case to support maintained giving levels and must continue to focus on broadening financial support.
- The Council will continue to raise money in a low profile, behind the scenes, quiet manner, utilizing top leadership.
- Cost effective fund raising is a priority. This is best accomplished through a leadership oriented development program.
- The Council does not use special events to raise money with the exception of The Sports Awards Breakfast. It is recognized that special events are not a cost effective way to raise money. Donors want to get the maximum return on their dollar.
- Product or commission sales to raise money are not to be utilized by the Council or districts. Units may use such methods, but the

Council's list of units and leaders is confidential and will not be shared with those promoting product or commission sales.

- The periodic need to run a genuine and justified capital campaign has been proven as extremely healthy for this organization.
- Based on our experience, and that of other highly successful development operations, outside counsel helps the staff and volunteers to establish a strong research program and organizational framework and provides campaign staff to augment the existing development office staff. Of greatest importance, the counsel keeps the larger priority issues in front of staff and volunteer leadership.
- It is recognized through our past experience, and the experience of many other successful institutions, that the capital/endowment program is the most expedient way to build the endowment fund.
- The Executive Committee adopted as a defensible need the endowment fund designed as an integral part of an overall, long-range financial plan for the Council. Specific uses of endowment income include: maintenance of a facility or support for elective programs. The Council leadership feels strongly that brick and mortar (capital) projects should not be undertaken without endowment funds to maintain those facilities.
- Based on a thorough analysis of our income budget we were to identify a major area where we feel attention must be focused. The area is sustaining membership or annual giving which constitutes an unusually high proportion of annual income budget. The percent (around 33%) is much higher than most of the Boy Scout Councils in America. This percentage is also much higher than other successful non-profit organizations we analyzed.

The solution to this problem of a high pressure annual campaign is to produce more income from two other areas. Since we feel the United Way is declining in its percent of support we must turn to ourselves to find other ways to generate operating dollars. The most important of course is the strong continual effort to build our endowment fund. This simply is the answer for our future financial stability. We have made enormous strides and must continue to do so.

- The planned giving effort is important to our future success, and the creation of viable programs to build the endowment over the next five to seven years is an integral part of our plan to take pressure off the annual fund.
- The other area we must work on is to produce more income from activities, camping, training and other events at a district and Council level. We believe in a philosophy of value for value and concurrently, we believe, based on the percentage of income being generated from program fees in other successful institutions, that we need to pass more costs on to our con-

stituency. We must never price ourselves out of the reach of the average Scouter's family. We also believe we should charge in terms of what it is worth. Scouting in Denver is in a traditional mode of charging less than full costs, a policy we must change gradually over the next few years. The pressure on the annual fund necessitates that a higher percentage of the income be generated from program events. We feel that increased usage of facilities and participation in activities supports the case for increased fees.

A special fund from increased revenues could be utilized to help those that are unable to participate.

- Public relations is a function of the development program of the Council, not to the exclusion of program and/or other Council services. This statement defines the priority.

This statement is probably one of a kind for Boy Scout Councils in America. Simply stated it is the positive development philosophy of the Denver Area Council.

Long Range Goals, Five-Year Plan

INTERFAITH COUNSELING SERVICE
Long-Range Goals
Five-Year Plan
(March, 1981)

Interfaith Counseling Service is a not-for-profit, church-related mental health agency with two major thrusts: to provide direct service counseling and psychotherapy on an ability-to-pay basis to people with social/emotional/spiritual problems of living, and second, to provide prevention, education, consultation, training and research services. Service is provided without regard to race, color, religion, sex, age, national origin or handicap.

Interfaith sees itself as a place where people come to learn new and more satisfying ways of living together in depth. Thus, community and spirituality are valued as well as scientific psychotherapeutic approaches in the healing of human emotional illness and disease.

Courtesy of the Interfaith Counseling Service, Inc., Scottsdale, AZ. Reprinted by permission.

In looking toward the future, Interfaith Counseling Service also sees itself as one particular model among many for what can be accomplished in the bridge-building process between the church and mental health communities (including a state mental health system). Furthermore, Interfaith is committed to maintaining strong loyalties to both of these communities as an authentic (though not normative) expression of their creative working together.

Goals and Objectives of Interfaith Counseling Service: A Long-Range Perspective

It is helpful for an organization to periodically and systematically spell out its long-range goals and objectives. During the past year, the Long-Range Planning Committee of the Board of Directors along with the Executive Director and other agency staff have met and considered relevant data along with individual goals and dreams for the agency. The following five-year goals are presented as the result of this year-long process.

The following paragraphs include the goals, objectives, and where necessary, the activities that outline these goals. For clarity and uniformity, the components are coded by a number system. The following format is used:

1. Goal
1.1. Objective
1.1.1. Activity (where required)

The first number at the left is the goal, the second number is the objective, and the final number (if utilized) is the activity. A coding such as 1.1.4. would indicate the second goal, the first objective under the goal, and the fourth activity listed under that objective. It should also be noted that the goals and objectives are listed in order of priority as they now appear.

Goal 1.   To provide direct help to people with social/emotional/spiritual problems of living through counseling/psychotherapy.

Objective   1.1. To effect a change in identity, life style, and interpersonal relationships of clients toward more satisfying ways of living in the community.

Activity   1.1.1. <u>Direct service counseling/psychotherapy</u>: Interfaith offers various kinds of counseling to meet particular needs of persons and problems. Included in direct service is individual, marriage, family, and group counseling. Increased emphasis will be placed upon family therapy and theme centered groups.

    1.1.2. <u>Crisis counseling</u>: It is staff policy to deal with emergency requests for service within seventy-two hours. Included in this kind of counseling is suicide, grief reactions, parent-child conflicts, marriage crises, and so forth.

    1.1.3. <u>Psychological testing and evalution</u>: Personality, vocational and other appropriate testing procedures are used to facilitate assessment and growth in the counseling process.

    1.1.4. <u>Client staffing</u>: An integral part of offering quality direct service counseling are regular clinical staffings of clients. Treatment plans are developed out of these weekly meetings so that clients may be helped in the briefest and most effective way.

    1.1.5. <u>Vocational evaluations</u>: Intensive vocational evaluation is offered to ministers and others in the greater Phoenix area. Personal/professional goals are evlauated and reevaluated for professional change and/or redirection.

    1.1.6. <u>Pre-seminary evaluations</u>: Personal/professional pre-seminary and pre-ordination evaluations are periodically requested by denominations, church judicatories, and seminaries. Interfaith considers this service an important one to the church at large in terms of assisting it to evaluate potential professional church workers.

    1.1.7. <u>Pastoral care/counseling for clergy and families</u>: Clergy and their families are experiencing greater amounts of stress than ever before. The pastoral care counseling activities help clergy and families to deal more effectively with the interrelationship of their personal and professional lives. Where appropriate, referral will be made to other regionally accredited vocational and psychological services.

            <u>Person responsible</u>: Clinical Coordinator
            <u>Time line</u>: Presently in effect
            <u>Added Cost</u>: Not anticipated

<u>Goal 2.</u>   To provide educational/prevention service to communities and churches in the areas of mental health and personal/spiritual growth.

Objective   2.1. To provide spring and fall prevention programs at convenient community locations, spring and fall workshops/conferences for helping professionals, a new family life education program, and periodic biofeedback and assertiveness classes.

Activity   2.1.1. Spring and fall programs of at least four classes each are to be offered each year at reasonable fees and in areas of staff expertise and community interest. These might include marriage enrichment, step-parenting and others.

2.1.2. An education program is to be developed and offered to organizations, schools, and congregations in the area of Family Wellness Training (operational by fall, 1981).

2.1.3. A yearly fall conference in the area of family therapy is to be offered to area professionals (continuous).

2.1.4. A yearly spring workshop for ministers is to be offered in conjunction with the annual corporation meeting (continuous).

2.1.5. Biofeedback and meditation, and assertiveness training programs are to be offered on a periodic basis throughout the year as prevention programs.

2.1.6. Periodic retreats for couples and other special interest groups will be conducted as time and resources permit.

2.1.7. A program of continued funding is to be developed to sustain a full-time person in the area of education/prevention work. (F.T.E.)

Person responsible: Education Coordinator
Time line: All in place except 2.1.2. to be operational fall 1981 and 2.1.7. to be operational spring 1982.
Added Cost: Approximately $7,000 to $12,000 per year.

Goal 3.   To provide training and consultation services for other mental health professionals, pastoral counseling residents, masters and doctoral level interns, and area ministers.

Objective   3.1. To offer a supervision and training program for AAMFT accreditation for area professionals, to reorient and strengthen the AAPC accredited residency program, to add one doctoral level ASU intern, to accept master's level interns on an individual basis, and to develop a certificated training program for area clergy on a part-time basis.

Activity   3.1.1. Structure, enact, and fund from fees an AAMFT accredited supervisory program for area professionals.

3.1.2. <u>Extend the use of supervisory tools</u> such as videotape in the residency program. Strengthen theoretical competencies of residents. Limit number of full-time residents in program to one per year.

3.1.3. <u>Develop funding</u> of approximately $4,500 per year to support an ASU doctoral level internship.

3.1.4. <u>Plan and implement</u> a two year, part-time pastoral counseling program for two local clergy in conjunction with the Garrett Theological Seminary D.Min. program. Such a program would include training in assessment, marriage counseling, family therapy, alcohol counseling, along with practicum section. Completion of this program would lead to AAPC certification at the Member or Fellow level.

3.1.5. Provide consultation/training to various community/Indian groups as at present upon request.

<u>Person responsible</u>: Training Coordinator
<u>Time Line</u>: 3.1.1. by 1982, 3.1.2. by 1981, 3.1.3. by 1983, 3.1.4. by 1982.
<u>Added cost</u>: $5,000 per year beginning in 1983

* <u>Goal 4.</u>   To extend Interfaith's program and services to other geographical sites in the greater Phoenix area where population needs dictate and local support will sustain.

Objective   4.1. Prepare proposal(s) by June 1982 for board approval for such location(s) as the executive director deems meet conditions of need and support.

Activity   4.1.1. To meet with local clergy, mental health centers and other appropriate service and funding sources in order to formulate specific proposals.

<u>Person responsible</u>: Executive Director
<u>Time Line</u>: As appropriate with no new satellite functional before approval by board of need, structure, and funding plans.
<u>Added cost</u>: $35,000 for each new center

<u>Goal 5.</u>   To increase funding of Interfaith programs and expansion in a manner adequate to meet present and future needs and at the same time to orient funding towards private sources.

---

* See Addendum

Objective   5.1. Funding efforts would be redirected as much as possible over the coming years away from governmental sources and increasingly toward direct donations by individuals, endowments, and corporate donations.

Activity   5.1.1. During 1981 support and organizational tasks necessary to redirect funding efforts in this direction would be undertaken. Direct funding efforts will begin in the spring of 1982 with major thrusts each year thereafter.

Person Responsible: Executive Director
Time Line: $35,000 in 1982, increasing by approximately $20,000 per year thereafter

Goal 6.   To provide administration and support to enable the agency to accomplish its goals and objectives.

The function of the administrative and support areas is to provide the administrative services necessary to enable the agency to accomplish its objectives.

Objective   6.1. Yearly evaluation of management and clinical staff.

Activity   6.1.1. Yearly evaluation of executive director's functioning shall be by the Executive Committee of the Board to be carried out in September of each year. The executive director shall evaluate clinical staff with the assistance of the Personnel Committee yearly.

Objective   6.2. Evaluation of support staff.

Activity   6.2.1. The evaluation should be completed on the anniversary date for each support staff.

Person Responsible: Executive Director

Goal 7.   To review fiscal information system development. Interfaith Counseling Service requires an adequate fiscal information and cost containment review to ensure that the cost benefit relationships of services to needs are maintained.

Objective   7.1. To have a fiscal information system that is responsive to both internal management and external needs.

Activity   7.1.1. Interfaith will continue to develop a complete budgetary and fiscal management information system. Such a system will relate to agency and other organizations that could require financial reports. Such a system will also provide information for the annual audit and such in-house reports as may be required for monthly board meetings.

Objective   7.2. To know the individual service costs and ensure
                  productive efficiency.

Activity   7.2.1. Interfaith will continue to conduct on-going cost finding
                  programs and cost and operation monitoring for reporting
                  at the board level.

                  Persons Responsible: Executive Director and Bookkeeper
                  who will channel information to the board of directors
                  through the finance committee
                  Time Line: Preliminary plan due spring, 1982
                  Added Cost: $3,000 per year

* Goal 8.   To continue long-range strategy and planning. Every
                  agency or organization must continue to do consistent
                  long-range strategy and planning to ensure the continuity
                  of the organization.

Objective   8.1. To provide direction, information, and consistency for the
                  participating organizations, the Board of Directors, the
                  Executive Director and the staff.

Activity   8.1.1. Interfaith's Long-Range Planning Committee will provide
                  an annual update of long-range planning to the Board in
                  April of each year.

                  Person Responsible: The Executive Director and the
                  Long-Range Planning Committee who will report to the
                  Board of Directors.

Goal 9.   To develop effective public relations responsibility. The
                  agency will have an effective and current public relations
                  document and policy by fall of 1981.

Objective   9.1. To provide responsible information and communication
                  with our community (supporting churches, clients, board,
                  etc.).

Activity   9.1.1. Public Relations Committee responsibility—to plan and
                  implement.

                  Person Responsible: Executive Director, Public Relations
                  Committee and Board of Directors
                  Time Line: Fall 1981
                  Cost: $3,500 over a two-year period

---

* See Addendum

Goal 10.   To assess overall agency functioning to provide a means of
                evaluation to be conducted from a number of perspectives:
                A. Accomplishment of goals and objectives: coordinators
                B. Service delivery process: through evaluations by staff,
                especially front office personnel
                C. Evaluation of service delivery: through community
                survey
                D. Cost efficiency and containment: through annual budget
                E. Quality assurance: clinical staff evaluations
                F. Consumer satisfaction: client survey
                G. Compliance with requirements of regulatory authorities,
                funding sources, etc.: through continued various
                accreditations.
                H. A third party evaluation

Objective   10.1. To provide an annual review of the agency

                Person Responsible : Executive Director and appropriate
                staff persons
                Time Line : Annually in fall with report to Board

ADDENDUM ONE

Demographic Considerations in Long-Range Planning

Interfaith Counseling Service was founded over ten years ago in
Scottsdale, Arizona by a number of churches concerned for the men-
tal health needs of the people in their communities. At that time,
Scottsdale was a developing area in terms of industry, business, and
housing. Although some development is still taking place in this area,
it is today a mature and less rapidly growing part of greater metro-
politan Phoenix. Future growth seems to be oriented more in the
North, West, and Southeast areas of the greater metropolitan area.
The direction of population growth may have implications for
Interfaith should it choose to expand.

A second important demographic factor in the greater Phoenix
area is the low population density per square mile. Of twelve similar
metropolitan areas, Phoenix ranked eleventh lowest in population
density per square mile. Thus, Phoenix area residents must travel
greater distances for services than residents of other similar metropolitan areas. This low population density may also have implications
for Interfaith should it choose to expand in the coming years.

A third important factor in looking at long-range goals for
Interfaith is utilization of mental health services by different age
groups. According to Arizona Department of Health Services data, by
far the single largest user of mental health services is the age group

25–34 years of age (this age group along with those 35–44 years of age constitute almost two-thirds of mental health service utilization at Interfaith in 1980). In light of this, it is interesting to note that the 25–34 year old age group comprises only 14% of the total population of Scottsdale. By comparison, this same age group comprises 24% of the population of Glendale, 29% in Tempe, and 30% in Mesa. The only group in Scottsdale that constitutes more than 30% of the total population is the 65 plus group.

Trustee Workshop Agendas

TWO-DAY TRUSTEE WORKSHOP

Objectives: (1) To explore the board's role and responsibilities and (2) to identify possible areas for improvement in its organization and performance.

Presiding: AGB Board-Mentor (trustee from a similar type of institution).

DAY ONE:

12:30 p.m.	Luncheon Session
	Discussion of workshop's objectives
	Self-introductions: (1) A little about your background and why you chose to serve on the board; (2) What do you see as some of the institution's (or board's) key objectives over the next five years? and (3) What expectations do you have for this workshop?
2:30–4:00	Review of trustee responses to *Self-Study Criteria*
4:00	Coffee Break
4:15–5:30	Reconvene for continued discussion of results of the *Self-Study*
6:30	Cocktails
7:00	Dinner (no agenda)
8:00–9:30	Evening Session
	Discussion of the board's role in institutional planning (AGB filmstrip)

"Sample Agendas," by Richard T. Ingram, pp. 8–10 in *Trustee Workshops and Retreats,* a booklet published by the Association of Governing Boards of Universities and Colleges, Washington, DC, 1978. Reprinted by permission.

DAY TWO:

8:00 a.m.   Breakfast Session

Discussion of the board's role in fundraising (AGB filmstrip and advance reading assignment)

9:30–11:00   Group Discussions (trustees assigned at random)

Purpose: To consider issues raised in earlier discussions and to identify objectives to strengthen the board's organization or performance.

Group I Leader: Chairperson of Finance & Budget Committee

Group II Leader: Chairperson of Education Committee

11:00   Coffee Break

11:15   Closing Session—What have we learned?

12:00 noon   Next Steps?

Brief reports by group leaders
Closing comments by Board-Mentor

Adjournment by Noon (Luncheon for those who can remain)

ONE-DAY TRUSTEE WORKSHOP

Objectives: (1) To explore issues of the board's role in the institution's planning and management of resources; and (2) to consider implications for possible committee reorganization.

Presiding: AGB Board-Mentor (trustee from a similar type of institution).

9:30–11:00 a.m.   Opening Session

Self-Introduction: (1) A little about your background and why you chose to serve on the board; (2) What do you see as some of the institution's (or board's) key objectives over the next five years? and (3) What expectations do you have for this workshop?

11:00   Coffee Break

11:15–12:30 p.m.   Institutional Planning

AGB filmstrip presentation, followed by discussion
Presiding: Board-Mentor

12:45 p.m.   Luncheon Session
Remarks: Chief Executive Officer of the institution

2:00–3:45   Management of Resources

AGB filmstrip presentation, followed by discussion
Presiding: Board-Mentor

3:45   Coffee Break

4:00–5:00   Group Discussions

Informal consideration of issues and suggestions raised in
earlier sessions

Group I—Discussion Leader: Chairperson of Finance &
Budget
Committee, Resource Person: Chief Executive Officer

Group II—Discussion Leader: Chairperson of Education
Committee, Resource Person: Board-Mentor

5:15–5:45   Closing Session

Presentation by leaders of discussion groups highlighting
the discussions: What are some apparent needs? Next
steps?

Adjournment by 5:45 (Cocktails and dinner for those
who can remain)

Annual Operating Budget (Simplified) for a Voluntary Health & Welfare Organization

	Program Services:		Support Services:		
ESTIMATED REVENUES:	Health Activities	Welfare Activities	Mgmnt. & General	Fund-raising	Total
Fees	$ 40,000	5,000	-	-	$ 45,000
Grants	64,570	7,000	10,000	5,000	86,570
Special Events	2,000	16,000	-	4,500	22,500
Memberships	1,000	-	1,000	-	2,000
TOTAL REVENUES:	$107,570	28,000	11,000	9,500	$156,070
BUDGETED EXPENSES:					
I. Personnel					
Salaries & Wages	30,000	25,000	30,000	20,000	105,000
Fringe Benefits	300	250	300	200	1,050
Consultants/ Contracts	-	-	500	500	1,000
SubTotals:	30,300	25,250	30,800	20,700	107,050
II. Nonpersonnel					
Occupancy	1,000	1,000	1,800	1,000	4,800
Equipment Rental	100	100	700	700	1,600
Printing & Publications	2,000	2,000	3,500	3,500	11,000
Supplies	4,420	4,450	3,300	2,150	14,320
Travel	1,500	1,500	2,500	4,500	10,000
Telephone	400	400	1,500	1,000	3,300
Other	350	550	650	450	2,000
Depreciation	-	-	2,000	-	2,000
TOTAL EXPENSES:	$40,070	35,250	46,750	34,000	$156,070

Board Self-Evaluation Instrument

TRUSTEE REPORT CARD
"FORDASH COLLEGE"

Note: Use sliding scale of points between arbitrary levels noted, if trustee performance does not fit point definitions provided.

Name_____

Date joined Board_____

Assignment on Board_____

Term, Class, or Category _____

1. Suitability As Trustee   (*Total possible, 20 points.*) _____
   20 pts. Fulfills an important role on the Board of Trustees. Represents in his own background a pertinent high degree of competence and experience and/or is in a position of unique influence with others critically important to the success of the institution. (These qualities do not merely duplicate, in a substantially lesser way, those possessed by other members of the Board.) Membership on the Board contributes to the rounding-out, in a major way, of the total trustee complex of strengths, abilities, and experience deemed necessary for major progress of the institution.
   12 pts. To a lesser degree meets criteria above but is not of optimum strength within the probable availability of such strength to the institution.

Excerpt from an article by Francis C. Pray, which first appeared in the Summer 1964 issue of *The Educational Record*, published by the American Council on Education, Washington, DC. This "Report Card" was reprinted with permission in *The Board Letter*, no. 4, published by Duca Associates, Denver, CO, 1981.

4 pts. Of some value as a member of the Board but largely duplicative of stronger relationships held by others and of areas of interest and competence represented by stronger members. Substantially below level of strength, competence, and experience of others conceivably available for Board membership.

0 pts. On a realistic basis, must be largely discounted as having any significant degree of ability to contribute to soundness of Board decisions or effectiveness of Board actions.

2. General Preparation As Trustee

(*Total possible, 20 points.*) _____

20 pts. Has briefed himself well on the institution's problems and needs. Visits campus. Has visited classes. Knows some faculty and students. Has visited other campuses and/or discussed problems with trustees of other institutions. Knows the institution's history, philosophy, and plans. Endeavors to keep abreast of national trends in education. Understands function of trustee—to guide policy, establish effective management, keep out of administration, and assist institution's growth.

12 pts. Generally knows the institution's philosophy and problems. Has conducted some independent self-education as trustee. Keeps up fairly well with general educational problems and problems of the institution. Understands role of trustee.

4 pts. Little knowledge but some interest in general problems of higher education. Only sporadic interest in self-briefing.

0 pts. Almost no knowledge of, and little demonstration of interest in, general problems of higher education or duties and opportunities and responsibilities of trusteeship.

3. Specific Preparation for Action As Trustee

(*Total possible, 20 points.*) _____

20 pts. Thoroughly prepares himself for trustee meetings. Has studied and understands reports and background materials. Asks probing and insightful questions at meetings, focused on policy. Demands and gets information necessary for major decisions.

12 pts. Generally prepared for discussion of problems at meetings. Has read briefing materials supplied by administration, and participates intelligently and constructively in discussion in a manner showing some prior thought and consideration.

4 pts. Some, but little, evidence of study of problems prior to meetings. Willingness to let most of leadership fall to others.

0 pts. No evidence of prior preparation for trustee meetings. Discussion participation, if any, often negative and unhelpful.

4. Ambassadorship   (*Total possible, 20 points.*) _____
   20 pts. Enthusiastic spokesman for purposes of college. Speaks often and with knowledge of the institution to others. Often uses contacts on behalf of the institution. Suggests ways he can use contacts on behalf of specific programs.
   12 pts. Friendly. Occasionally uses own contacts on behalf of the institution. Mentions it constructively to others.
   0 pts. Apathetic. No evidence of active ambassadorship.

5. Participation in Development Program of the College
                                     (*Total possible, 20 points.*) _____
   20 pts. Makes own financial contribution in amount meaningful in terms of own resources. Active in planning, helps identify prospects for development program and, where possible, personally helps win financial support of others, through direct and indirect personal participation. Has made arrangements for long-range gifts.
   12 pts. Makes meaningful financial contribution. Occasionally helps enlist aid of others.
   4 pts. Nominal financial contribution. Little or no personal participation in program.
   0 pts. Does not participate even nominally in financial support program.

6. Committee Activity   (*Total possible, 20 points.*) _____
   20 pts. Serves usefully on one important committee and is active on committee assignments. Suggests ideas. Carries out duties. Uses own abilities and influence constructively.
   12 pts. Nominally loyal to committee responsibilities. Carries out some duties.
   4 pts. Attends committee meetings fairly regularly. Little or no activity outside of meetings.
   0 pts. Little or no activity or sense of responsibility in committee assignment, or refuses committee assignment.

7. Attendance   (*Total possible, 20 points.*) _____
   A. Board Meetings   B. Committee Meetings

   10 pts. Attends all or has valid   *10 pts.* same criteria
   excuse. Shows interest in
   attending and makes effort
   to do so.

6 pts. Attends majority of meetings or has valid excuse.	*6 pts.* same criteria
2 pts. Sporadic attendance.	*2 pts.* same criteria
0 pts. Poor attendance; no valid excuses.	*0 pts.* same criteria

8. For Chairman of Board or Chairman of Board Committees
   (Total possible, 20 points.) _____

  20 pts. Prepares carefully for meetings. Insists that reports from and by administration are properly prepared and to the point. Clearly distinguishes between material for information only and that which requires action. Keeps emphasis on major policy matters. Insists summaries and visuals are available where interpretation will be aided thereby. Considers with president or appropriate administrative officer (in case of committee chairman) the broad problems of trustee information and motivation and endeavors to make each meeting an interesting and (hopefully) exciting experience.

  12 pts. Adequate moderator and some (but not extensive) interest in considerations noted above.

   4 pts. Adequate Moderator, but little interest in facing problems of Board management and trustee motivation.

   0 pts. Moderator only, but little, if any, other participation. Leaves most of problems to the president. Does not encourage and motivate trustee participation in policy decisions, or exercise leadership in motivation of trustee interest.

9. Special Service   *(Total possible varies.)* _____
   If service of trustee in a single special significant way is of vital importance to the college, even though scores in other areas are low, a special score may be added here. In other words, a rare special situation might arise where attendance at Board meetings is realistically difficult, but where a trustee relationship makes possible distinguished service of a nature not easily had by the institution from another person who would also serve more usefully in normal trustee relationships. In this case, a special score might be given here to override the deficit in one or more of the other above categories where lack of score is to be forgiven because of the special service. Note, however, that if this service would occur or be available whether or not the individual is a member of the Board, no credit should be given here as trustee.

REPORT CARD SUMMARY

Name of Trustee:	*Points*
Suitability as Trustee	_____
General Preparation	_____
Specific Preparation	_____
Ambassadorship	_____
Participation in Development	_____
Committee Activity	_____
Attendance	
Total (100 is passing)	_____
Chairman	
Total (115 is passing)	_____
Special Service (see Report Card)	_____

Evaluations:
☐ Excellent (115 or more points)
☐ Good (100-115 points)
☐ Fair (60-100 points)
☐ Poor (22-60 points)
☐ Hopeless (under 22 points)

Minutes Using Paragraph Heading Format

EXECUTIVE BOARD/ADVISORY COUNCIL MEETING
Tuesday, January 25, 1983
Denver Athletic Club
7:15 A.M.

Minutes

Attendance:

Officers

James G. Nussbaum, Council President
Glen L. Ryland, Chairman of the Board
William H. Weiskopf, Council Treasurer
Philip F. Roan, Council Commissioner
P.K. Ware, Vice President
Grant T. Alley, Vice President
Robert A. Backus, Vice President
Richard F. Walker, Vice President
Robert B. Decker, Member at Large
George G. Priest, Member at Large
William R. Kephart, Scout Executive

Executive Board/Advisory Council

Preston Adams	Richard W. Cunningham	A. Dean Lund
Linda Alvarado	Father Neal Dow	Jon McNutt
Mike H. Barrett	Bonnie Downing	Edward Nelson
John S. Berge	Larry Farnum	Robert Palmer

Ron Blanding	George S. Granger	Dr. Fred Pundsack
Robert Briggs	Carol Green	Alfred V. Rodriguez
Dr. Joseph E. Brzeinski	William V. Haberer	James L. Weist
Helen Carroll	N. Berne Hart	Challen H. Wells
Earl E. Clark	Harry Henke, III	
Ralph F. Cox	Leo W. Kraemer	

Guests

Roger Knight	Robert Shanahan
Colonel Kowakowski	David Rockoff

Staff

A. Ely Brewer, Jr.	Dave McFarland	Norton Rainey
Lori Lynch	Paul Needham	

The meeting was called to order by James G. Nussbaum, President, with a quorum in attendance.

A. SUMMARY OF ACTION TAKEN
   1. Approval of Executive Board minutes of November 6, 1982.
   2. Approved endorsing Project 1,000 for the 1983 Summer Camping season.
   3. Approval of the December Treasurer's Report and Properties' Report as presented by Council Treasurer, William Weiskopf.
   4. Approval of Herrick Roth serving as our 1983 Silver Beaver Chairman.
   5. Approval of Jim Baxter serving as Chairman of our 1983 Investments' Committee.
   6. Approval of Richard Walker serving as Chairman of our 1983 Resolutions' Committee.
   7. Approval of the Council forming a Long Range Planning Update Committee with Fred Pundsack serving as Chairman, Joseph Brzeinski and Ely Brewer/Membership Study, Bob Backus and Paul Needham/Program Study, Bob Lee and Norton Rainey/Finance Study, and Dick Walker and Bill Kephart/Organization and Manpower Study.
B. SUMMARY OF DISCUSSION
   1. Bob Shanahan, Executive Vice President of the Denver Post, reported for Lee Guittar that there are 71 table sponsors to date with 15 major sponsors signed-up. He urged members not already hosting a table to sign-up now.

2. Earl Clark presented Eagle belt buckles to: Mike Barrett, Jim Nussbaum and Bill Kephart for joining the Council's Heritage Trust Fund. Earl also noted that Max Goodwin was a new member but unable to attend the meeting. Jim Nussbaum in turn presented Earl a belt buckle and thanked him for all his work in developing this new program.

3. Council Commissioner, Phil Roan, reported that the average time a boy spends in Scouting is six months. In 1982 there were 1,049 Tiger Cubs, 13,098 Cub Scouts, 6,380 Boy Scouts, 3,416 Exploreres, 493 Units that rechartered on time and 416 top leaders trained. He also reported that there is a total of 277 Commissioners in our Council which makes one Commissioner available for every two units. Our goal for 1982 was one Commissioner for every three units. Recruitment efforts are underway for 1983 in order to have one Commissioner for every unit.

   Phil also reported that the Council's Trading Post sales have increased 150% since September and also our distributors' sales have increased by 47%.

4. Bob Backus, Vice President/Program, presented Roger Knight, 1982 Scout Show Chairman and Chairman of the Board and President of Metro Bank, a small token of the Council's appreciation for his efforts in the Scout Show. The Council netted a record $28,000 compared to $14,000 last year. There was a total of 87,000 tickets sold and approximately 8,000 sold in concessions making the 1982 Scout Show the most successful ever.

5. Bill Haberer, Chairman of the Outdoor Program Executive Committee, reported that 613 Scouts attended Peaceful Valley Scout Ranch last summer which is less than half from a year ago. He stated that one of the reasons in the decline is last year our Council went into a cooperative effort with the other Councils in Colorado to promote all the camps available to Scouts in the area. The Council had a net income of $3,900 at the end of the camping season. Bill noted the goal for 1983 is 1,000 boys and that we need 250 boys a week to break even.

6. Dean Lund, Chairman of Properties/Facilities Committee, reported the farming operation and forest thinning project both brought in good revenues for 1982.

7. Berne Hart, Chairman of the Capital Campaign, reported we reached 14% of our goal so far and that Don Jansen is in charge of contacting Board members for their contributions. He indicated that we are in the process of contacting nine foundations in hopes of raising 2½million. Drawings were on display of the new facilities Peaceful

Valley Scout Ranch will soon have after the completion of this successful campaign; lake, dining hall, family camping area and handicapped camping area.

C. ANNOUNCEMENTS
1. February 6, 1983 - Francis S. Van Derbur Scout Service Center dedication.
2. March 1, 1983 - Sports Awards Breakfast at Regency Inn - 7:00 A.M.
3. March 22, 1983 - Executive Board Meeting - Denver Athletic Club - 7:15 A.M.

There being no further business, the meeting was adjourned.

Respectfully submitted,

DENVER AREA COUNCIL
BOY SCOUTS OF AMERICA

_____

James G. Nussbaum
Council President

_____

William R. Kephart
Scout Executive

Minutes Using Narrative Format

MINUTES OF THE MEETING OF THE BOARD OF DIRECTORS
October 15, 1981

Members present were: David French, Buck Lamb, Paul Flores, Jim Sample, Pat Barajas, Bob Foland, Phil Greenberg, Gale Terry, Gary Moore, Bob Short, Mike McCune, Dick Brindle, Steve Sander
Staff present were: Terry Miller, Jim Olmstead, Tom O'Leary, John Mancha, Craig LaVigna, Helen Quelch
The meeting was called to order by President Bob Short at 4:40 PM. New Board member Mike McCune was introduced and welcomed.
The minutes of the September meeting were approved as mailed, and the list of new volunteers was approved.
Bob Short reported that technical plans for the office addition have been submitted for issuance of a building permit, and it is hoped that a final price for the addition and the permit will be issued by November 1st. He added that the United Bank of Denver may grant us a two-year construction loan. Contacts are needed for the possible donations or sale at cost of concrete, lumber, windows, doors and floor coverings. Anyone with possible contacts in these areas is asked to speak to Bob as soon as possible.
Helen Quelch reported for the staff that Big Brothers will have a billboard display at 8th & Lincoln for one month beginning in late November. This has been arranged through a new Big Brother who works for Gannet Outdoor Advertising. We will have the option to purchase additional space at $50 each, a fraction of the market cost.
John Mancha reported on several new committees that are or will be functioning soon. A Minority Recruitment Committee has 5 members and will devise ways to increase recruitment of minority

---

volunteers. An Activities Committee of 13 members will plan and implement activities and programs for Big and Little Brothers. A Big Brother who is a student at DU is developing a Speakers Bureau to provide public speakers for the program.

Terry Miller reported that we have received recent gifts from Marathon Oil Company ($1,000), and the Swan Foundation for the Hogan Project, matching funds ($2,500) and our contract with DialAmerica for July and August ($1,275).

Steve Sander reported for the PR/Marketing Committee that all the plans are set for the 1st Annual Big Brother Olympics to be sponsored by the Reach Club at DU, on Saturday, October 17th. At present, 38 matches have signed up to participate. T-shirts will be given, and refreshments provided.

Annotated Bibliography

This is a representative list of what the author considers some of the best literature applicable to the field of nonprofit management. This list is divided by topic area for easy reference.

GENERAL READINGS

Connors, Tracy D., ed. *The Nonprofit Organization Handbook.* New York: McGraw-Hill, 1980.
    A good collection of contributed articles on a variety of subjects relative to nonprofit management.

Conrad, William R., and Glenn, William R. *The Effective Voluntary Board of Directors: What It Is and How It Works.* Chicago: The Swallow Press, 1976.
    The authors use a mythical nonprofit throughout for illustration purposes. The work includes many charts and graphs, some of which are helpful, some of which are redundant.

Flanagan, Joan. *The Successful Volunteer Organization.* Chicago: Contemporary Books, Inc., 1981.
    Geared toward the start-up organization.

Montana, Patrick J., and Borst, Diane, eds. *Managing Nonprofit Organizations.* New York: AMACOM, 1977.
    Well-organized series of articles covering both the theory and practice of nonprofit management.

O'Connell, Brian. *Effective Leadership in Voluntary Organizations.* New York: Walker and Company, 1976.
    The author stresses the importance of the role of the volunteer and claims the role of staff is a subordinate one. The 16 chapters do not offer an in-depth treatment of the topics. Worth reading for a different perspective.

O'Connell, Brian, ed. *America's Voluntary Spirit.* New York: The Foundation Center, 1983.
    A book of readings on volunteerism with a very extensive bibliography.

Trost, Arty, and Rauner, Judy. *Gaining Momentum for Board Action.* San Diego, CA: Marlborough Publications, 1983.
    Useful worksheets and checklists that can be reproduced for board training activities. The large typeface used in this book is annoying.

EVALUATION

Hatry, Harry; Winnie, Richard E.; and Fisk, Donald M. *Practical Program Evaluation for State and Local Government Officials.* 2d ed. Washington, DC: The Urban Institute, 1981.
   Covers more than program evaluation; discusses impact and cost benefits. Practical and easy to understand, with wide application.

Morris, Lynn Lyons, and Fitz-Gibbons, Carol Taylor. *Evaluator's Handbook.* Beverly Hills, CA: Sage Publications, 1978.
   Useful step-by-step guide to the process of program evaluation; includes worksheets.

Weiss, Carol H., ed. *Evaluating Action Programs: Readings in Social Action and Education.* Boston, MA: Allyn and Bacon, Inc., 1972.
   Collection of articles with limited practical application. However, the overview by the author is valuable, and the article on educational evaluation is particularly useful. Includes a comprehensive bibliography.

FUND DEVELOPMENT

American Association of Fund-Raising Counsel, Inc. *Giving USA,* 1984 Annual Report. New York: American Association of Fund-Raising Counsel, Inc., 1984.
   Compilation of facts and trends in philanthropy.

Brakeley, George A., Jr. *Tested Ways to Successful Fund Raising.* New York: AMACOM, 1980.
   Fundamentals of fund-raising campaigns by a well-respected professional.

Crimmins, James C., and Keil, Mary. *Enterprise in the Nonprofit Sector.* New York: The Rockefeller Brothers Fund and Partners for Livable Places (Washington, DC), 1983.
   A first of its kind and a real contribution to the expanding field of nonprofit entrepreneurialism. The case studies presented are most interesting.

Flanagan, Joan. *The Grassroots Fundraising Book.* Chicago: The Swallow Press, Inc., 1977.
   A collection of fund-raising events with how-to's.

Frantzreb, Arthur C., ed. *Trustee's Role in Advancement.* New Directions for Institutional Advancement, no. 14. San Francisco, CA: Jossey-Bass, Inc., 1981.
   Worthwhile articles on trustees' responsibilities; focused on the trustees of colleges and universities.

Kotler, Philip. *Marketing for Nonprofit Organizations.* 2d ed. Englewood Cliffs, NJ: Prentice-Hall, Inc., 1982.
   A widely read book on this topic. Looks and reads like a textbook; worth the effort. Includes useful illustrations.

Montana, Patrick J., ed. *Marketing in Nonprofit Organizations.* New York: AMACOM, 1978.
A collection of 26 articles, some on marketing mix and targeting are a bit technical for most organizations.

Schneiter, Paul H., and Nelson, Donald T. *The Thirteen Most Common Fund-Raising Mistakes and How to Avoid Them.* Washington, DC: Taft Corporation, 1982.
Useful, common sense approach and fun reading.

Seymour, Harold J. *Designs for Fund-Raising.* New York: McGraw-Hill, 1966.
Considered the classic of fund-raising literature and widely quoted. The author's concepts are as valid today as they were nearly 20 years ago.

White, Michelle J. *Nonprofit Firms in a Three Sector Economy.* COUPE (Committee on Urban Public Economics), Papers on Public Economics. Washington, DC: The Urban Institute, 1981.
Collection of readings regarding the value of nonprofit organizations.

White, Virginia P. *Grants, How to Find out about Them and What to Do Next.* New York: Plenum Press, 1975.
Good basic references on the grants application process. Focused on government grants; specifics on types of grants now outdated.

GROUP DYNAMICS, HUMAN RELATIONS, AND VOLUNTEERISM

Cialdini, Robert B. *Influence.* New York: William Morrow and Company, Inc., 1984.
Useful for understanding the psychological concepts related to leadership.

Cohen, Allan R.; Fink, Stephen L.; Gadon, Herman; and Willits, Robin D. *Effective Behavior in Organizations.* Rev. ed. Homewood, IL: Richard D. Irwin, Inc., 1980.
Basic introduction to managing human behavior in organizations.

Schindler-Rainman, Eva, and Lippit, Ronald. *The Volunteer Community.* 2d ed. San Diego, CA: University Associates, 1978.
Thoroughly readable overview of volunteers and their place in American society. Emphasizes the value of training and evaluating volunteers.

Tropman, John E. *Effective Meetings: Improving Group Decision-Making.* Sage Human Service Guide, vol. 17. Beverly Hills, CA: Sage Publications, 1980.
Indispensable for anyone responsible for meetings.

————. *The Essentials of Committee Management.* Chicago: Nelson Hall, 1979.
Exhaustive presentation of the types and functions of committees.

————. *Meetings: How to Make Them Work for You.* New York: Van Nostrand, 1984.

Weiner, Bernard. *Human Motivation.* New York: Holt, Rinehart and Winston, 1980.
Basic text on the subject.

Zander, A. *Making Groups Effective*. San Francisco, CA: Jossey-Bass, Inc., 1982.

LEGAL AND ACCOUNTING

Arthur Anderson & Co. *Tax Economics of Charitable Giving*. 8th ed. Chicago: Arthur Anderson & Co., 1982.
An important booklet outlining methods for individual charitable gifts.

Gross, Malvern J., Jr. *Financial and Accounting Guide for Nonprofit Organizations*. 2d ed. New York: Ronald Press, 1974.
A highly useful guide to nonprofit accounting. However, budgeting is not covered.

Hopkins, Bruce R. *Charitable Giving and Tax-Exempt Organizations*. New York: Ronald Press, 1982.
Thorough discussion of the impact of the 1981 Tax Act.

———. *The Law of Tax-Exempt Organizations*. 4th ed. (with *Supplement*). New York: Ronald Press, 1983.
Helpful volume of regulations, rulings, cases, and literature on the subject of tax-exempt law by a preeminent expert in the field.

Lane, Marc J. *Legal Handbook for Nonprofit Organizations*. New York: AMACOM, 1980.
An easy-to-understand overview of a nonprofit's legal opportunities and pitfalls.

Oleck, Howard L. *Nonprofit Corporations, Organizations, and Associations*. 4th ed. Englewood Cliffs, NJ: Prentice-Hall Inc., 1980.
Most extensive work on the legal aspects of nonprofits. Includes the "Proposed Uniform Nonprofit Organizations Act."

Olenick, Arnold J., and Olenick, Philip R. *Making the Non-Profit Organization Work: A Financial, Legal and Tax Guide for Administrators*. Englewood Cliffs, NJ: Institute for Business Planning, 1983.
Good discussion on budgets, with sample formats. Legal section is an overview but offers a how-to on filing tax forms.

PLANNING AND MANAGEMENT CONTROL

Anthony, Robert, and Herzlinger, Regina. *Management Control in Nonprofit Organizations*. Rev. ed. Homewood, IL: Richard D. Irwin, Inc., 1980.
Comprehensive and useful treatment of the subject.

Borst, Diane, and Montana, Patrick J. *Managing Nonprofit Organizations*. New York: AMACOM, 1977.
Good discussion of the topic—and practical.

Drucker, Peter F. *Management: Tasks, Responsibilities, Practices*. New York: Harper & Row, 1974.
Much can be applied to the nonprofit organization.

Grayson, Leslie E., and Tompkins, Curtis J. *Management of Public Sector and Nonprofit Organizations.* Reston, VA: Reston Publishing Co., 1984.

Hardy, James F. *Corporate Planning for Nonprofit Organizations.* New York: Association Press, 1972.
Includes various models for a long-range planning process. Special attention is given to the roles of the board and staff.

Mager, Robert F. *Preparing Instructional Objectives.* 2d ed. Belmont, CA: Fearon Publishers Inc., 1962.
A how-to-write measurable program objectives with a focus on educational programs.

Morris, Lynn Lyons, and Fitz-Gibbons, Carol Taylor. *How to Deal with Goals and Objectives.* Beverly Hills, CA: Sage Publications, 1978.
A succinct how-to with a focus on educational programs.

Ramanathan, Kauasseri V., and Hegstad, Larry P. *Readings in Management Control in Nonprofit Organizations.* New York: John Wiley & Sons, Inc., 1982.
Useful collection of articles, in particular those dealing with the complex subject of cost benefits.

Steiner, George. *Strategic Planning.* New York: Free Press, 1979.
Excellent overview of the value of planning, with principles and procedures applicable to the nonprofit organization.

———. *Top Management Planning.* New York: Macmillan Publishing Co., 1969.

Index

by Linda Webster

Accountability, 105
Accountants, 27–28
Accounting, 103–04, 220
Accreditation, 105
Achievement motivation, 71–72, 75
Ad hoc committees, 25, 31
Administrative boards, 19, 35, 43
Administrative policies, 40
Advisory boards, 17–21, 35, 139,
  142, 190
Agenda, 115–20
Alcoholic beverages, 8
AMC Cancer Research Center, 20
Annual reports, 5–6, 14
Arizona Theater Company, 65–66
Arkansas, 12
Athletic license, 8
Atkinson, John, 71
Attorney general offices, 12, 13
Audit, 28

Bankruptcy, 1, 3
Big Brothers, Inc., of Denver (CO),
  214–15
Bingo games, 7
Blind, employment of, 6
Board development committee,
  29–30
Board members
  cash contributions to
    organization, 95–97
  commitment, 68–71
  conflict of interest, 3
  evaluation, 136–43, 205–09
  expressions of appreciation,
    72–74, 75

financial expertise, 2
fraud, 1
fund raising, 93–98
hidden roles, 109–10
honesty with, 74
honorary, 151
inactive members, 70
incentives, 72–74, 75
insurance, 4
job description, 172–73
liability, 1–4
maximizing participation,
  149–54, 158
moral obligations, 4–5
motivation factors, 67–69, 74–75
motivation techniques, 68–74, 75
qualification, 58–60, 65–67,
  140–41
recruitment, 55–67, 74
recruitment form, 174–75
rotation, 151–52, 158
terms of office, 149–52
time factors, 58–59, 64
Board of directors
  Colorado survey, 15–16, 83, 92
  discussion techniques, 152–54,
    158
  evaluation, 32, 136–43, 205–09
  financial mismanagement, 3
  friction with staff, 43
  goals and objectives, 32
  legal obligations, 2–4
  planning documents, 188–90
  relation with executive director,
    144–46, 158

responsibilities, 1–2, 23–24, 44, 53
  size, 15–18, 35
  types, 18–23, 35
Board officers, 32–35
Bonding, 12, 104, 107
Bookkeeping, 28, 34
Boxing license, 8
Boy Scouts, 15–17, 176–92, 210–13
Boys Clubs of America, 88
Brainstorming, 51, 153. *See also*
  Discussion techniques
Budget
  contingency budget, 100
  definition, 99
  finance committee's
    responsibility for, 27
  formats, 102–03
  sample, 204
Budgeting
  evaluation, 100–01
  methods, 101–02
  steps, 99–101, 107
Building permits, 8
Bulk mailing, 8
Business income, 6–7, 14, 98–99, 105, 107
Bylaws
  attendance requirements, 16
  committees, 25
  compensation of trustees, 2
  dissolution procedures, 13
  executive committee, 26
  legal ramifications, 4
  policy setting, 41
  samples, 163–69, 170–71

California, 12
Camp Fire Council (Phoenix, AZ), 25, 65, 172–75
Cancer Research Center, 20
Cash flow analysis, 100
Certified public accountant, 28
Charitable giving, 10–12, 14, 95–97.
  See also Fund raising
Charitable organizations. *See*
  Nonprofit organizations
Child care centers, 105
*Christian Echoes National Ministry,
  Inc. v. United States*, 9
Churches, 10, 98, 105

Colleges and universities, 20, 22, 27, 80, 88, 98, 105, 163–69
Colorado, 13, 52–53, 83, 92, 95
Colorado Association of Fund
  Raisers, Inc., 15, 19
Committees, 16, 24–31, 35, 79, 170–71
Community colleges, 88. *See also*
  Colleges and universities
Community relations committee, 30–31
Community services audit, 133
Conflict management, 154–56, 158
Conrad, William R., 43, 145
Consultants, 87–89, 141–43
Controller, 27, 28
Cost-benefit analysis, 130, 132
Counseling services, 25, 192–200
Craig Rehabilitation Hospital, 15

Decision making, 45, 110–11, 114–15, 120–22, 125–26. *See
  also* Planning
Delaware, 12
Denver (CO) Area Council of Boy
  Scouts, 15–17, 176–92, 210–13
Denver (CO) Big Brothers, 214–15
Denver (CO) Girls Club, 61–62, 79–80, 104
Denver (CO) hospital, 15
Denver (CO) medical research
  center, 20
Denver (CO) Regional
  Transportation District, 76
Denver (CO) schools, 18
Director. *See* Executive director
Discussion techniques, 152–54, 158
Dissidents. *See* Conflict
  management
Dissolution of nonprofit
  organizations, 12–14
Drucker, Peter, 44–45, 52, 110

Economic Recovery Act (1981), 10–11
Educational institutions. *See*
  Colleges and universities;
  Elementary schools
Elementary schools, 18
Emergency shelter, 66

Employee benefits, 105, 107
Endowment fund, 20, 21
Evaluation
  bibliography, 218
  board of directors, 32, 136–43,
    205–09
  budgeting, 100–01
  costs, 132
  difficulties, 130–31
  executive director, 133–36, 142
  meetings, 120–22, 125–26
  planning, 52, 53
  program evaluation, 129–33, 142
  report, 132
  training programs, 87
Executive committee, 18, 26, 79,
    170, 189
Executive director
  evaluation of board, 139, 142–43
  evaluation procedures, 133–36,
    142
  finance committee and, 27–28
  hiring of, 28, 147–49
  new board members, 78, 79
  personnel committee and, 28–29
  planning responsibilities, 53
  policy responsibilities, 41
  relationship with board, 144–46,
    156, 158

Facility planning, 183–85
Facility policies, 40
Family service agency boards, 16
Fidelity bonding, 4, 104, 107
Finance committee, 27–28, 100,
    102
Financial development. *See also*
    Charitable giving; Fund raising
  attitudes toward, 92–95, 106
  bibliography, 218–19
  board giving, 95–97
  board member involvement,
    93–98
  misconceptions, 91
  resource development committee,
    29
Financial planning, 190–92
Financial policies, 40
Financial reports, 27–28, 34
Fiscal control, 103–07
Fiscal year, 99

Food sales, 7–8
Formative evaluation, 132
Foundation boards, 21–22, 35
Fraud, 1
Freud, Sigmund, 71
Fund raising
  advisory board activities, 19–20
  attitudes toward, 92–95, 106
  bibliography, 218–19
  board giving, 95–97
  board member involvement,
    93–98
  misconceptions, 91
  permits, 105
  regulations, 11–12

Gift shops, 7, 98
Gilpin Elementary School, 18
Girl Scouts, 88, 98
Girls Club of Denver, Inc., 61–62,
    79–80, 104
Glenn, William R., 43, 145
Goals and objectives, 32, 127, 129,
    193–99
Governing board. *See* Board of
    directors
Grantsmanship Center, 88
Grievance committee, 170

Hardy, James H., 46
Haugen, Chuck, 77
Herzberg, Frederick, 72
Higher education. *See* Colleges and
    universities
Historian, 34
Hospitals, 7, 15, 16, 21, 27, 105
Human service agencies, 16, 25, 27,
    50–52, 66–67, 192–200

Impact evaluation, 129. *See also*
    Evaluation
Income taxes. *See* Tax-exempt
    status
Inflation, 101
Inservice training. *See* Training
    programs
Interfaith Counseling Service of
    Scottsdale, AZ, 25, 192–200
Internal Revenue Service, 2, 5, 9,
    14, 98, 105, 107. *See also*
    Tax-exempt status

Investment opportunities, 34
Investment tax credit, 11

Kellogg Foundation, 88
Kentucky
    fund-raising regulations, 12
Kiritz, Norton, 88

Leadership, 156–58
Legal obligations, 2–4, 41, 220
Legislative activity, 8–10
Liability, 1–4
Licensing, 7–8, 12, 14, 105, 107
Liquor license, 8
Litigation expenses, 2
Loans, 3, 104
Lobbying, 8–10, 14, 105
Long-range planning, 31, 44,
    176–200. *See also* Planning

Mail-order catalog, 98
Mailing permits, 8
Management, 220–21. *See also*
    Board of directors; Budgeting;
    Fiscal control; Planning;
    Policy
Maricopa (Phoenix, AZ) Camp Fire
    Council, 25, 62, 172–75
Marketing policies, 40
Mathiasen, Karl, 41, 127, 150
Meetings
    agenda, 115–20
    attendance by prospective board
        members, 62
    decision rules, 110–11
    deterrents to effectiveness,
        108–12, 125
    evaluation, 120–22, 125–26
    minutes, 122–26, 210–15
    new business, 114, 119
    preparation for, 111–12
    president's responsibilities, 32
    principles and rules for
        effectiveness, 112–22, 125
    reports, 113–14, 119
    time keeping, 119–20
Mental health associations, 23. *See
    also* Social service agencies
Metropolitan Museum of Art, 98
Middleton, Melissa, 145
Minnesota, 12

Minutes
    approval, 124–25
    committee meetings, 171
    information contained, 122
    relationship with agenda, 124
    responsibility for, 33–34, 122
    samples, 123, 210–15
Moral obligations, 4–5
Motivation, 67–75
Museums, 16, 98

Naisbett, John, 110
National Association of Mental
        Health Agencies, 88
National boards, 22–23, 35, 163–69
National Industrial Conference
        Board, 37
National Information Bureau, Inc.,
        140–41
National Mental Health
        Association, 23
Nelson, Donald T., 97
New York, 3, 12, 13
Newsletters, 7, 94
Nominating committee, 29–30,
        62–64, 65, 174–75
Nonprofit organizations. *See also*
        headings beginning with Board
    bibliography, 217
    business income, 6–7, 98–99,
        105, 107
    Colorado survey, 52–53, 95
    dissolution, 12–14
    incorporation, 2
    licenses and permits, 7–8
    loans, 3
    public support rules, 6
    tax-exempt status, 2–10, 98, 105,
        107
Notary, 34

Objectives. *See* Goals and
        objectives
O'Connell, Brian, 22–23, 43
Officers. *See* Board officers
Ohio, 3, 12
Oklahoma, 12
Organizations. *See* Nonprofit
        organizations
Orientation, 30, 33, 76–80, 89

Paltridge, James G., 139
Parliamentarian, 34
Pennsylvania, 12
Performance measures. *See*
    Evaluation
Permits. *See* Licensing
Personnel committee, 28–29, 170
Personnel policies, 28–29, 40
Philanthropy. *See* Charitable giving;
    Fund raising
Phoenix (AZ) Camp Fire Council,
    25, 65, 172–75
Planning
    benefits, 47–48, 53
    bibliography, 220–21
    characteristics, 45–46
    definition, 44–45
    evaluation, 52, 53
    example, 50–52
    relationship to budgeting, 100
    resistance to, 46–47
    sample documents, 176–200
    steps, 48–52
    versus policy, 38
Planning committee, 49–50, 53
Planning task force, 31, 50–52
Policy
    approval, 1
    board responsibilities, 41–43
    definition, 37–38, 53
    implementation, 43–44, 53
    program services committee, 27
    pyramid, 39
    review of, 42
    staff responsibilities, 41–44
    types, 38–41
    versus operating procedures, 38
    versus planning, 38
    versus strategies, 38
Policy manual, 42
Policymaking boards, 18–19, 35
PONPO, 145
Postal rates, 8
Pray, Francis, 140
President, 32, 79, 156–58, 208
Process evaluation, 129. *See also*
    Evaluation
Profit-making enterprises. *See*
    Business income
Program budgeting, 101–02, 107.
    See also Budget; Budgeting

Program evaluation, 129–33, 142.
    See also Evaluation
Program on Non-Profit
    Organizations, 145
Program policies, 40
Program services committee, 27
Psychoanalytic theories, 71
Public relations committee, 30–31,
    170
Public relations policies, 40–41

Recruitment, 55–67, 74, 78, 174–75
Reports, 5–6, 113–14, 119
Resource development committee,
    29, 97
Retreats, 30, 33, 85–87, 90
Robert's Rules of Order, 34
Rumford, Mrs. Lewis III, 151

Schaumburg case, 12
Schindler-Rainman, Eva, 84
Schneiter, Paul H., 97
Schooler, Dean, 137
Scottsdale (AZ) Interfaith
    Counseling Service, 25,
    192–200
Scouts. *See* Boy Scouts; Girl Scouts
Seattle (WA) youth employment
    center, 43
Secretary, 33–34, 122
Secretary of state, 12, 13
Self-assessment, 136–43, 205–09.
    See Evaluation
Sierra Club, 98
Smithsonian Institution, 98
Social service agencies, 16, 25, 27,
    50–52, 66–67, 192–200
Solicitation. *See* Charitable giving;
    Fund raising
South Dakota, 12, 13
Staff. *See also* Personnel committee
    friction with board members, 43
    fund raising, 94
    planning documents, 186–87
    policy implementation, 43–44, 53
    policy recommendations, 41
    relationship with board, 144–46
    relationship with executive
    director, 158
Standing committees, 25, 170

State attorney general offices, 12, 13
State laws, 1, 12
State Supreme Court, 13
Stein, Mindell, 124
Steiner, George, 38–39, 45
Strategic planning. *See* Planning
Summative evaluation, 132. *See also* Planning
Symphonies, 98

Tacoma (WA) Rescue Mission, 15, 18
Task force, 31. *See also* Committees; Planning task force
Tax deductions for charitable giving, 10–11
Tax Reform Act (1976), 9
Tax-exempt status, 2–10, 14, 98, 105, 107
Theaters, 65–66, 98
Thrift shops, 7, 98
Ticket sales, 7, 94, 98
Tompkins, Curtis J., 52
Trainers, 87–89
Training programs, 30, 33, 83–90, 201–03
Transportation district, 76
Treasurer, 27–28, 34, 102–04
Tropman, John, 124, 125

Trustees. *See* headings beginning with Board

UNICEF, 98
U.S. Supreme Court, 12
United Ways, 88, 140
Universities. *See* Colleges and universities
University of Utah, 20, 163–69

Vice-president, 33, 84
Village of Schaumburg v. Citizens for a Better Environment, 12
VOLUNTEER, 88
Volunteers
  assumptions about, 84–85
  fund-raising activities, 97–98
  importance of, 81, 89
Voting memberships, 22–23, 35

Weber, Joseph, 17–18, 43
Windfall profit tax exemption, 11
Workshops, 85–87, 90, 201–03
Wrestling license, 8

Youth service agencies, 16

Zander, A., 109
Zero-based budgeting, 102. *See also* Budget; Budgeting
Zoos, 16